I0814852

The War for Middle-earth

J. R. R. Tolkien and C. S. Lewis Confront the Gathering Storm, 1933–1945

JOSEPH LOCONTE

An Imprint of Thomas Nelson

The War for Middle-earth

Published in Nashville, Tennessee, by Nelson Books, an imprint of Thomas Nelson, 501 Nelson Place, Nashville, TN 37214, USA. Nelson Books and Thomas Nelson are registered trademarks of HarperCollins Christian Publishing, Inc.

Thomas Nelson titles may be purchased in bulk for educational, business, fundraising, or sales promotional use. For information, please email SpecialMarkets@ThomasNelson.com.

HarperCollins Publishers, Macken House, 39/40 Mayor Street Upper, Dublin 1, D01 C9W8, Ireland (https://www.harpercollins.com)

ISBN 978-1-4002-5144-5 (ITPE)

Library of Congress Cataloging-in-Publication Data

Names: Loconte, Joseph, 1961- author.

Title: The war for Middle-earth : J.R.R. Tolkien and C.S. Lewis confront the gathering storm, 1933-1945 / Joseph Loconte.

Description: Nashville, Tennessee : Thomas Nelson, 2024. | Summary: "In the years leading up to the Second World War, authors J. R. R. Tolkien and C. S. Lewis--who both fought in the trenches of WWI--saw the world descending once again into a human catastrophe. This book tells the story of how the crucible of war brought them together in friendship and inspired them to engage their Christian imagination to confront the darkest forces of their age"-- Provided by publisher.

Identifiers: LCCN 2024026648 (print) | LCCN 2024026649 (ebook) | ISBN 9781400247936 (hardcover) | ISBN 9781400247769 (ebook)

Subjects: LCSH: Tolkien, J. R. R. (John Ronald Reuel), 1892-1973--Criticism and interpretation. | Tolkien, J. R. R. (John Ronald Reuel), 1892-1973--Religion. | Lewis, C. S. (Clive Staples), 1898-1963--Criticism and interpretation. | Lewis, C. S. (Clive Staples), 1898-1963--Religion. | Christianity and literature--History--20th century. | Literature and society--History--20th century. | LCGFT: Literary criticism.

Classification: LCC PR6039.O32 Z6918 2024 (print) | LCC PR6039.O32 ebook) | DDC 823/.912--dc23/eng/20240617

LC record available at https://lccn.loc.gov/2024026648

LC ebook record available at https://lccn.loc.gov/2024026649

Printed in the United States of America

26 27 28 29 30 LBC 7 6 5 4 3

For my nephews and niece, who have enriched my life in so many beautiful ways: Nicholas, Joey, Avery, Michael John, and Christopher.

And for the children of Ventotene, Italy.

CONTENTS

INTRODUCTION

Minds Lit by Fire

A man, to be greatly good, must imagine intensely and comprehensively; he must put himself in the place of another and of many others. . . . The great instrument of moral good is the imagination.
—Percy Shelley

Halfway through the Great War, on November 30, 1916, a small group of European leaders managed to attend the funeral of Franz Joseph, ruler over the Austro-Hungarian Empire. In a ceremony scripted by the emperor before his death, the Grand Cortege carrying his coffin halted outside the Capuchin Monastery in Vienna, where all the Hapsburg emperors were laid to rest.

What transpired was a whisper from an earlier era, a nod to the transcendence of God and the frailty of men. The herald, on behalf of the emperor, knocked on the monastery door.

"Who is knocking?" shouted the abbot inside.

"I am Franz Joseph, emperor of Austria, king of Hungary."

"I don't know you."

Again the herald shouted: "I am Franz Joseph, emperor of Austria, king of Hungary, Bohemia, Galicia, Dalmatia, Grand Duke of Transylvania, Duke of—"

"We still don't know who you are," interrupted the abbot.

At this moment the herald fell on his knees and in front of all assembled declared, "I am Franz Joseph, a poor sinner, humbly begging God's mercy."

"Enter then," the abbot said. And the gates opened.

The funeral of the Austro-Hungarian emperor symbolized an outlook already in an advanced stage of decay. Settled beliefs about the religious dimension to human life were becoming unsettled. Assumptions about the moral life, about the existence of good and evil, seemed to have vanished into the killing fields of the 1914–18 war. By the end of the war, the emotional and spiritual lives of millions of ordinary Europeans were caught up in a no-man's-land of doubt and disillusionment.

Two of the most influential writers of the twentieth century, J. R. R. Tolkien and C. S. Lewis, were soldiers in the Great War. They fought in the trenches in France, what one contemporary called "the long grave already dug."[1] They emerged from the mechanized slaughter of that conflict physically intact—just barely.

No man could pass through the fires of the Somme and Arras and remain unchanged. For Tolkien, his war experience created an enduring sense of sadness. Yet he found that his imaginative cast of mind, his early taste for fantasy, was "quickened to full life by war." For Lewis, the conflict deepened his youthful atheism: the growing conviction that if God existed, he was a sadist. Paradoxically, the war years launched Lewis on a spiritual quest, a desire for "Joy," which ultimately led him on a remarkable journey of faith.

The lives of these two men intersected after the war as they were launching their academic careers at Oxford University. They soon formed a bond of friendship that, given the reach and influence of their novels, must rank as one of the most consequential friendships of modern times.

There was nothing inevitable about it. Tolkien was a devout Catholic; Lewis an Ulster Protestant and lapsed Anglican. At their first English faculty meeting, they circled each other like tigers in the wild. Yet they soon discovered that they loved many of the same things: ancient myths, epic poetry, medieval stories of honor, chivalry, sacrifice, and war.

The theme of war would become a defining feature of their professional and literary lives. Their personal lives would be upended by two global conflicts. Barely twenty years after surviving what was the most devastating conflict in history, Tolkien and Lewis would watch in anguish as new forces of aggression gathered and dominated the geopolitical landscape of Europe.

In 1938, a year before the outbreak of the Second World War, author H. G. Wells terrified millions with a radio broadcast based on his novel *The War of the Worlds*, in which an imaginary Martian invasion devastates the earth. Art would imitate life. As British historian Niall Ferguson observes, "men proved that it was quite possible to wreak comparable havoc without the need for alien intervention. All they had to do was to identify this or that group of their fellow men as the aliens, and then kill them."[2] This was the terrible pattern in the aftermath of the First World War. Communism, fascism, Nazism: all produced political systems that drew their strength from their hatreds.

The totalitarian states of Europe and Asia, despite their differences, shared another unifying characteristic: a contempt for the democratic and religious ideals of the West. Their ambitions made another global conflict almost inevitable.

"If the first great war was the seminal catastrophe," argues historian Sir Ian Kershaw, "the second was the culmination of this catastrophe—the complete collapse of European civilization."[3] Living and working in Oxford, England, Tolkien and Lewis found themselves at the storm front of this tragedy. Like no other conflict in Britain's long history, the Second World War created an existential crisis. For many months the political survival of their island nation was an open question.

It was in the crucible of this experience that Tolkien and Lewis sought each other out. The horror of the First World War instigated a cultural backlash, setting loose forces that tore at the moral and spiritual foundations of Western civilization. Both men were determined to fight back. They formed the nucleus of a group of like-minded writers, all resolved to establish a beachhead of resistance in the war of ideas that was raging around them.

The onset of the Second World War created a profound sense of urgency. Tolkien and Lewis came to believe that the soul of their neighbor, as well as the soul of their civilization, hung in the balance. In ways not fully appreciated, the 1939–45 war utterly transformed their lives and literary imaginations. Their most beloved works—including *The Hobbit*, *The Lord of the Rings*, *The Screwtape Letters*, *Mere Christianity*, and *The Chronicles of Narnia*—were conceived in the shadow of this conflict.

"Talent alone cannot make a writer," observed Ralph Waldo Emerson. "There must be a man behind the book."[4] Behind the extraordinary works of Tolkien and Lewis stood a cloud of witnesses: individuals whose contributions to the literary canon of Western civilization provided the inspiration for their epic novels. Both authors instinctively looked to this inheritance and were nourished by it in wartime.

As a result, they acquired something that our modern era has mostly abandoned: perspective. By being rooted in the great books of the Western tradition, they knew where to look for wisdom, virtue, courage, and faith. Intimate knowledge of the past braced them for the crisis years of 1933–45. In this, they reinforced each other's best instincts. "My entire philosophy of history," Lewis once told Tolkien, "hangs upon a single sentence of your own."[5]

Could an entire philosophy of history be summed up in a single sentence? What sentence? It is from a passage in *The Lord of the Rings*, when Gandalf the Wizard explains to Frodo Baggins something of the ancient struggle for Middle-earth. "There was sorrow then, too, and gathering dark, but great valor, and great deeds that were not wholly vain." Here is an approach to history—to the terrible history of the twentieth century—that invites reflection.

The lives of Tolkien and Lewis, after all, were embedded in this story when another disastrous war unleashed upon the earth a storm of human misery unsurpassed in the catalogue of world catastrophes. "Middle-earth, I suspect, looks so engagingly familiar to us, and speaks to us so eloquently," writes biographer John Garth, "because it was born with the modern world and marked by the same terrible birth pangs."[6] We cannot fully appreciate the achievement of these two remarkable authors until we try to see the world as they experienced it. They possessed a deep awareness of life's sorrows.

Yet this is only part of their story. Their experience of suffering was held in check by something stronger: gratitude. The Roman statesman Marcus Tullius Cicero called this quality "not only the greatest of virtues, but the parent of all the others." Like no other authors of their age, they used their imagination to reclaim—for their generation and ours—those deeds of valor and sacrifice and love that have always kept a lamp burning even in the deepest darkness.

CHAPTER 1

THE END OF ILLUSIONS

The world is out of joint.
—William Shakespeare, *Hamlet*

They began to feel that all this country was unreal, and that they were stumbling through an ominous dream that led to no awakening.
—J. R. R. Tolkien, *The Lord of the Rings*

If you've been up all night and cried till you have no more tears left in you—you will know that there comes in the end a sort of quietness. You feel as if nothing is ever going to happen again.
—C. S. Lewis, *The Lion, the Witch and the Wardrobe*

The agreement that officially ended the First World War has borne an impossibly heavy burden. The harsh terms of the Treaty of Versailles, signed on June 28, 1919, embittered Germany and set the stage for the rise of Nazism and the Second World War. This is the conventional account of the aftermath of the 1914–18 crisis, but it is mostly a myth. It was the Great War itself, not the treaty that concluded it, that set loose the forces and ideologies that would convulse Europe and initiate another global conflict. In fact, the year 1919—when J. R. R. Tolkien and C. S. Lewis both returned to Oxford after surviving the trenches at the Western Front—was a catalytic moment in world history.

In January 1919, the German Workers' Party, the fiercely nationalistic and anti-Semitic precursor to the Nazis, was launched in Munich—nearly six months *before* the terms of the Versailles treaty were ratified. Political leaders claimed that Germany had been "stabbed in the back" by cowards, communists, socialists, and Jews. The real betrayal, however, was the fictional narrative of victory concocted by Germany's military leaders. Even after the terrible losses during their failed spring offensive in 1918, even after American troops began pouring into France at the rate of 200,000 a month, the German people believed that their army was invincible. No treaty could have undone the psychological damage the German leadership inflicted upon its own citizens.

In March, Benito Mussolini, a war veteran, founded what became the Fascist Party. Three years later he was swept into power. Thus, Italy—one of the *victors* of the First World War—was the first European state to dispense with constitutional government and embrace the fascist vision. Mussolini's aim was to restore Italy's rightful place on the world stage. "My objective is simple," he said. "I want to make Italy great, respected, and feared."[1] The key to Italy's renewal was empire building, which required a martial culture and a militarized economy. "War alone keys up all human energies to their maximum tension," he said, "and sets the seal of nobility on those peoples who have the courage to face it."

Also in March, fifty-one representatives from two dozen countries met in Moscow at the Founding Congress of the Communist International. Long before Versailles, the other great totalitarian ideology of the twentieth century, Marxism-Leninism, was on the move.

In Russia, after two years of a vicious civil war, the Red Army was poised to install the first communist regime in Europe: the Bolshevik Party, led by Vladimir Lenin. Lenin's *Appeal to the Toiling Masses* was widely circulated in Great Britain; infiltration of the nation's working class was viewed as the key to a political revolution. British communists, embracing Lenin's creed, sent delegates to the 1919 meeting: "It is essential for the Communist Party that it should be intimately and continuously associated with the mass of workers, that it should be able to carry on constant agitation among the workers, to take part in every strike, to answer all the questions that agitate the minds of the masses."[2]

C. S. Lewis encountered quite a few communists among the student body at Oxford. As he wrote to his father:

> I think we have now arrived at the point where a wise man can do no more than wait for the end with what grace he can: and it is hard to summon much grace if you meet as many traitors and cranks in our own class as I do here, hankering for the blessing of Soviet rule. Only boys of course, as you will say: but it is usually a few fools who start the shooting which the wise heads cannot stop.[3]

The catastrophe of the Great War left a hungry void. Communist predictions of the self-immolation of capitalist societies seemed to be stunningly validated. Fascist warnings about a "sickness" in the racial stock of European society found support in educated circles, where the new "scientific" theory of eugenics was already established. No treaty, no matter how just or generous, could puncture the fantastical dreams that were displacing the political and religious ideals of entire populations. Writes historian Ian Kershaw: "The war had destroyed political systems, ruined economies, divided societies, and opened vistas onto radically utopian visions of a better world."[4]

DAYS OF DISILLUSIONMENT

On June 29, 1919, a day after the signing of the Versailles Treaty, Lewis wrote to his father to express his misgivings about the international situation. "The town is expecting the news of the peace and preparing for it with all kinds of modern fireworks which 'make a noise exactly like a heavy shell.' I don't know that I am very fond of that kind of noise," he wrote. "Meanwhile they are starving and torturing in Russia and the Polish women are out digging trenches against Hindenburg's invasion. Should one laugh—or cry?"[5]

When he returned to Oxford after the war, Lewis worried that he might be called back into active service—such was the ongoing political violence in Europe. "We have all been much amused here by the historic insolence of the German delegates at Versailles," he wrote. "I am afraid however that the matter has a very serious side, and some are already beginning to hint that we may be back in uniform again before it is all over."[6] Daisy Dunn, author of *Brideshead Revisited: Oxford Between the Wars,* also describes an unsettled postwar mood: "There were a lot of rumors spreading around Oxford University that even though peace was declared in 1918, it wouldn't last."[7]

There were yet deeper anxieties: a kind of emotional vertigo that harassed many war veterans and others who were damaged by the conflict. The artist Wyndam Lewis, reflecting on his return home from the Western Front, said that "a state of emergency came to mean for me, as for most soldiers, a permanent thing."[8] Barbara Tuchman, author of *The Guns of August,* observes that men had kept fighting, despite monstrous and futile offensives, because "the mirage of a better world glimmered beyond the shell-pitted wastes and leafless stumps that had once been green fields and waving poplars."[9] Yet, in the end, it was an illusion. The watchword of the postwar years, in fact, was "disillusionment."

How could it be otherwise?

Multitudes of young men set off for the front lines thinking they were headed for an adventure, a chance for heroism and distinction. "No man in the prime of life knew what war was like," writes British historian A. J. P. Talor. "All imagined that it would be an affair of great marches and great battles, quickly decided."[10] Instead, the mighty armies of Europe, equipped with new weapons of destruction, built thousands of miles of trenches and settled into a stalemate that lasted for nearly four unremitting years.

The result: empires collapsed; national economies were shattered; entire populations were starved to death; refugees were scattered across Europe. Ten million soldiers died in the conflict, twenty million were severely wounded, and another eight million came home permanently disabled—and for what? Nearly everything associated with the ideals and institutions of Western civilization, including traditional religion, was thrown into doubt. It was, after all, the "liberal," "Christian," and "enlightened" nations of Europe that had engaged in what amounted to a mutual suicide pact.

The shock waves were felt all over Europe, but uniquely in Great Britain, which had dominated the global scene throughout the Victorian era.

"The sheer scale of the slaughter made it impossible after the armistice to return to the world of 1914," writes historian J. M. Winter. "It was not only that the promise of talented men was thrown away; it was also that the war gave a powerful shock to an elite whose self-confidence was based on continuity and their supposed mastery of domestic and world affairs."[11] Winston Churchill, who fought in the Great War, wrote somberly about its aftermath. "Is this the end? Is it to be merely a chapter in a cruel and senseless story? Will our children bleed and gasp again in devastated lands?"[12]

THE THEFT OF YOUTH

The most poignant message that emerges from the letters and diaries of young people caught up in the war is the sense of loss: the grief not only over friends and intimates who died in battle but also over *the loss of time.*

Vera Brittain, who interrupted her studies at Oxford to serve as a nurse with the British military, wrote to her brother about it: "Dear Edward, shall we ever be young again, you and I? It doesn't seem much like it; the best years are gone already, and we've lost too much to stop being old, automatically, when the war stops—if it ever does."[13] Richard Aldington, who fought on the Western Front, captured this mood through the character of Winterbourne in his novel *Death of a Hero.* He was "slipping backwards" during those years "which should have been the most energetic and formative and creative of his whole life. . . . These lost War months, now mounting to years, were a knock-out blow from which he could not possibly recover."[14]

Tolkien battled against the same emotional headwinds. During his student days at Exeter College, he had begun to pursue in earnest his love for languages and mythologies. When war broke out, he still had a year left of studies and took the controversial step of deferring his enlistment. "It was a nasty cleft to be in," he recalled, "especially for a young man with too much imagination and little physical courage."[15]

On November 27, 1914—as the massive armies on both sides of the front were racing toward a deadlock—Tolkien read a poem to the Exeter College Essay Club, "The Voyage of Earendel," about a traveler who sails over the rim of the world chasing the sun. A friend asked him what the poem was about. "I don't know," Tolkien told him. "I'll try to find out." John Garth, in *Tolkien and the Great War*, suggests that Tolkien's decision to delay his enlistment influenced its composition, since the mariner "follows a wayward path among the fixed stars."[16] Garth calls the poem "an Odyssey in embryo."[17]

If so, the onset of the war caused a long gestation. On March 16, 1916, just before departing for France, Tolkien attended his graduation ceremony for Exeter College. He began writing a poem called "The Wanderer's Allegiance," in which wartime Oxford is portrayed as a shadow of the carefree and joyous university that Tolkien had known up until 1914: "Along thy paths no laughter runs / While war untimely take thy many sons."[18]

Tolkien formed a tight circle of literary-minded friends—Christopher Wiseman, Geoffrey Bache Smith, and Robert Gilson—who dubbed themselves the Tea Club and Barrovian Society, or the TCBS, since they often met for tea at the Barrow's department store in Oxford. All four were thrust into the conflict.

Tolkien was commissioned as a second lieutenant, as a signals officer, and was sent into the Somme Offensive, which had begun on July 1, 1916. With nearly twenty thousand men killed, it was the single deadliest day in British military history. In his angry memoir, *Civilization: 1914–1917*, French army surgeon Georges Duhamel recalls the makeshift field hospitals treating the wounded. "If the human material is not absolutely worthless, they patch it up carefully, so as to get it back into service at the first opportunity," he writes. "Then the factory would continue to rumble like a Moloch whose appetite has merely been awakened by the first fumes of the sacrifice."[19]

When Tolkien got the news that Gilson was killed in action at the Somme, he turned an emotional corner. He confessed that "the spark of fire" of his inner circle of friends—with their mission "to testify for God and Truth"—seemed to have died. "So far my chief impression is that something has gone crack." Years later, Tolkien described the sense of theft, the feeling that his imaginative powers were somehow diminished during this time. "I was pitched into it just when I had things to learn and stuff to write, but never picked it all up again."[20]

Junior officers like Tolkien took the lead in military operations and attacks, making them much more vulnerable at the front lines. By 1916, everyone knew the attrition rate was dismal. Of the 771 young men from Exeter College, 141 died, or nearly 1 in 5. Trench fever removed Tolkien from the war in 1917, and he never returned to the front. His battalion, the 11th Lancashire Fusiliers, was hurled into the second massive German offensive of 1918. As Garth notes, "nothing was heard from them again."[21] Tolkien's battalion was officially disbanded in July. "By 1918," Tolkien said, "all but one of my close friends were dead."

Lewis had just begun his studies at Oxford in April 1917 when he was commissioned as a second lieutenant. With little training, he was shipped off to France in November and endured months of intense trench warfare. "Everyone you met took it for granted that the whole thing was an odious necessity," he recalled, "a ghastly interruption of rational life."[22] In an assault at Riez du Vinage, he was struck by a mortar shell, which obliterated his sergeant standing nearby.

Had Lewis not been injured and taken out of harm's way, he probably would have perished. His college, University College, endured one of the highest casualty rates during the war. Of the 770 who fought, 175 were killed, nearly 1 in 4. "If you looked at the freshmen at University College in 1912 and 1913, between a quarter and a third of all our freshmen were killed during the First World War," explains Robin Darwall-Smith, archivist for the college. "Think of the freshmen from your generation from college and losing over a quarter of them. That's the First World War at this college."[23]

In a letter to his father, written from his hospital bed in Bristol, Lewis mourned the loss of one of his closest friends, Laurence Johnson, whom he met during military training at Oxford. Lewis had entered the war as an atheist, but Johnson was edging toward theism, "a man of conscience," whose personal integrity challenged his own malleable ethics.

> Nearly all my friends in the Battalion are gone. Did I ever mention Johnson who was a scholar at Queens? I had hoped to meet him at Oxford some day, and renew the endless talks we had out there. . . . I had him so often in my thoughts, had so often hit on some new point in one of our arguments, and made a note of things in my reading to tell him when we met again, that I can hardly believe he is dead.[24]

Walter Hooper, who served as Lewis's personal secretary near the end of his life, spoke with him about the war. Many of Lewis's friends, he told Hooper, were "convinced they would survive the war, they would be winners in this. Jack Lewis remembered hearing all of them talk." It was not to be. "He once said 'I think some of the best friends I will have made were those soldiers that I trained with, and that I expected to see afterwards, but you know, nearly every one of them was killed.'"[25]

Simon Horobin, an instructor in English Language and Literature at Oxford and author of *C. S. Lewis's Oxford*, believes that Lewis's war experience affected him throughout his life. "I came across this while reading his copy of the works of Geoffrey Chaucer," Horobin explains. "Lewis himself has written in the margin in black ink: 'What do you know about serving in a war? Have you ever faced an enemy? Have you ever fired a gun?' It's a very private moment. But it suggests something about someone who felt deeply affected by that personal experience."[26]

Lewis returned to University College in 1919 to complete his studies in classical literature and philosophy. Ordinary college life was reviving—lectures, debates, clubs—but there were many reminders of the trauma of the previous four years. The Radcliffe Quadrangle, requisitioned and transformed into a hospital to treat wounded soldiers, was still being refurbished. At the first meeting of a literary club to which Lewis belonged before his deployment, the minutes of the last meeting—from 1914—were read aloud. It had a jarring effect. "I don't know any little thing that has made me realize the absolute suspension and waste of these years more thoroughly."[27]

THE RETURN OF THE MYTHMAKER

After he was demobilized, Tolkien was desperate to pick up where he left off—at Oxford. Even before the armistice, when he was on sick leave, Tolkien traveled to the university to look for work. The prospects of an academic post, however, were dim; the war cut deeply into the financial resources of the university.

Tolkien reached out to a tutor, William Craigie, who had taught him Icelandic, now on staff at the New English Dictionary. Knowing Tolkien's skills in philology, Craigie secured him a job as an assistant lexicographer. It was a very exclusive club: a small team of experts dedicated to producing the most comprehensive dictionary of the English language to date. "I learned more in those two years," Tolkien said later, "than in any other equal period of my life."[28]

In early 1919, Tolkien moved into rooms on St. John's Street in Oxford with his wife, Edith, and his infant son, John. Although the British economy was recovering, Tolkien had to supplement his income from the New English Dictionary and began tutoring Oxford students in Anglo-Saxon. Importantly, he reconnected with Exeter College. He rejoined the Essay Club and was asked to deliver a paper on the topic of his choice. Even so, he failed to produce the paper on time. He began his talk, on March 10, 1920, by confessing sheepishly that "circumstances have prevented me from writing a critical paper."[29]

His procrastination, though, apparently triggered a creative turning point in his life. Unable to extricate himself from his promise, he was left with one choice. "Therefore, I must read something already written, and in desperation I have fallen back on this Tale." The tale in question was *The Fall of Gondolin*, widely regarded as the first real story of his epic mythology. He began writing it when, as he put it, he was a soldier thrust into "the carnage of the Somme."[30] It describes how the Elvin city of Gondolin is betrayed into the hands of Morgoth. Men of courage must confront orcs, dragons, balrogs, and a Dark Lord.

> There at the end of a weary night in the grey of dawn they halted, and Voronwë was dismayed, looking about him in grief and fear . . . he saw a land defiled and desolate. The trees were burned or uprooted; and the stone-marges of the pool were broken, so that the waters of Ivrin strayed and wrought a great barren marsh amid the ruin. All now was but a welter of frozen mire, and a reek of decay like a foul mist upon the ground.[31]

Tolkien's description of "a land defiled" might have been lifted from the journals of any number of soldiers of the Great War with a literary bent. Here, it seems, is a memory of no-man's-land, the death zone separating enemy trenches and decimated by high explosives. Thus, an Oxford literary club provided Tolkien with his first public audience for a full-blown story from Middle-earth. John Garth calls this "Tolkien's first prose mythological narrative, an epic of war."[32]

The author was clearly anxious about its reception:

> It has, of course, never seen the light before but it was not written maliciously for your annoyance but in past days for my own amusement. A complete cycle of events in an Elfinesse of my own imagination has for some time past grown up (rather than been constructed) in my mind. . . . This is not the best of them, but it is the only one that has so far been revised at all and insufficient as that revision has been, I dare read aloud.[33]

As the club secretary reported in the minutes, the story was enthusiastically received. Tolkien is described as "a staunch follower of tradition"—the Romantic tradition of William Morris and George MacDonald, authors beloved by another Oxford student and future friend, C. S. Lewis. As noted in the minutes: "The battle of the contending forces of good and evil . . . was very graphically and astonishingly told, combined with a wealth of attendance to detail interesting in extreme." In the audience that evening were Nevill Coghill and Hugo Dyson, authors who would join the literary group founded by Lewis and Tolkien in the 1930s known as the Inklings.

With the harrowing memories of combat still fresh, Tolkien had created a rough template for *The Lord of the Rings*. What began as a short, imaginative story about a battle for a hidden city, a tale written for Tolkien's own amusement, would form the basis for his story of an existential struggle for an entire civilization. Though compared to "the typical Romantics" of an earlier age, Tolkien would redefine the meaning of epic fantasy for the modern era.

THE RETURN OF THE ATHEIST POET

Before being admitted to Oxford, Lewis had studied under William Kirkpatrick, a retired headmaster in Great Bookham. In addition to classical authors such as Homer and Virgil, Lewis was introduced to the writings of a wide circle of English authors—some of them works of fantasy, many of them deeply Christian: Spenser's *Faerie Queene*; William Morris's *The Well at the World's End*; Shelley's *Prometheus Unbound*; John Bunyan's *The Pilgrim's Progress*; and John Milton's *Paradise Lost*.

Although Lewis had declared himself an atheist to his closest friends, he was continually drawn to these authors, none more enduringly than the nineteenth-century Scottish novelist George MacDonald. His first encounter with MacDonald occurred in 1916, halfway through the Great War and shortly before he enlisted for combat. Waiting for a train to Great Bookham, Lewis picked up a copy of *Phantastes* at the station bookstall. "A few hours later," he recalled, "I knew I had crossed a great frontier." At the time, Lewis was "waste deep in Romanticism" and, although MacDonald's story was also a romance, it possessed a different quality.

> Nothing was at that time further from my thoughts than Christianity, and I therefore had no notion what this difference was. I was only aware that if this new world was strange, it was also homely and humble; that if this was a dream, it was a dream in which one at least felt strangely vigilant; that the whole book had about it a sort of cool, morning innocence.[34]

Phantastes explores what at first seems to be a young man's search for feminine beauty but becomes something much more profound, an exploration of the human longing for transformation. "I should have been shocked in my teens," Lewis admitted, "if anyone told me that what I learned to love in *Phantastes* was goodness."[35] If Lewis's spiritual quest did not begin with *Phantastes*, it was quickened by MacDonald's infusion of fantasy with his moral and religious outlook on life.

Nevertheless, Lewis's experience of combat was an event of "deep theological significance" for him. "Many would say that Lewis's atheism was reinforced by this seeming pointlessness, the devastation of the Great War," explains biographer Alister McGrath. "If there was a God, why was this trauma happening? Why on earth was all this violence there? And you can see Lewis beginning to feel that his horrible experiences in the First World War cemented and reinforced and consolidated his fundamental belief there is no God and there can be no God."[36]

A collection of his poems, written mostly during the war years and published in 1919, bears witness to his deepening cynicism. Calling it *Spirits in Bondage*—a line from Milton's *Paradise Lost*—Lewis described the poems as "mainly strung around the idea . . . that nature is wholly diabolical and malevolent and that God, if He exists, is outside of and in opposition to the cosmic arrangement."[37]

"In Prison," for example, expresses a "bitter wrath" against a "hopeless life" caught up forever "in a circling path." In "Satan Speaks," God is portrayed as a cosmic sadist, indifferent to humankind with its "loathing for the life that I have given / A haunted, twisted soul for ever riven." In "De Profundis," the echoes of Milton's portrait of Satan—"It is better to reign in hell than serve in heaven"—are unmistakable:

> Come let us curse our Master ere we die,
> For all our hopes in endless ruin lie.
> The good is dead. Let us curse God most high. . . .
> Yet I will not bow down to thee nor love thee,
> For looking in my own heart I can prove thee,
> And now this frail, bruised being is above thee.[38]

Yet the atheist poet never quite abandoned hope. The intense longing for a faraway country, a place of beauty and noble purpose, was not extinguished. In "World's Desire" he seeks after "the sacred court, hidden high upon the mountains," where "lovely folk" are found "breathing in another air, drinking of a purer fountain," where "there's a place for you and me."[39]

Lewis's spiritual instincts, however, sat uneasily with his materialism—and they were not winning the argument going on in his mind. After his conversion to Christianity, looking back on this period, Lewis described a brutal contest between his imaginative life and the life of his intellect: "The two hemispheres of my mind were in the sharpest contrast. . . . Nearly all that I loved I believed to be imaginary; nearly all that I believed to be real I thought grim and meaningless." A letter to his brother, Warren "Warnie" Lewis, captures his ambivalence: "The trouble about God is that he is like a person who never acknowledges one's letters and so, in time, one comes to the conclusion either that he does not exist or that you have got the address wrong."[40]

PSYCHOANALYSIS AND SOCIAL DECAY

Either God does not exist or we have the wrong address. It would be hard to write a more concise lament to describe the intellectual mood in the years immediately after the First World War.

The new discipline of psychoanalysis, pioneered by Sigmund Freud, had much to do with this. Like no one before him, Freud categorized religious belief as an irrational and neurotic desire: a condition to be treated through therapy.

Freud emphasized the primal urges of the unconscious, where the symptoms of phobia, fanaticism, and neurosis are found. People typically repressed, or "sublimated," emotions that had no healthy or acceptable outlet, and the unconscious mind became the place where they found safe haven. Moreover, the sexual impulse, Freud claimed, was at the root of nearly all forms of human behavior. Psychoanalysis would liberate people from unhealthy guilt and repression.

By 1914, Freud was already well-known in psychiatric circles, thanks in part to his book *The Interpretation of Dreams* (1899). But it was the novel experience of widespread war trauma—the "shell-shocked" veteran—that created his celebrity status.

In Great Britain alone, tens of thousands of war veterans were granted pensions for psychiatric disability; many were considered permanently insane. Electric shock therapy and other cruel treatments employed in military hospitals outraged many families, and in 1920 the Vienna General Hospital prodded the Austrian government to set up a commission of inquiry. Freud was called in to advise. The controversy made him a household name. "But even more spectacular, and in the long run far more important," writes historian Paul Johnson, "was the sudden discovery of Freud's works and ideas by intellectuals and artists."[41]

Lewis was introduced to Freud's outlook in an intensely personal way. Keeping a promise to a friend, Edward Francis "Paddy" Moore—who was killed at the Battle of the Somme—he brought Moore's mother and daughter into his home to live with him. Through them, Lewis met and befriended Mrs. Moore's brother, "the Doc," a combat veteran who suffered a sudden attack of war nerves during a visit in February 1923.

"He was here for nearly three weeks, and endured awful mental tortures,"

Lewis wrote to his friend Arthur Greeves. A psychoanalyst and neurological specialist examined the Doc and explained to Lewis that "every neurotic case went back to the childish fear of the father." Freud's techniques in this case evidently resulted in failure. After Lewis spent many nights trying to console him, the Doc was admitted to a hospital and died a short time later. "He had the delusion that he was going to Hell. Can you imagine what he went through and what we went through?"[42]

In his book *The Twilight Years: The Paradox of Britain Between the Wars*, Richard Overy argues that psychoanalysis presented itself as a scientific-therapeutic cure for the disorientation of modern society. Like the advocates of eugenics, who promised to rescue humanity from racial degradation, "the early pioneers of psychoanalysis promised to save civilization from the menace of their own imagining."[43]

This salvation scheme, however, had little use for religion. Freud's entire approach to human personality was thoroughly secular. As biographer Peter Gay puts it, "Freud was a convinced, consistent, and aggressive atheist."[44]

Just as Freud made a lifelong effort to give scientific respectability to psychoanalysis, he also sought to discredit religious belief as an irrational state of mind, untethered from reality. "The riddles of the universe reveal themselves only slowly to our investigation; there are many questions to which science today can give no answer," he wrote in *The Future of an Illusion* (1927). "But scientific work is the only road which can lead us to a knowledge of reality outside ourselves."[45] Like the Enlightenment philosophers of the eighteenth century, writes Gay, Freud believed that "religion and science are mortal enemies and that every attempt at bridging the gap between them is bound to be futile."[46] Thus, in his clinical practice, Freud regarded the religious experiences of his patients as symptoms of a neurosis.

The "wish-fulfillment" argument against religion, however, despite its claims to rationality, was vulnerable to calm reason. Why couldn't the Freudian accusation be turned against Freud himself? Wouldn't many people find it convenient to their personal lives to dispense with a God who might make moral demands upon them? Despite the question-begging quality of the psychological approach to religion, many writers, educators, and intellectuals in the 1920s and '30s took its conclusions for granted.

Lewis was among them. His attitudes toward religion during this period parroted the popular social-psychological view. In a striking passage in a letter to Arthur Greeves, Lewis explained why he rejected all religious beliefs. "There is absolutely no proof for any of them. . . . All religions, that is, all mythologies, to give them their proper name, are merely man's own invention—Christ as much as Loki." He went on:

> Primitive man found himself surrounded by all sorts of terrible things he didn't understand—thunder, pestilence, snakes, etc.: what more natural than to suppose that these were animated by evil spirits trying to torture him. These he kept off by cringing to them, singing songs and making sacrifices, etc. Gradually from being mere nature-spirits these supposed being[s] were elevated into more elaborate ideas, such as the old gods: and when man became more refined he pretended that these spirits were good as well as powerful. Thus religion, that is to say, mythology, grew up. . . . Now all this you must have heard before: it is the recognized scientific account of the growth of religions.[47]

Here is the spirit of the age: Religious belief is a primitive illusion designed to help people cope with a dangerous world. *This was the recognized scientific account of the growth of religions.* As such, it had no truth value, no connection to reality. Freud's influence was wide and deep.

After Lewis's conversion to Christianity, in his first work of theological fiction, he will go after Sigmund Freud with an axe. He will conclude that Freud's theories, by dismissing man's deepest longings as illusions, led ordinary people into a state of despair.[48]

The advocates of Freudian psychology, however, claimed to offer a pathway out of despair: nothing less than the hope of redemption in the face of the modern threats to humanity.[49] The grandiosity of its claims, allegedly rooted in science and thoroughly materialistic, gave Freudianism a militant quality. The very last sentence of *The Future of an Illusion*, for example, finds the author impervious to alternative theories. "No, our science is no illusion. But an illusion it would be to suppose that what science cannot give us we can get elsewhere."[50]

As Paul Johnson observes, critics of Freudian psychology were treated as heretics. "Freud betrayed signs, in fact, of the twentieth-century messianic ideologue at his worst—namely, a persistent tendency to regard those who diverged from him as themselves unstable and in need of treatment."[51] In this, Freud personified the modern secular zealot.

THE WASTELAND OF THE WEST

The embrace of Freudian psychology in educated circles coincided with the deepening materialism of European society after the First World War. The stage was thus set for the rise of a new artistic and literary movement: an outlook that rejected the traditional understanding of the human person as a rational, responsible, and moral being.

The Modernist Movement was a prewar phenomenon. But the cataclysm of the Great War appeared to shatter nearly all conventional restraints.[52] New artistic movements such as Dadaism and Surrealism seemed to project Freudian ideas about man's primal instincts onto the artist's canvas. The emphasis was on "the absurd, the nonsensical, the illogical and the irrational."[53]

Author Herbert Read, a contemporary observer, described what had happened in the field of art with figures like Picasso. His critique applies as well to the poetry and literature of the period:

> There have been revolutions in the history of art before today. . . . But I do think we can already discern a difference in kind in the contemporary revolution: it is not so much a revolution, which implies turning over, even a turning back, but rather a break-up, a devolution, some would say a dissolution. Its character is catastrophic.[54]

Historians and literary critics have described a moment in which a generation of authors and artists effectively checked themselves into a madhouse.[55] The Modernist outlook, write Malcolm Bradbury and James McFarlane, can be viewed as the result of "the destruction of civilization and reason in the First World War." In a world reinterpreted by Marx, Freud, and Darwin, there arose an "existential exposure to meaninglessness or absurdity."[56]

It was an outlook steeped in doubt, utterly disconnected from traditional religion. Writing in the late 1920s, journalist Walter Lippmann observed the sea change: "To walk through a museum of Western European art is to behold a peculiarly vivid record of how the great themes of popular religion have ceased to inspire the imagination of modern men."[57] Though not a person of faith, Lippmann lamented the "feverish experimentation" of the modern artist "to find an adequate substitute for the organizing principle of the religion which he lost."[58]

Whatever form Modernism took—in art, theater, film, or literature—the emphasis was on exposing the chaos behind the façade of order, rationality, and convention. The effect of the movement on English literature was profound. In 1922, the appearance of James Joyce's *Ulysses*—in which the concepts of human agency and morality dissolve into subjectivity—was the literary equivalent of the splitting of the atom.[59]

No author captured more poignantly the sense of fragmentation and dissolution than T. S. Eliot. His great Modernist poem, *The Waste Land* (1922), laments the decay of Western civilization, instigated by technology and mass culture and accelerated by the war.[60] The collective effect of Eliot's stark language—"a heap of broken images," "the dead tree gives no shelter," and "I will show you fear in a handful of dust"—was a vision of a civilization in irreversible decline. The old certainties and virtues were obsolete.

Author J. P. Hodin recognized a literary culture with only thin remnants of a rational conception of the world: "A world collapsed, became rubble."[61] In his book *Modern Heroism*, Roger Sale argues that for Eliot, traditional concepts such as faith, courage, heroism, and virtue "now produce deceit, unnatural vices, and impudent crimes." The individual who seeks a heroic destiny "is deceived, and dangerous."[62]

MYTHS AND THE MEDIEVAL KNIGHT

This was the temper of the generation of Tolkien and Lewis as they launched their academic careers. They both thought of themselves chiefly as poets, yet they were repulsed by the Modernist trends in literature, typified by Joyce and Eliot.[63] "They thought Eliot—with his 'heap of broken images'—was infected with chaos, rather than fortifying others against it," explains Oxford scholar Michael Ward. "Yes, many images were broken, and rightly so. But you couldn't just live in an iconoclastic graveyard."[64]

In their own distinctive ways, Tolkien and Lewis launched a counterattack: a literary campaign they would sustain over the course of their careers.

After studying a volume of Eliot's verse for the first time, Lewis recruited his Oxford friends Frank Hardie and Nevill Coghill in a somewhat outlandish anti-Eliot scheme. The plan was to write a parody of the kind of modern poetry for which Eliot had become famous and send it to *The Criterion*, the magazine Eliot edited. They hoped to get their poem published as serious poetry, thus exposing the absurd quality of the Modernist literary movement. "If he falls into the trap," Lewis wrote in his journal, "I will then consider how best to use the joke for the advancement of literature and the punishment of quackery."[65] In the end, the plot evaporated and their poetry—"very sad and desperate and disillusioned, cheap as dirt"—was never sent.[66]

Like Lewis, Tolkien's literary tastes were firmly grounded in the heroic code found in medieval works such as *Beowulf*, *Sir Gawain and the Green Knight*, and *Le Morte d'Arthur*. There was a self-absorption to Modernist literature that Tolkien disliked intensely. He denounced the "manhandling of English" that was justified "in the name of art" or "personal expression."[67] According to John Garth, Tolkien was aware of how literary "realism" had combined itself with Modernism, producing an "overbearing, intolerant, and denunciatory orthodoxy." This new outlook scorned the older literary traditions as "archaic" and "medieval."[68]

On the contrary, Tolkien insisted, language whose meaning is clear and is "filled with the memory of good and evil, is an achievement, and its possessors are richer than those who have no such tradition."[69] In the new literary orthodoxy, however, there was no memory of the concepts of good and evil, no place for heroism or noble sacrifice. Tolkien rejected this outlook in part because of his authentic Catholic faith. Equally important, his literary passions were effectively at war with the Modernist spirit.

In 1925, for example, Tolkien published a new edition of the fourteenth-century English poem *Sir Gawain and the Green Knight*, coedited with

E. V. Gordon. It was aimed at college students, especially those who lacked a background in Old and Middle English. Tolkien's objective, he wrote in the introduction, was to provide "a sufficient apparatus for reading this remarkable poem with an appreciation as far as possible of the sort which its author may be supposed to have desired."[70]

This aim deserves attention, because Tolkien understood the historical and moral dimensions of the story—and he was determined to transmit its lessons to the next generation. The author of *Sir Gawain* drew upon an ancient past as the basis for his storytelling. "Antiquity," Tolkien explained, "like a many-figured back-cloth hangs ever behind the scene." The author's story is not about these older things, "but it receives part of its life, its vividness, its tension from them." Tolkien held up *Sir Gawain* as an example of what a great fairy-story should do. "There is indeed no better medium for moral teaching than the good fairy-story," and by that Tolkien meant "the real deep-rooted tale."[71]

There is no better medium for moral teaching than a good fairy-story. Whatever else motivated Tolkien as he constructed his many stories about the struggle for Middle-earth—his legendarium—the moral objective must not be ignored.

The moral teaching of *Sir Gawain* involves, among other things, fidelity to God in the face of sexual temptation. Indeed, the temptation and confession of Gawain form "the very nub of the poem." In medieval Europe, the romantic chivalric tradition, though a product of Christendom, had idealized love and transformed it into a game of the court. Elaborate rules were established that justified adultery and loveless marriages. Gawain, in obedience to conscience, to "eternal and universal values," resists sin and retains his honor.[72]

In describing the core values of the story, Tolkien reveals something of his own:

> The noblest knight of the highest order of Chivalry refused adultery, places hatred of sin in the last resort above all other motives, and escapes from a temptation that attacks him in the guise of courtesy through grace obtained by prayer. That is what the author of *Sir Gawain and the Green Knight* was mainly thinking about, and with that thought he shaped the poem as we have it.[73]

At the very beginning of his academic career, Tolkien was also thinking about these things. They would shape his approach to his most epic fairy-story, *The Lord of the Rings*, a fantasy infused with moral seriousness. He will place a knight—Aragorn, a Ranger of the North—close to the center of the story. Like the author of *Sir Gawain*, Tolkien will build upon "antique material" to express his own "stern and uncompromising moral view."[74] As in *Sir Gawain*, his story will be illuminated by his distinctive vision of Christian knighthood.

Tolkien was passionate about communicating these ideals to his students. "The highlight of each lecture was when Tolkien would move away from his lectern and pace back and forth at the front of the room, his black academic gown billowing round his shoulders, as he recited whole sections of the poem," recalled Adele Vincent, one of his students. "One sonorous line would follow rapidly after another, now rippling like a running stream, now roaring like a raging torrent."[75]

Nothing could be further from the Modernist view: a belief in "eternal and universal values"; in the enduring worth of a "deep-rooted tale"; in the "hatred of sin" and the power of prayer; and in the value of medieval chivalry, transformed by "Christian knighthood." In the intellectual climate of the postwar years, Tolkien's commitment to retrieving these concepts for his own age was nothing less than revolutionary.

BEOWULF AGAINST A HOSTILE WORLD

In the same year that he published *Sir Gawain and the Green Knight*, Tolkien began translating *Beowulf*, the story of a Scandinavian hero from the sixth century. *Beowulf* was written by a Christian monk looking back before Christianity had fully penetrated the West. He was celebrating the ancient virtues of bravery and sacrifice, while framing them in a Christian context. Tolkien considered it one of the greatest poems of English literature.

It is a poem about war. Beowulf, coming to the aid of the king of the Danes, must fight a monster called Grendel. "Straightway that master of evil deeds perceived that never had he met within this world in earth's four corners on any other man a mightier gripe of hand," writes the author of *Beowulf.* "In heart and soul he grew afraid, yet none the sooner could escape."[76] After defeating Grendel, Beowulf fights and kills Grendel's mother. Fifty years later he battles a dragon and defeats it, but is mortally wounded in the encounter.

In his foreword to Archibald Strong's 1925 translation of *Beowulf*—which Tolkien read and studied carefully—R. W. Chambers wrote that "the whole spirit of Beowulf is Christian" and that "the poet is careful to avoid anything incompatible with the Christian faith and morals."[77] His aim was to harmonize the pagan and Christian elements of European society.

"He looks back on those warriors, he sees that what they were struggling for, what they were trying to do was noble, but ultimately was doomed," explains Stuart Lee, author of *The Keys of Middle-earth.* "And I think in *The Lord of the Rings* and in *The Hobbit*, you see Tolkien playing this out quite a bit—particularly in *The Lord of the Rings*, where the allies are faced with pretty much a hopeless task. And even at the end they march right to the gates of Mordor, knowing they are going to perish, just in that vain hope, to try to give Frodo a bit more time," Lee says. "But it's that choice, just carrying through, completing the task to the end, even if you think it's going to be doomed."[78]

No other epic poem so absorbed Tolkien's attention. In addition to his own translation, he studied it intently, lectured on it regularly throughout his career, and delivered a scholarly address in 1936 that transformed the entire approach to Beowulf studies. As one scholar summarizes it, the story supplied "a seemingly inexhaustible source for his scholarly speculation and creative inspiration."[79] That's no exaggeration. In a letter to his friend W. H. Auden, Tolkien revealed an aspect of the story that he still found compelling decades after he first read it: the existence of radical evil and the obligation to resist it.

> The overthrow of Grendel makes a good wonder-tale, because he is too strong and dangerous for any ordinary man to defeat, but it is a victory in which all men can rejoice because he was a monster, hostile to all men and to all humane fellowship and joy.[80]

Ignored or despised by the *literati* of the 1920s, the theme of heroic sacrifice would nevertheless define Tolkien's academic and literary career.

Indeed, the exultation of valor in the struggle against evil—even in the face of certain defeat—informed Tolkien's entire legendarium of Middle-earth.

VIRGIL AND *THE AENEID*

Although Lewis shared Tolkien's attachment to these medieval ideals, he also found inspiration in an older tradition, that of classical Rome. No ancient work held a firmer grip on his imagination than Virgil's *Aeneid.* An epic story about war, courage, perseverance, and sacrifice, it has been called "the single most influential literary work of European civilization for the better part of two millennia."[81]

Lewis first encountered Virgil during his studies with Kirkpatrick, in part to hone his skills in Latin. His appetite was whetted.

In February 1918, when Lewis was in a British Red Cross hospital in France, recovering from trench fever before returning to the front line, he ordered "a couple of books of Virgil from my bookseller in London."[82] In June 1920, after returning to University College, he wrote to Arthur: "I am also, in the evening, reading Virgil through again."[83] In August 1922, after completing his studies, he began his own translation of the poem, a task he worked on through the 1930s and '40s. Lewis would use his translation of *The Aeneid* in several of his works, including *The Pilgrim's Regress, The Problem of Pain,* and *Preface to Paradise Lost.* Toward the end of his life, Lewis was asked by a magazine editor, "What books did the most to shape your vocational attitude and your philosophy of life?" He put Virgil's *Aeneid* near the top of the list.

The Aeneid is also a story about origins—the founding myth of ancient Rome—written by Rome's greatest poet when his nation was in the throes of an identity crisis. The Roman people had discarded their republican form of government in favor of an empire run by autocrats. Virgil sought to give Rome a revived sense of its civilizing mission in the world: to somehow reconcile the ideals of the republic with the fearsome realities of the empire. Thus, the mission of Aeneas is to establish a new civilization: "Roman, remember by your strength to rule Earth's peoples—for your arts are to be these: to pacify, to impose the rule of law, to spare the conquered, battle down the proud."

As Lewis saw it, Virgil transformed the meaning of the word "epic," telling a story not simply about individual heroism to protect one's family or tribe but rather one of civilizational significance. "It is this which gives the reader of the *Aeneid* the sense of having lived through so much," he wrote. "No man who has once read it with full perception remains an adolescent."[84]

Aeneas accepts his calling reluctantly, sensing the hazards that lie ahead. When he wavers—as when he falls in love with Dido of Carthage and convinces himself that Carthage, not Rome, can be the new home for the Trojans—he invites disaster. It is only when Aeneas submits unreservedly to the divine calling that he achieves his stature as a great and heroic leader.

Classical scholar A. T. Reyes, noting the impact of the story on Lewis, draws attention to his personal experience of war. "For Lewis, a veteran of the First World War, the beauty and fascination of Virgil's poem lay in its expression of waste and loss. What affected him most was Virgil's need to depict the human tragedy within war," he writes in *C. S. Lewis's Lost Aeneid*. "Costliness is the key. As a young man, Lewis had served in combat, and in middle age he taught the young as they headed to the battlefields of Europe. He not only understood, but felt, the truth of Virgil's description of war and death."[85]

It is not only the sense of loss, however, that was important to Lewis. One of Virgil's chief themes is *pietas*, which signifies duty and devotion: honoring one's binding commitments regardless of the personal costs. In the early lines of the poem, Aeneas is called "a man outstanding in his piety." Without this quality, he cannot fulfill his calling. "It is the nature of a vocation to appear to men in the double character of a duty and a desire, and Virgil does justice to both," Lewis wrote. "To follow the vocation does not mean happiness: but once it has been heard, there is no happiness for those who do not follow."[86]

Classicist Daisy Dunn observes that Lewis's distinctive translation of *The Aeneid* itself reveals much about his views of the poem and its classical values. "He translated it in a very consciously archaic, elevated, lofty style that is far removed from everyday language," she explains. "It's as if he was saying, 'Here is a poem that is higher than anything else we have. This is a poem that is like a holy book, something that we need to more than just read. It is something we need to connect with, something we need to follow.'"[87]

The Aeneid became for Lewis what *Beowulf* was for Tolkien: a bitterly realistic story not only about war but also about the supreme importance of fortitude and courage in the fog of war. Indeed, the moral necessity of war—as a check against a great evil—would emerge as a dominant theme common to the works of both authors.

As we'll see, the First World War created a backlash of antiwar sentiment, which expressed itself in both the literature and the politics of the 1920s and '30s. The antiwar poets of this era focused almost exclusively on the horrors of modern warfare. Tolkien and Lewis rejected the pacifist assumptions that were in vogue up until the outbreak of the Second World War. Though both men had reasons to despise what Tolkien called "the utter, stupid waste of war," they both were rooted in literary traditions that offered a more complex perspective on war and the human condition.

AN ANGLO-SAXON TRIUMPH

Although Tolkien had already established himself as a promising young scholar at the University of Leeds, his imaginative mind—formed and enriched by his early friendships as much as his studies—seemed bound up with Oxford. Whether through the chance circumstances of academic life or, perhaps, the hand of Providence, Tolkien was offered the opportunity to return and pursue his passion for linguistics. He became a top candidate for the newly vacated Rawlinson & Bosworth Professorship of Anglo-Saxon at Oxford.

Established in 1755, it was a venerable post filled by first-rate scholars. In his application letter to the university, Tolkien highlighted his efforts at Leeds to strengthen the link between English literature and the study of ancient and medieval languages. "Philology, indeed, appears to have lost for these students its connotations of terror if not mystery," he wrote. His mission at Oxford, he proclaimed, would be "to advance, to the best of my ability, the growing neighborliness of linguistic and literary studies" and to encourage "philological enthusiasm among the young."[88]

Tolkien prevailed: On July 21, 1925, facing a split vote by the board of electors, the university vice chancellor cast the deciding vote for Tolkien. Outside of Oxford, it is difficult to imagine another academic setting where

Tolkien could have pursued his desire to give England a mythology "of its own"—an epic story worthy of its role in the history of Western civilization. Considering the enduring appeal of *The Hobbit* and *The Lord of the Rings*, Tolkien's love not only for old languages but *for inventing new ones* would inspire "philological enthusiasm" in ways he could not have imagined.

To celebrate his Oxford appointment, Tolkien took Edith and his three sons—John (age eight), Michael (age five), and baby Christopher—to the seaside town of Filey, in Yorkshire, where they stayed at a cottage overlooking the sea. During their trip, Michael lost his cherished toy dog on the beach. To console him, Tolkien invented a story about a dog named Rover, who was turned into a toy by a nasty wizard. Rover encounters a friendly wizard who sends him on a quest to become a real dog again and be reunited with his owner.

There is plenty of danger: black spiders, "glass-beetles with jaws like steel traps," and "nasty, creepy things in the bog." Tolkien's tale becomes *Roverandom*, a children's story that contains myth, legend, and even history.[89]

Even here, in a picturesque town by the sea, there were reminders of the First World War. Before they left, the family took a long walk to see the remains of a German submarine, the UC-47, which was sunk by the British near Flamborough Head.[90] Throughout most of the war, the German U-boats wreaked havoc upon the British Navy and merchant ships, almost bringing Great Britain to its knees. As Tolkien noted, his son John was "conceived and carried during the starvation-year of 1917 and the great U-boat campaign."[91]

The UC-47 sub had sunk fifty-six United Kingdom and Allied ships in just over a year. Its end came on November 18, 1917, when a British patrol boat, by pure luck, spotted the U-boat shortly before dawn. Within fifteen seconds a Royal Navy vessel rammed the sub. All twenty-six of her crew perished along with her.[92]

"A TOWER OF DREAMS"

After a year of intense study in English Language and Literature, Lewis was ready to sit for his final examinations. In the months leading up to this ordeal, he was in a rough patch emotionally. "After my last entry," he wrote, "there followed a period so busy and on the whole so miserable that I had neither time nor heart to continue my diary, nor poetry, nor pleasant effort of any sort."[93] Pleasant or not, intense effort was required. Candidates had to demonstrate competent knowledge of English literature and of the English language at all periods, including Old and Middle English.

On July 16, 1923, Lewis's examination results were published. He achieved First Class Honors, a rare "Triple First." In Oxford's prewar days, students like Lewis would have been assured an academic posting. But there was a postwar glut of graduates looking for jobs, and his employment prospects were slim. Lewis felt strongly that there were no real alternatives for him.

"But I think I know my own limitations," he wrote his father, "and am quite sure that an academic or literary career is the only one in which I can hope ever to go beyond the meanest mediocrity."[94] Lewis had no illusions about his chances to become an Oxford don, and he even resigned himself to the prospect of becoming a headmaster at a public school. "I should not be a son of yours if the prospect of being adrift and unemployed at thirty had not been very often present to my mind."[95]

In the meantime he was supporting Mrs. Moore (whom he called "Minto") and her daughter while struggling to pay his bills, facts he was concealing from his father. He secured a temporary post teaching philosophy to undergraduates at University College and acted as an examiner, grading countless high school papers. He continued to rely on his father to supplement his income.

Nevertheless, Oxford had captured his heart. Amid the gloomy verses of *Spirits in Bondage* is a beautiful poem called "Oxford," a stirring tribute to the intellectual and cultural legacy of the university during the ravages of wartime:

> It is well that there are palaces of peace
> And discipline and dreaming and desire,
> Lest we forget our heritage and cease
> The Spirit's work—to hunger and aspire:
> Lest we forget that we were born divine,
> Now tangled in red battle's animal net,

Murder the work and lust the anodyne,
Pains of the beast 'gainst bestial solace set.
But this shall never be: to us remains
One city that has nothing of the beast,
That was not built for gross, material gains,
Sharp, wolfish power or empire's glutted feast.
We are not wholly brute. To us remains
A clean, sweet city lulled by ancient streams,
A place of visions and of loosening chains,
A refuge of the elect, a tower of dreams.
She was not builded out of common stone
But out of all men's yearning and all prayer
That she might live, eternally our own,
The Spirit's stronghold—barred against despair.

Of the many influences on Lewis's journey to faith, Oxford University itself—which still took seriously the quest for truth and beauty—must rank high. Lewis described the university's historic mission as "the Spirit's work" and "the Spirit's stronghold." Not even the chaos of war, of a world "tangled in red battle's animal net," could divert Oxford from its transcendent purpose. It remained "a refuge of the elect" and "a tower of dreams" built upon "all men's yearning." The university seemed to embody the search for transcendence.

"We should never underestimate the importance of Oxford as a place to these writers," says Daisy Dunn, "even if it doesn't feature explicitly and overtly in their work." The university, she explains, provided the underpinning of their thinking, the intellectual and spiritual environment in which they produced their works. As the third-oldest university in Europe, Oxford communicates in myriad ways—through its libraries, churches, architecture, art, portraits—its connection to a much older literary and cultural inheritance. "Oxford has always been quite an otherworldly place," Dunn observes. "It is a place that feels far removed from everywhere else, where everything feels magnified."[96]

Lewis dared to hope that he might become part of this remarkable community. After years of internal debate, Magdalen College announced in April 1925 that it intended to establish a Fellowship as Tutor in English

Language and Literature. The college president told Lewis he was "the strongest and most acceptable candidate." The only stipulation was that, in addition to English, he should be available to teach philosophy (a subject that Lewis once thought would be his career choice). "I need hardly say," he recorded in his journal, "that I would have agreed to coach a troupe of performing bagbirds in the quadrangle."[97]

Lewis telegrammed his father the news, in one of the warmest exchanges in their difficult relationship:

> My dear Papy, First, let me thank you from the bottom of my heart for the generous support, extended over six years, which alone has enabled me to hang on till this. . . . You have waited, not only without complaint but full of encouragement, while chance after chance slipped away when the goal receded furthest from sight. Thank you again and again. . . . Once more, with very hearty thanks and best love, your loving son, Jack.[98]

Lewis was not exaggerating the importance of his father's support. Although his intellectual talents were remarkable from a young age, without his father's help at key moments of his life, Lewis would have been adrift. His father made possible "the one course of life which gave the opportunity for the full expression of his genius."[99] Oxford would have remained an unfulfilled fantasy.

Father and son had endured much together: the loss of Lewis's mother, the outbreak of the Great War, the anxieties and fears of Jack's deployment to the Western Front, and his close brush with death. The immense significance of this opportunity to Lewis's career was not lost on the father. "I went up to his room and burst into tears of joy," Albert Lewis wrote in his diary. "I knelt down and thanked God with a full heart. My prayers had been heard and answered."[100]

THE SUMMER OF 1925

Thus, in the summer of 1925, two literary men of immense imagination, both veterans of the Great War, were planning to make Oxford their academic home. Both had extraordinary gifts, which those closest to them sensed would be put to great effect. Christopher Wiseman, one of Tolkien's inner circle, made a brazen proclamation about him in 1916: "If you do come out in print, you will startle our generation as no one has yet."[101] Albert Lewis made a similar prediction about his son. "If Oxford does not spoil him . . . he may write something that men would not willingly let die."

Having endured great suffering and loss, they were determined to press ahead with their lives and vocations. Their futures seemed bright.

And the world was at peace. The prospect of war, in fact, was not even dimly on the horizon. The major European leaders were contemplating a new round of treaty negotiations to prevent another conflict. Seven countries would soon send delegations to a conference in Locarno, Switzerland: Belgium, Britain, Czechoslovakia, France, Germany, Italy, and Poland. By persuading Germany to formally accept its obligations under the Versailles Treaty and its new boundaries with France, the Locarno Pact would be called a diplomatic triumph. The "spirit of Locarno" would mark a moment of great hope for the creation of a peaceful political order.

Yet the summer of 1925 also brought darker omens.

Just a few days before Tolkien received news of his appointment at Oxford, a publishing event quietly occurred in Germany. On July 18 the first volume of Adolf Hitler's *Mein Kampf* appeared in bookstores in Berlin. Subtitled "A Reckoning," it is a four-hundred-page diatribe on the alleged ills afflicting Germany: the ongoing threat of France, the need for more lebensraum, or "living space"—expanding Germany's borders eastward—and the degenerative effects of "mongrel" races on the German character. The superiority of the German race—and the imperative to maintain its "purity"—is the dominant note. "All the human culture, all the results of art, science, and technology that we see before us today," Hitler declared, "are almost exclusively the creative product of the Aryan."

Even in this early work, Hitler's anti-Semitism was on full display as he set the Jewish people in violent opposition to the Aryan race:

> No, the Jew possesses no culture-creating force of any sort, since the idealism, without which there is no true higher development of man, is

> not present in him and never was present. . . . Not through him does any progress of mankind occur, but in spite of him. . . . He is and remains the typical parasite, a sponger who like a noxious bacillus keeps spreading as soon as a favorable medium invites him. And the effect of his existence is also like that of spongers: wherever he appears, the host people die out after a shorter or longer period.[102]

A philosophical autobiography, *Mein Kampf* offered a blueprint for the nascent Nazi Party and a glimpse into the racist nightmare that would haunt and terrorize Europe from 1933 to 1945.

Tolkien will personally confront Hitler's racist outlook when, in the late 1930s, he is approached by Nazi publishers for the rights to translate and publish *The Hobbit* in Germany. It could be argued that one of Tolkien's objectives in *The Lord of the Rings* was to repudiate the racist narrative of Nazism and the militarism that supported it. For his part, Lewis will skewer Hitler for his anti-Semitism and will conceive of his diabolical satire, *The Screwtape Letters*, after hearing a radio broadcast of one of Hitler's speeches over the BBC.

THE CRISIS OF THE WEST

These two Oxford dons, in fact, were launching their academic careers at a moment of civilizational crisis. "As the years went by and youth departed and remembrance grew dim," observed Vera Brittain, "a deeper and ever deeper darkness would cover the young men who were once my contemporaries."[103] John Maynard Keynes, writing in 1919, lamented that the European states were "at the dead season of our fortunes." Quoting from *Prometheus Unbound*, he concluded: "Never in the lifetime of men now living has the universal element in the soul of man burnt so dimly."[104] J. P. Hodin saw a generation of writers and artists eager to sweep away social, political, and religious norms, while offering nothing of substance to replace them. "Everything sentimental and trivial was destroyed, but together with it everything that was vital."[105]

The disorientation of the postwar years took various forms in politics, philosophy, and the arts. In literature, however, it became "a cult of despair," a rejection of any solid basis for the worth and dignity of the human person.[106]

Support for this gloomy outlook came from many sources. Darwinian evolution seemed to make human choice and responsibility meaningless: a random product of biology. Herbert Spencer, and his social philosophy of "the survival of the fittest," left no room for selfless and heroic sacrifice. Sigmund Freud reduced religious belief to an infantile delusion. In the literature of the postwar years—especially in the English-speaking world—the idea of human life having a transcendent purpose was being abandoned.

Indeed, the hollowing out of human personality, a process begun in the mud and the trenches and the barbed wire of the Western Front, became a distinguishing feature of early twentieth-century man. Under these circumstances, the artist "confronted the world without any accepted understanding of human life," observed Walter Lippmann. "He has had to improvise his own understanding of life. That is a new thing in the experience of artists."[107] Literary editor R. Ellis Roberts discerned the same moral vacuum. "In such a world the artist can work only by his recollection of an older universe in which he has ceased to believe," he wrote. "Of all men, the artist needs God most."

As a person of faith, Tolkien perceived the dilemma of the modern mind. He believed that the artist functioned as a "sub-creator," whose talents and purposes were bound up with a purposeful Creator. "Fantasy remains a human right," he explained. "We make in our measure and in our derivative mode, because we are made: and not only made, but made in the image and likeness of a Maker."[108] Seen in this way, the fantasy story can illuminate truths about the real world and man's place in it. Without this anchor of belief, Modernist thinkers "must make a new God. And they offer us the artist himself."[109]

Lewis was wrestling with the same contradiction as his materialism collided with his imagination. His experiences of beauty were too profound to be despised. By the early 1920s, he had abandoned the cold rationalism that once kept him from admitting a spiritual dimension to reality. "It will be a comfort to me all my life," he wrote his father, "to know that the scientist and the materialist have not the last word: that Darwin and Spencer undermining ancestral beliefs stand themselves on a foundation of sand;

of gigantic assumptions and irreconcilable differences an inch below the surface."[110]

As he set out on his academic journey, Lewis rejected both the "shallow optimisms" and the "shallow pessimisms" that characterized his generation. Yet a question, which would appear in many forms in his writing, haunted him: "The sweetest thing in all my life has been the longing—to reach the Mountain, to find the place where all the beauty came from. . . . Do you think it all meant nothing, all the longing? The longing for home?"[111]

CHAPTER 2

ENEMIES OF THE PERMANENT THINGS

And now death, grim death, is looming up beside me. No longer far away, my doom has come upon me. Let me not then die without glory, without a struggle. But let me first do some great thing that shall be told among men hereafter.

—Homer, *The Iliad*

I will not walk with your progressive apes,
erect and sapient. Before them gapes
the dark abyss to which their progress tends.

—J. R. R. Tolkien, *Mythopoeia*

Their prison is only in their own minds, yet they are in that prison; and so afraid of being taken in that they cannot be taken out.

—C. S. Lewis, *The Last Battle*

For nine days in May of 1926, a national strike thrust England into a state of chaos. A million coal miners, protesting a cut in wages, walked off their jobs. They were soon joined in solidarity by tens of thousands of other workers from different industries: Transportation and dock workers, people working in iron, steel, construction, gas, electricity, and newspaper printing all stopped work. Students from the University of Oxford either joined picket lines or volunteered at strike committees to help keep supplies moving.

C. S. Lewis, a lecturer in English Language and Literature, wrote to his father about it: "Nearly all my pupils went off during the strike to unload boats or swing batons or drive engines." Lewis's brother, Warnie, "had some ugly adventures in London, but if he has not told you, perhaps they are not to be committed to the *written* word."[1]

There were quite a few ugly moments during the strike, which stretched from May 3 to 12 and affected nearly the entire population. The political left, advancing rapidly in postwar Britain, saw an opportunity. Their activities helped to make the strike one of the largest—and most violent—industrial disputes in British history. In London, vehicles were set on fire and others thrown into the Thames. There were fierce street battles, attacks on buses, trams, and rail stations. Mobs destroyed property in cities around the country.

During the 1918 election campaign, Prime Minister David Lloyd George had promised to make England "a fit country for heroes to live in." But for many returning soldiers, the economic impact of the Great War made his pledge look hollow. Postwar Britain faced mass unemployment, inflation, and revolutionary violence. In their influential book *The Decay of Capitalist Civilization* (1922), Beatrice and Sidney Webb delivered a withering critique of Britain's capitalist system that framed the socialist argument for the next two decades. "Capitalism need not hope to die quietly in its bed," they wrote. "It will die by violence, and civilization will perish with it."[2]

Their argument was years in the making. Britain had led the industrial revolution in the nineteenth century, which created unprecedented economic growth and technological advances. But it also attracted a mostly rural population into cities—into the factories—where they encountered disease, squalor, crime, and working conditions that made their lives extremely difficult.

Thus, the Communist Party of Great Britain was formed in 1920, with the long-expected death of the capitalist system in view. Its initial membership was modest but composed of true believers. They took their cues from Moscow and formed their own "revolutionary elite." By 1922, with financial support from the Soviet Union, communists were infiltrating trade unions and winning seats to Parliament.

During the 1926 General Strike, Soviet leader Joseph Stalin predicted that the British working class would realize that "Parliament, the constitution, the king and other attributes of bourgeois rule are nothing but a shield of the capitalist class against the proletariat." British Prime Minister Stanley Baldwin called the crisis "a challenge to the Parliament" and "the road to anarchy."

A FATEFUL FACULTY MEETING

On May 11, 1926, at the peak of the strike, as social radicals were hoping to shape the nation's political and economic future, members of Oxford's English faculty were meeting to discuss, among other things, the future of the English curriculum. Founded in the eleventh century, Oxford University set the standard for the study of classical literature and languages. But it was not until the nineteenth century that the university considered the study of English literature a legitimate academic discipline. It was a work in progress.

Among those attending the meeting in Merton Hall were R. F. W. Fletcher, George Gordon, Margaret Lucy Lee, and two recent additions to the faculty, J. R. R. Tolkien and C. S. Lewis. This was their first known encounter.

It got off to a bumpy start, not least because Tolkien was a Catholic and Lewis an Ulster Protestant. As Lewis recalled later: "At my first coming into the world, I had been (implicitly) warned never to trust a Papist, and at my first coming into the English Faculty (explicitly) never to trust a philologist. Tolkien was both."[3]

They were on opposite sides of the curriculum debate. Lewis was nourished on the works of English poets such as Edmund Spenser. He believed that English was best taught through literature dated after Geoffrey Chaucer (ca. 1400), or decidedly postmedieval. Tolkien wanted more attention to ancient and medieval English texts, requiring students to master Old and Middle English. "The English School here is a battleground," he told a former student, "and there is small peace and little sense to it."[4]

The two men spoke again after the meeting. "Your literature, Mr. Lewis, was written for the amusement of men between thirty and forty years old," Tolkien said. "If you think about it clearly, you really ought to vote yourselves out of existence."[5] Writing in his diary, Lewis complained that Tolkien's "pet abomination" was the idea of "liberal" studies, meaning a curriculum that did not demand the study of ancient and medieval languages. "He is a smooth, pale, fluent little chap. . . . There's no harm in him: only needs a smack or so."

Such was the start of their relationship: a typically contentious exchange in the academy over proposed changes in the curriculum. Yet given the profound influence these two academics would have on each other—and on generations of readers around the world—it must rank as one of the most important faculty meetings in the history of Oxford.

THE DECLINE OF THE WEST

Oxford could not shield itself from the forces of disorder that were mounting in the postwar years. Britain's national strike was just a symptom of the unrest that characterized much of Europe in the mid-1920s. Writing during this period, Percy Dearmer, an Anglican leader and author, saw troubling echoes of the previous century, when Europe was convulsed after the end of the Napoleonic Wars. "The parallel with our own moment is remarkable: a period of postwar exhaustion had begun, in 1815, as in 1918, with its social antagonisms and moral confusion, and civil disturbances more violent than anything we have known this time in England or America."[6]

The mind shaped by the trauma of the Great War was shell-shocked: Public intellectuals as well as ordinary citizens had become disoriented, disillusioned, and despairing. Many no longer believed in the concepts of individual virtue and heroism; many abandoned the ideals and institutions of European civilization. German philosopher Oswald Spengler had begun writing *The Decline of the West* shortly before the outbreak of the First World War. Germany's military collapse in 1918, however, plunged

Spengler into despair and deepened his cynicism about politics, morality, and religion.

"There are no eternal truths," Spengler proclaimed. "Every philosophy is the expression of its own and only its own time."[7] For Spengler, Pilate's question to Jesus is forever on the lips of the politician: What is truth? "The born statesman stands beyond true and false," he wrote. "He has convictions, certainly, that are dear to him, but he has them as a private person; no real politician ever felt himself tied to them when in action."[8] In the end, Spengler's approach to political life was indistinguishable from that of Machiavelli in *The Prince*.

Spengler identified symptoms of decline nearly everywhere: in politics, art, music, philosophy, economics, and religion. Like other civilizations, the West had experienced a period of cultural flourishing that was destined to come to an end. Its survival was "strictly limited and defined," extending over a few centuries, which could be "calculated from available precedents."[9] In this, Spengler replaced the Greek concept of fate with a pseudoscientific determinism. The West was at the end of its tether. "We have to reckon with the hard cold facts of a late life, to which the parallel is to be found not in Pericles' Athens but in Caesar's Rome."[10]

The Decline of the West touched a nerve. Similarly gloomy prognostications about European civilization began appearing. Based on a 1922 lecture series at Oxford, the distinguished missionary Albert Schweitzer published *The Decay and Restoration of Civilization*. "We are living today under the sign of the collapse of civilization," he warned. "It is clear now to everyone that the suicide of civilization is in progress." Public lecture programs with dark and anxious titles drew large crowds: "Can Civilization Be Saved?"; "The Tragedy of Human Existence"; "The Decay of Moral Culture"; and "Shortcuts to the Millenium." The Fabian Society, a socialist think tank, sponsored a series of 1923 lectures under the title "Is Civilization Decaying?"[11]

In *The Twilight Years: The Paradox of Britain Between the Wars*, Richard Overy argues that the popular theories of "impending decline and collapse" influenced nearly all cultural activities: intellectual, artistic, literary, scientific, and philosophical. "The fear that civilization was under threat," he writes, "was a promiscuous and enduring hallmark of the two decades that separated the first great war from the second."[12] Likewise, historian David

Reynolds observes that although authors such as T. S. Eliot provided a jarring literary response to the chaos after 1918, "the future of civilization was intensely debated by intellectuals all through the 1920s."[13]

Among the most important, especially in Great Britain, was H. G. Wells. Today we think of Wells as a pioneer in science fiction, author of works such as *The War of the Worlds*, *The Time Machine*, and *The First Men in the Moon*. But Wells had other interests, namely, an intense concern for the future of Western civilization. His materialist philosophy of history is on display in *The Outline of History* (1920), another sweeping reflection on Western society that emerged from the ashes of the Great War.

Wells got involved with the League of Nations Union, a group formed in 1918 in Britain to promote international peace and security. He was struck by the "brutal nationalism" that had not only fueled the First World War but was also still thriving in European capitals.[14] Wells sought to replace the "narrow, selfish, and conflicting nationalist traditions" taught in schools with a universal history of mankind.

> The essential task of men of goodwill in all states and countries remains the same, it is an educational task, and its very essence is to bring to the minds of all men everywhere, as a necessary basis for world co-operation, a new telling and interpretation, a common interpretation of history.

This was his prime motivation behind *The Outline of History*. In Wells's "new telling" of world history, the upward evolution of mankind depended, among other things, upon the transformation of traditional religion—namely, Christianity—into a world religion with an ethical code embraced by virtually everyone. Doctrines discredited by the science of Darwinism, such as original sin, should be put to rest. "And if there had been no fall, then the entire historical fabric of Christianity . . . collapses like a house of cards."[15] And not a moment too soon, Wells appeared to be saying. The "next stage of history," he wrote, was "a federation of all humanity" living harmoniously in a "World State."

The Outline of History became a publishing sensation, selling over 100,000 copies in its first year, and was quickly reprinted with a revised and illustrated edition soon to follow. All of this suggests that an emotional cleft had opened between the prewar generation and the generation of the 1920s and early '30s. Perhaps no thinker more powerfully exemplified this division than philosopher and historian Arnold Toynbee, whose monumental work, *A Study of History*, made him the English equivalent of Oswald Spengler. Like other authors of his day, his grand narrative of the rise and decline of civilizations had its roots in the 1914–18 war.

Toynbee worked for the British Foreign Office during the war and was a delegate to the 1919 Paris Peace Conference. He began to question the prewar assumptions about the progress and permanence of Western civilization. The result was the ten-volume *A Study of History*, in which Toynbee traces the trajectory of twenty-six civilizations. His prognosis for the West was gloomy. "The human race's prospects of survival were considerably better when we were defenseless against tigers than they are today when we have become defenseless against ourselves." Reviewers praised the book as "the greatest work of our time."

Historian H. R. Trevor-Roper, however, complained that Toynbee "seems to undermine our will, welcome our defeat, gloat over the extinction of our civilization. . . . It is a doctrine of messianic defeatism."[16] Through his lectures and radio broadcasts, Toynbee frequently compared the crisis in the West to the final crisis of the Roman Empire. "It is difficult to think of any intellectual of comparable public standing," writes Richard Overy, "who did more to undermine confidence in the survivability of Western civilization."[17]

A LITERARY COUNTEROFFENSIVE

The West seemed to carry the seeds of its own destruction: such was the intellectual mood. It produced a backlash, however, from an unlikely source. In ways largely unappreciated, J. R. R. Tolkien and C. S. Lewis became determined to reclaim and revitalize the cultural and spiritual ideals of Western civilization. They vigorously rejected the interpretations of human history currently in vogue.

In this task, Tolkien and Lewis drew strength from the literary traditions that had shaped the intellectual and cultural history of the West, from ancient Greece through the Middle Ages and the Renaissance. From their classical education, they learned how the Athenians were nurtured on the values exalted in *The Iliad* and *The Odyssey*, just as Romans were taught the heroic ideals expressed in *The Aeneid*. In their youth, both men were drawn to what Tolkien called "that noble northern spirit," evident in the literature of the Old North. The Norse myths and legends, dating back a millennium or more, drew upon an oral tradition of storytelling: tales of desperate battles and clashing armies.

"The most striking feature of Northern mythology, to the classically educated and Christian readers of early modern Europe, was that it was hopeless," writes Tom Shippey. Men march out to fight giants and monsters with no hope of victory—and yet remain unyielding and defiant. Thus, for Tolkien, the most stirring moment in *The Lord of the Rings* occurs when Gandalf, riding Shadowfax, confronts the Lord of the Nazgûl at the Gate of Gondor. The battlelines are drawn, and there is no question of negotiation, appeasement, or turning back. Suddenly, Gandalf hears "the Great horns of the North wildly blowing." Against all hope, the armies of Rohan had arrived at last.[18]

It was the Christian thinkers of the Middle Ages—the authors of works such as *Beowulf, The Divine Comedy*, and *Paradise Lost*—who built upon the pagan stories and offered a distinctly Christian vision of human life.

Tolkien and Lewis admired the medieval capacity to combine the highest ideals of paganism with Christianity: the cardinal virtues of justice, temperance, wisdom, and courage alongside the Christian virtues of faith, hope, and love. Thus, in *Beowulf,* Tolkien discerned a "theory of courage" that moved him deeply. "Let us by all means esteem the old heroes: men caught in the chains of circumstance or of their own character, torn between duties equally sacred, dying with their backs to the wall."[19] The earliest story of Tolkien's legendarium of Middle-earth, *The Fall of Gondolin*, written when he was a soldier on the Western Front, uplifts this heroic outlook. "Then did dread fall more heavily still upon the Gondothlim at the death of Rog and the loss of his battalion . . . and Penlod perished there in a lane with his back to the wall."[20]

The steely devotion to duty, despite the prospect of a dreadful defeat, was arguably a distinctive quality of the English soldier during the Great War. No one could forget the famous directive issued by Field Marshal Sir

Douglas Haig on April 11, 1918, anticipating the horrific spring offensive by the German Army:

> There is no other course open to us but to fight it out. Every position must be held to the last man: there must be no retirement. With our backs to the wall, and believing in the justice of our cause, each one of us must fight on to the end. The safety of our homes and the freedom of mankind depend alike upon the conduct of each one of us at this critical moment.[21]

The medieval mind anchored these ideals in a belief in spiritual realities that permeated the natural world. "He is like a man being conducted through an immense cathedral," wrote Lewis, "not like one in a shoreless sea."[22] In an increasingly secular age, Tolkien and Lewis devoted themselves to transmitting this Christian vision through their scholarship, lectures, tutorials, and, of course, through their imaginative literature. Their collaboration in this grand project began in 1926, shortly after their first encounter. It began with a somewhat eccentric reading club.

Earlier in the year, Tolkien launched a literary club for Oxford dons interested in translating and reading aloud Icelandic sagas.[23] Tolkien called his club the Kolbitars, an Icelandic word for people who sit so close to the fire that they seem to be "biting the coals." He invited Lewis to join them. It marked a turning point in their relationship.

One of the works they read together was the Völsunga saga, a story about a dragon-slayer named Sigurd on a quest to save Princess Signy from a wicked king.[24] Of all his childhood reading, Tolkien enjoyed this story from "the nameless North" the best. "Such lands," he said, "were pre-eminently desirable."[25] This "strange and glorious tale," he declared during his student days at King Edward's School, embodied "the highest epic genius struggling out of savagery into complete and conscious humanity."[26] Not long after Tolkien joined the English faculty at Exeter College, he began delivering his own weekly lectures on the story. In other words, the Völsunga saga was very close to Tolkien's heart.

Considered one of the most important examples of the heroic sagas of Germanic legend, the Völsunga saga extols the concepts of honor, loyalty, and glory. "When men encounter enemies in the fight," its author advises, "a robust heart is better than a sharp sword." An important element in the story is a golden ring, which brings a curse upon all who possess it. There is also the recurring appearance of Odin, a Norse deity often depicted as a hooded old man and associated with wisdom and war. Consciously or not, Tolkien's thorough embrace of this ancient story almost certainly inspired elements of his own epic tale, *The Lord of the Rings.*

Given their contentious introduction, why did Tolkien invite Lewis into his group? He must have sensed a kindred spirit, and he was exactly right: Lewis's early discovery of *The Ring of the Nibelung* had awakened "an insatiable appetite for Nordic mythology."[27] It never left him. "For Lewis, it was a great opportunity, something he always wanted to do, which was to read the great myths of the ancient North in the original language," says Simon Horobin. "He loved these stories since he was a child."[28] As Lewis explained to Arthur Greeves: "You will be able to imagine what a delight this is to me and how, even in turning over the pages of my Icelandic Dictionary, the mere name of a god or giant catching my eye will sometimes throw me back fifteen years into a wild dream of northern skies."[29]

Tolkien and Lewis both believed that these tales upheld ancient virtues that were worth recalling, preserving—and defending. In this they were at odds with a literary establishment that had consigned these virtues to the dustbin of history.

THE LOGIC OF EUGENICS

To grasp the nature of their dissent, consider the dominant cultural and political responses to the trauma of the Great War: the radical schemes to rescue Western civilization from collapse and reconstruct it on an entirely new moral and ideological foundation.

For some, salvation would be achieved by using the tools of science to improve the genetic stock of humanity. In a journal entry dated June 13, 1926, Lewis noted, "Started reading G. Chesterton's Eugenics and Other Evils." For a time, the Catholic thinker G. K. Chesterton stood nearly alone among public intellectuals in his opposition to eugenics, what he called "terrorism by tenth-rate professors." In *Eugenics and Other Evils,*

Chesterton declared that the ideology of eugenics must be destroyed if human freedom was to be preserved. The eugenic idea, he wrote, "is a thing no more to be bargained about than poisoning."

British anthropologist Francis Galton, who coined the term "eugenics"—from the Greek for "good birth"—was among the first to argue that scientific techniques for breeding healthier animals should be applied to human beings. To many intellectuals the catastrophe of the First World War, in addition to the worsening problems of poverty, crime, and social breakdown, suggested a sickness in the racial stock. Book titles in the 1920s reveal the fear of a biological crisis in the making: *Social Decay and Degeneration*; *The Need for Eugenic Reform*; *Racial Decay*; *Sterilization of the Unfit*; and *The Twilight of the White Races.*

Perhaps the most revealing description of the eugenic mindset comes from Julian Huxley, a celebrity zoologist and the grandson of Thomas Huxley, a disciple of Charles Darwin. To the so-called scientific community, the "unfit" represented an existential threat to civilization:

> What are we going to do? Every defective man, woman and child is a burden. Every defective is an extra body for the nation to feed and clothe, but produce little or nothing in return. Every defective needs care, and immobilizes a certain quantum of energy and goodwill which could otherwise be put to constructive ends. Every defective is an emotional burden—a sorrow to someone, and in himself, a creature doomed, when unassisted, to live an incomplete and sub-human existence. Not only that, but if their numbers continue to increase, the burden . . . will gradually drag us down.[30]

The fear of perpetual racial decline—particularly among educated whites—was one of the factors driving the early birth control movement. Margaret Sanger, founder of Planned Parenthood and one of the movement's pioneers, was brutally frank about the stakes involved. In *The Pivot of Civilization* (1922), she regards "stern" birth control measures as a pathway to a new humanity, "flowering into beautiful expression."

More importantly, eugenic techniques would serve as a prophylactic against a degenerative humanity:

> The emergency problem of segregation and sterilization must be faced immediately. Every feeble-minded girl or woman of the hereditary type, especially the moron class, should be segregated during the reproductive period. Otherwise, she is almost certain to bear imbecile children, who in turn are just as certain to breed other defectives. . . . Moreover, when we realize that each feeble-minded person is a potential source of an endless progeny of defect, we prefer the policy of immediate sterilization, of making sure that parenthood is absolutely prohibited to the feeble-minded.[31]

In his preface to Sanger's book, H. G. Wells praised the author for her "extraordinary breadth of outlook" and "the real scientific quality of her mind." He was not alone. The anxiety over "race suicide" drove public debates in Great Britain and the United States: marriage laws banning the union of those considered defective; restrictions on immigration of undesirable races; and sterilization to prevent the propagation of the "unfit." Those considered to be "degenerates," "imbeciles," or "feeble-minded" would be targeted. By the late 1930s, thirty states enacted sterilization laws, and tens of thousands of people were sterilized, most of them against their will.[32]

"The concept appealed," explains Richard Overy, "because it gave to the popular malaise a clear scientific foundation."[33] More than that, it offered a "scientific" solution to the malaise.

It is hard to overstate the degree to which eugenics captured the imagination of the medical and scientific communities in the 1920s and '30s. Eugenics societies were supported by Nobel Prize–winning scientists. Premier scientific organizations, such as the American Museum of Natural History, and academic institutions, such as Harvard and Princeton, preached the eugenics gospel. They held conferences, published papers, provided research funding, and advocated for sterilization laws.

In "The Case for Eugenics," published in *The Sociological Review* in 1926, Julian Huxley exulted in the fact that, thanks to new discoveries in the "laws of heredity," the concept of eugenics was "no longer a fantastic or monstrous idea, but a practicable and indeed urgent piece of applied science."[34] Triumphalism in human potential, backed by scientific techniques, was the keynote. "With Darwin and the acceptance of the theory of

Evolution," Huxley declared, "the human race realized, in a way impossible to it before, that man was in control of his own destinies, and could effect alterations in his own nature."[35]

In *Eugenics and Other Evils*, Chesterton explained that at the heart of the eugenics movement was an utterly materialistic view of the human person: man as laboratory rat. "Materialism is really our established Church," he wrote, "for the Government will really help it to persecute its heretics." The shocking reality of this moment was that the scientific establishment had become an ally in this campaign.

As we'll see, Tolkien and Lewis fiercely resisted this materialist outlook. They infused their novels with spiritual qualities, bestowing upon their characters a transcendent source of worth and dignity. Indeed, the dehumanization of the individual, through the abuse of science and technology, emerges as a major theme in their works. Think of the mutant orcs in *The Lord of the Rings*, who are designed to serve as tools of Sauron and the kingdom of Mordor. Or consider the villains in Lewis's *Ransom Trilogy*, determined to achieve human perfectibility at all costs. "Man has got to take charge of man," declares Lord Feverstone in *That Hideous Strength*. "That means, remember, that some men have got to take charge of the rest."[36]

THE FASCIST DISEASE

Racial theories about the decline of Western civilization not only propelled the pseudoscientific movement of eugenics. The fear of race degeneration galvanized an entirely new political movement: fascism. Under the fascist view, the West had become weak and corrupt, and its rejuvenation depended upon an intensely muscular and racial form of nationalism.

The ideology of fascism was thrust upon the world stage by Benito Mussolini, who despised what he called "the putrid corpse" of liberal democracy. "Liberalism denied the State in the name of the individual," he proclaimed. "Fascism reasserts the rights of the State as expressing the real essence of the individual."

His was an unlikely success story. In Italy's general election of November 16, 1919, Mussolini and his fascist allies suffered humiliating losses. Meanwhile, the socialists won roughly 1.8 million votes and claimed 156 seats in the Chamber of Deputies, making them the largest political party. The left-wing paper, *Avanti!*, declared Mussolini a political corpse; his coffin was paraded through the streets of Milan, along with dirge-singing demonstrators.

The funeral celebrations were premature. Efforts to reconvert Italy's war economy were flailing; strikes and riots over the cost of living accelerated. Trains, banks, and public buildings were attacked by mobs all over Italy. Fascism appeared to be the only way to stem the communist tide. Writes Christopher Hibbert in *Mussolini: The Rise and Fall of Il Duce*: "The Fascists put themselves forward as saviors of the country, the only force by which Bolshevism could be checked and strangled."[37]

In the end, Mussolini did not have to seize power; he was offered it by King Victor Emmanuel III. Immediately after forming a coalition government, he demanded from the Chamber of Deputies unrestricted authority to implement his reforms. He was granted these powers by a majority of 275 votes to 90. By 1926, Mussolini had outlawed all opposition parties.

Remarkably, he did not try to conceal the totalitarian nature of his vision of the state:

> The Fascist conception of the State is all embracing; outside of it no human or spiritual values can exist, much less have value. Thus understood, Fascism is totalitarian, and the Fascist State—a synthesis and a unit inclusive of all values—interprets, develops, and potentiates the whole life of a people.

Although his fascist revolution would captivate Adolf Hitler—who would eclipse him on the world stage—it was Mussolini's Italy that introduced the fascist virus into the bloodstream of Europe. And the virus spread rapidly. Before the end of the decade, fascist or quasi-fascist groups appeared in Austria, Germany, Greece, Hungary, Poland, Portugal, and Spain.

Like the other great totalitarian project, Soviet communism, fascism was built upon a personality cult and sustained through fear, political cant, and propaganda. "The political idea of the man who is able to persuade mass movements to do appalling things was a huge factor in the 1920 and 1930s," explains British author Julia Golding. "Other literary figures of their day were attracted to it. Tolkien and Lewis were never taken in by it."[38] Persuasive speech turned toward evil ends, in fact, will play a role in the totalitarian societies envisaged in their novels. "And ever Wormtongue's whispering was in your ears," writes Tolkien in *The Lord of the Rings*, "poisoning your thoughts, chilling your heart, weakening your limbs, while others watched and could do nothing, for your will was in his keeping."[39]

It is chilling to recall that the seminal Nazi propaganda film of the 1930s was entitled *Triumph of the Will.* The wills of countless millions, already being captured by the sweet promises of political messiahs, would soon be caught up in a whirlwind of violence and suffering.

THE PROMISE OF PEACE

Throughout the 1920s, however, the shadows cast by the totalitarian project were barely visible to most Europeans, and even less so to their American counterparts. The political slogan of the hour was "disarmament."

The push for massive cuts in the size of national armies began even before the end of World War I. It was one of President Woodrow Wilson's "Fourteen Points" upon which he hoped to build a new international order. The American president wanted national armaments "reduced to the lowest point consistent with domestic safety." Virtually the exact language from Wilson's January 1918 speech to Congress was inserted into the Treaty of Versailles.

Fears of another arms race led to a series of international peace conferences, where delegates pledged arms reductions and the elimination of warships. For the first time in Western history, an international peace movement came into existence.

Peace organizations soon attracted many thousands of members on both sides of the Atlantic. The British No More War Movement, for example, sponsored a press conference in Geneva with Albert Einstein, who urged disarmament. Members of the clergy drove much of the activity. They had given the Great War their eager blessing; many had turned it into a holy crusade. By the 1920s, churches across all denominations were passing resolutions renouncing war. Surveys of clergymen found that most would not support any future war or serve as military chaplains in wartime.

Although the Great War was originally described as "the war to end war" and "the war for civilization," anxieties about another global conflict—with weapons of even greater destructive power—deepened throughout the decade. In a speech in January 1927, Stanley Baldwin, a future British prime minister, asked starkly: "Who in Europe does not know that one more war in the West, and the civilization of the ages will fall with as great a crash as that of Rome?"[40]

These fears culminated in an unprecedented diplomatic moment in the summer of 1928, when signatories from sixty-five nations agreed to abandon war as a foreign policy option. Known as the Kellog-Briand Pact of Paris (named after the American and French diplomats who led the negotiations), the agreement united "the civilized nations of the world in a common renunciation of war as an instrument of their national policy." Even the US Senate, usually in an isolationist mood, ratified the treaty.

The Paris Pact raised hopes that a new global spirit of peace was on the move, championed by the League of Nations. As Gilbert Murray, the British classicist, expressed it at the time, the covenantal language of the League marked "the Great Repentance" or renunciation of war.

In his book *The Ordeal of This Generation* (1929), Murray offered a detailed defense of the key provisions of the League and the necessity of disarmament. Nations that resorted to war, he intoned, "must be treated as an enemy of civilization."[41] Before the end of the decade, antiwar novels such as *All Quiet on the Western Front, Goodbye to All That,* and *A Farewell to Arms* became bestsellers. Authors and activists such as Vera Brittain persuaded many Britons disillusioned by the carnage of the Great War to embrace pacifism. "If only now, *now,* while we were still young, we could oust the old men and women, the worshippers of precedent, privilege and property, whose minds had been set before the War!"[42]

TOLKIEN'S TRAGIC HEROES

While Great Britain and much of Europe were working feverishly to keep the peace, Tolkien was delivering lectures on medieval tales of war. His weekly lectures in 1928 included *Beowulf*, *The Fight at Finnesburg*, and *The Battle of Maldon*. Each of these stories not only upholds the virtues of the heroic warrior; each also touches upon some tragic dimension of war and the human condition. Together they helped shape Tolkien's imagination as he constructed his mythic story about an existential struggle for the civilization of Middle-earth.

Beowulf contains numerous references to the collective history of the Germanic tribes that occupied northern Europe during the Dark Ages. For Tolkien, one of the most tantalizing was *The Fight at Finnesburg*, only a fragment of which survives.

The "episode," as it is called, is mentioned after Beowulf defeats the monster Grendel in the mead hall of King Hrothgar the Dane. To mark the victory, the king's bard sings in celebration: It is a story about Finn, king of the Frisians, a border people caught between the Danes to the north and the mighty Franks to the south. Finn and his soldiers survive a brutal attack. He makes peace with his adversaries but is later killed, his hall burned to the ground, and his queen and treasure taken away.

"The tragic hero of this drama is Finn, caught up in conflicts not of his own making and destroyed by his own generosity," writes Oxford scholar Malcolm Godden. For the generation that endured the 1914–18 war, he observes, this story of ancient grievances instigating a preventable war sounded eerily familiar. When Tolkien delivered his first lectures on the poem, barely a decade after the end of the First World War, "it can have lost nothing from its echoes of recent events, with its picture of two great powers anxious to maintain peace and dragged into ruinous conflict by resentful exiles from smaller nations, pursuing their old vendettas."[43]

Tolkien's other significant lecture topic, *The Battle of Maldon*, caught his interest when he was an Oxford undergraduate. Written in the tenth century, the poem commemorates a decisive battle between the Anglo-Saxons and the invading Vikings in 991. There is a religious subtext to the poem, as the Anglo-Saxons are described as God-fearing, pitted against the pagan Vikings.

> Then they went forth, they cared not for their lives; fiercely did the men of his household put them into the fight, those grim wielders of

> the spears, and God they prayed that they might avenge their lord and patron, and compass a slaughter among their foes.[44]

Some scholars believe that next to Beowulf, *The Battle of Maldon* should rank as "the Old English poem that most influenced Tolkien's fiction."[45] That may be right. In his introductory notes, Tolkien extols the value of the poem in illuminating the history and character of the English people. "And this thing preserved (by chance?!) survives to overthrow the text-book estimate of the England of Æthelred," he writes, "and lets in more light than any other document upon the grievous struggles and disasters and the heroism of the English."[46]

Tolkien liked to quote its lines describing the fortitude of the English even in defeat: "We shall be the sterner, heart the bolder, spirit the greater as our strength diminishes." As Malcolm Guite explains, "The good guys lose, but that doesn't matter. It's just a question of being on the right side. And the right side is not the winning side. The right side is *the right side*."[47]

PROMETHEUS: BOUND AND UNBOUND

The concept of heroic sacrifice for a noble cause—even with little or no hope of success—held the same powerful allure for Lewis. As Tolkien was lecturing on medieval war stories, Lewis turned his attention to one of the most influential of Greek tragedies, *Prometheus Bound*. Over the course of a long evening on January 25, 1927, Lewis and his friend Owen Barfield read and translated the poem together. It seemed to have a catalytic effect.

Written by the poet Aeschylus in the fifth century BC, the story of *Prometheus Bound* could be described as a civil war: a contest between mankind, represented by the sacrificial god Prometheus, and Zeus, the supreme god of the Greeks and portrayed as a tyrant and enemy of humanity.

In this retelling of an ancient myth, Prometheus—against the wishes of Zeus—gives fire to mankind to prevent their destruction by the gods. "I gave them hope," declares Prometheus, "and so turned away their eyes from death." As punishment, Zeus chains Prometheus to a remote rock, where he is taunted and tortured. What follows is a series of speeches in which the overwhelming power of Zeus is pitted against the immovable will of Prometheus.

As the play unfolds, Prometheus explains the extent of his help to mankind. He not only brought fire but awakened the light of reason, showed them how to discern the movements of the stars, and taught them medicine, mining, sailing, and more. "Hear the sum of the whole matter in the compass of one brief word—every art possessed by man comes from Prometheus."[48]

As Lewis knew quite well, the character of Prometheus has been both admired and feared among Western writers and revolutionaries. Karl Marx called him "the most eminent saint and martyr in the philosophical calendar."[49] Percy Shelley, in his masterwork *Prometheus Unbound* (1820), portrayed him as the champion of humanity against every form of tyranny and oppression.[50] Shelley's wife, Mary Shelley, however, took a dimmer view, warning of the corrupting influence of science and technology. Her science fiction classic, *Frankenstein: The Modern Prometheus* (1818), delivered a stark rebuke to mankind's impulse to play God. Mary Shelley, it seems, was prophetic: In *Mein Kampf*, Hitler refers to the Aryan race as "the Prometheus of mankind from whose bright forehead the divine spark of genius has sprung at all times."

Several themes appear in Aeschylus's story, all of which were being contested in the postwar era: the idea of progress, human achievement, resistance to tyranny, and the value of religious authority. In doubting the justice of Prometheus's punishment, and in laying bare the painful moral choices he had to face, the play ranks as one of the first great tragedies of Western literature. "At issue is the justice, or not, of his punishment for rebelling against the supreme deity on behalf of mankind," writes classical scholar Joel Agee. "In his protest against cruel abuses of power . . . Prometheus speaks for us and to us."[51]

The mythic story seemed to speak to Lewis in a fresh and powerful way. As we've seen, Lewis's experience in the First World War deepened his skepticism; he'd become something of a moral cynic. Yet by the late 1920s, he had shaken off his atheism. One of the human links in the chain was Owen Barfield.

The two men first met in 1919; both had returned to Oxford after the war to study English literature.[52] A Christian and a fierce anti-materialist,

Barfield was drawn into a debate with Lewis, still an atheist, beginning in 1923—they called it "the Great War"—about the existence of God and transcendent realities. Barfield recalled the exchange vividly: "He didn't believe that any access to the spiritual or supernatural world was possible for the human mind, and that any human mind that supposed that it had such access was living in a world of fantasy."[53]

Barfield's grandson, Owen Barfield, emphasizes their contrasting views of human imagination: "For Lewis, the imagination was a tool to be used and delighted in. But for Barfield, imagination was a route to truth."[54] For his part, Lewis admitted to Barfield "the extent to which your views occupy my mind when I am not with you" and "the animosity I feel towards them."[55] Nevertheless, they developed a great respect for each other and a close friendship blossomed.[56] The argument continued, in letters and in person, throughout the 1920s.

The two men made it a custom to spend weekends together reading the great books: the works of Homer, Virgil, and Dante. On January 25, 1927, they set out to tackle *Prometheus Bound*. Traveling from his home in London, Barfield met up with Lewis in Oxford to translate the work together. As Lewis recorded in his journal,

> It was delightful to see him. After a confused chat of philosophy and jokes, we settled down to read Aeschylus' *Prometheus* together, as we had promised ourselves to do. After an hour or so we went out and dined at the Town & Gown. Coming back we sat up till half past one to finish our play, sometimes convulsed with laughter at our own literal translation. . . . I understood the play better this time. The wild defiance at the end must definitely (for a Greek) have stamped Prometheus as one of "the former mighty ones."[57]

The two spent the next morning together, discussing "whether the death of a person one really cares about would abolish the horror of the supernatural or increase it." They no longer argued intensively about these ultimate questions; something had changed. "I was sorry to see him go," Lewis wrote. "These meetings are always beyond expectation."[58]

The effect of Barfield's visit lingered. "Felt better in my mind than I have done for ages," Lewis wrote later that day. As Lewis headed for bed, he went to the window. "Pulled up my blind to see the stars, thought suddenly of Bergson: then of how I have been playing the devil with my nerves by letting things I really don't believe in and vague possibilities haunt my imagination," he noted. "I had a strong conviction of having turned a corner."[59]

If, when Barfield arrived, Lewis had nurtured doubts that there was a reality behind his spiritual intimations, he apparently put them to rest. Why did Lewis think immediately of Bergson?

Henri Bergson had challenged Lewis's materialism a decade earlier, when Lewis read *Creative Evolution* from his hospital bed during the war. Bergson's objection to the randomness of evolution strengthened Lewis's belief that his experiences of beauty were not senseless events, that there was something authentic about them. In his annotated copy of Bergson's work, he noted that strict Darwinism "has to lean on a marvelous series of accidents."[60]

By his own description, Lewis "turned a corner" in his outlook on life that evening. In this instance, great literature, deep friendship, and a taste of beauty all seemed to play a role. He was still a good distance from coming to faith in Jesus Christ. But he could no longer accept the idea of an indifferent universe in which the experiences of joy, love, and longing carried no ultimate meaning.

If this is true, it helps to explain the much more dramatic moment in Lewis's journey to faith that occurred, by his own account, during Oxford's Trinity term of 1929 (between April 28 and June 22). It involved both an emotional and intellectual surrender—"total surrender, the absolute leap in the dark, were demanded"—but not yet to the person of Jesus.

> You must picture me alone in that room in Magdalen, night after night, feeling whenever my mind lifted even for a second from my work, the steady, unrelenting approach of Him whom I so earnestly desired not to meet. That which I greatly feared had at last come upon me. . . . I gave in, and admitted that God was God, and knelt and prayed: perhaps that night, the most dejected and reluctant convert in all England.[61]

Lewis's conversion was to theism, a genuine belief in a sovereign, all-powerful Creator. Many voices—from classical and romantic literature, from his experiences of longing, from his growing circle of Oxford friends—had propelled him along the way. Lewis recalled the moment: "Everyone and everything had joined the other side."

BEREN AND LÚTHIEN: A HEART EXPOSED

Relationships were crucial. In his book *The Four Loves*, published near the end of his life, Lewis reflected on the meaning of friendship. Real friendship begins, he wrote, when two people discover that they "are on the same secret road" in their pursuit of truth or beauty. If a date could be placed for when this realization dawned upon Lewis and Tolkien, it probably would be November 18, 1929.[62]

Lewis took the initiative. After they attended a university club meeting together, he invited Tolkien to his rooms at Magdalen College. Lewis lit a fire, and over the course of the evening, they realized that great myths moved them in the same way.

They talked about the tales of Asgard, the dwelling place of the gods in Norse mythology, roughly akin to Mount Olympus in Greek mythology. One of the most prominent stories is about Balder, which Lewis first encountered in a poem by Henry Wadsworth Longfellow. It describes Balder's death, a moment of shocking revelation that the gods were mortal: "I heard a voice that cried / Balder the beautiful / Is dead, is dead!" The words stirred Lewis deeply, uplifting him "into huge regions of northern sky. . . . I desired with almost sickening intensity something never to be described."[63] He called the story "a great myth, a thing of inexhaustible value."[64]

Tolkien had made the study of Norse mythology one of his private passions. Perhaps like none of Lewis's other friends, he was able to embrace, with nearly equal enthusiasm, pagan literature and Christian belief. For Tolkien, a committed Catholic, there was no essential quarrel between myth, imagination, and the historic Christian faith. Lewis must have found this outlook deeply appealing, especially after his conversion to theism.

It is easy to imagine the two men quoting lines from these ancient stories, catching the gleam of excitement in each other's eyes as the fire crackled beside them. As Lewis described their meeting in a letter to Arthur Greeves, dated December 3, 1929, "One week I was up till 2:30 on Monday, talking to the Anglo-Saxon professor Tolkien, who came back with me to College from a society and sat discoursing of the gods and giants of Asgard for three hours, then departing in the wind and rain—who could turn him out, for the fire was bright and the talk good."

Their evening together—immersed in an intense discussion of evocative, epic literature—made a deep impression on both men. A few weeks later, Tolkien shared with Lewis a long narrative poem that he had begun writing in 1925 and had been working on ever since. Tolkien had just completed another collection of verses, and he wanted his friend's opinion. It is considered the most personal story in all of Tolkien's mythology: the tale of Beren and Lúthien.

> Among the tales of sorrow and ruin that come down to us from the darkness of those days there are yet some in which amid weeping there is joy and under the shadow of death light that endures.[65]

The inspiration for the story, first known as the *Lay of Leithian*, occurred when Tolkien was a soldier in the Great War. He was on leave, recovering from trench fever, when he and Edith slipped away to the countryside, to a woodland glade in Yorkshire. Edith danced for him in the sunlight. In his story, Tolkien imagines Edith as Lúthien, an immortal Elvish princess, and casts himself as Beren, the mortal man. He calls Beren "the outlawed mortal" who, with the help of Lúthien, "penetrates the stronghold of the Enemy" and acquires one of the precious Silmarilli, the jewels of light, from the Iron Crown. He succeeds in his quest—"where all the armies and warriors have failed"—and is rewarded with the hand of Lúthien. The first marriage of mortal and immortal is achieved.[66]

It would be a mistake, though, to regard the *Lay of Leithian* exclusively as a love story. The capture of the Silmaril leads to catastrophe, as the desire for the jewels brings disaster upon all the kingdoms of the Elves. As Tolkien later explained, this initial contact of Men and Elves foreshadows the events of the later Ages. "Here we meet, among other things, the first example of the motive (to become dominant in Hobbits) that the great policies of world history, 'the wheels of the world,' are often turned not by the Lords and Governors, even gods, but by the seemingly unknown and weak."[67]

Remarkably, Tolkien has shared with his friend a story that will play an immensely important role in his legendarium of Middle-earth. We are introduced to Morgoth, "the Black Enemy," and Sauron, bent on the destruction of Middle-earth. We learn of the land of the Elves and their shared lineage with Men. Tolkien himself called it "the chief of the stories of the *Silmarillion*."[68] It was the one that Tolkien loved best of all his stories, in part because it was modeled on his relationship with Edith.

Julia Golding, director of the Oxford Center for Fantasy, sees it as a courageous decision for Tolkien to share his unfinished poetry with Lewis. "This was an odd thing if you think about it. These are two grown-up men, both professors at Oxford, very serious stuff. And Tolkien shares his little love story about elves," she says. "Lewis understood that Tolkien was exposing his breast, that he's saying, 'stab me here.' That's what he's saying when he offers this story to him."[69]

The response from his friend must have struck Tolkien like a bolt from the heavens. Lewis not only praised the poem but offered an initial critique to help improve it.

> I can honestly say that it is ages since I have had an evening of such delight. . . . Two things that come out clearly are the sense of reality in the background and the mythical value: the essence of a myth being that it should have no taint of allegory to the maker and yet should suggest incipient allegories to the reader. . . . Detailed criticisms (including grumbles at individual lines) will follow.[70]

Lewis fired off at least fourteen pages of critique with no shortage of "grumbles." He approached Tolkien's text as if it were "an ancient and anonymous work" that required an academic commentary. This was a deliberate strategy on Lewis's part: a way to deliver justified praise as well as tough-minded criticism. Tolkien incorporated many of Lewis's proposed modifications into his next draft of the story.

Thus, a moment of vulnerability that could easily have ended badly—throwing a wet blanket on their relationship—would prove to be a turning point in both their lives.[71]

A CONSPIRACY OF THE DONS

Soon after this exchange, Tolkien and Lewis decided to lead an effort among like-minded faculty to reform the Oxford English School. They called their group The Cave, after the Cave of Adullam in the Old Testament book of 1 Samuel where David sought refuge from Saul, who was trying to kill him. The Cave of Adullam became a base of operations for David, "the implication being," explains biographer Humphrey Carpenter, that the Tolkien-Lewis faction was "conspiring against . . . the reigning party in the English School."[72] Members included Nevill Coghill and Hugo Dyson, as well as female faculty sympathetic to the cause. They met regularly and shared ideas over casual dinners.

The conspirators prevailed, reinforcing the principle that the development of English, as both a living and a literary language, should be studied from its earliest roots.[73] The Old and Middle English parts of the curriculum were made more appealing to undergraduates, but the study of Victorian literature effectively fell by the wayside. Anything published after 1832 was ruled out. Jane Austen and Percy Shelley made the grade, but authors such as Emily Brontë and Charles Dickens were rejected. Lewis was triumphant. "This is a great feather in my cap," he wrote to his brother, "especially as next year is the first exam held under the syllabus, which my party and I have forced upon the junto after much hard fighting."[74]

It's important to realize what the collaboration between Tolkien and Lewis in the curriculum debate represented. This was not merely the triumph of an idiosyncratic attachment to old languages. It was another skirmish in their campaign to preserve the classical Christian inheritance of the West.

From their youth both men had been nourished by the languages and literature of ancient and medieval Europe. Through it they were introduced to a *moral universe*: life-and-death contests over noble causes, where honor was won or lost on the field of battle, where the concepts of sacrifice, valor, fidelity, and faith carried weight. Both men sensed that these ideals were under a modern assault—a "great divide," as Lewis would call it—which had begun in earnest in the nineteenth century and was reaching a fearsome climax in their own day.

They were determined to fight back, through the content of the English curriculum as well as through their imaginative writing. "I think they saw in the ancient resources they had, in the older books they were reading, not an irrelevant world into which you could escape, but curiously enough exactly the diagnostic tool they need to critique the world they were in," explains Malcolm Guite. "And they did so to devastating effect."[75]

FAITH, MYTH, AND GEORGE MACDONALD

The deepening friendship between Tolkien and Lewis—now as co-conspirators to defend the Western literary tradition—provides the emotional backdrop for their famous conversation at Oxford's Addison's Walk on September 19, 1931.

Lewis had invited Tolkien and Hugo Dyson to dine with him at Magdalen College, and after dinner they walked the footpath that snakes along the River Cherwell. Their talk focused on the nature and meaning of myths and their relationship to the Christian faith. For many years Lewis had taken for granted the accepted academic view of Christianity: the idea that, although Jesus existed as a historical figure, "all the other tomfoolery about a virgin birth, magic healings, apparitions and so forth is on exactly the same footing as any other mythology."

Tolkien insisted that Lewis was mistaken in believing that the pre-Christian myths contained nothing in the way of universal truth. Ancient tales of a semidivine figure who is killed and then reborn appeared across cultures: Adonis among the Greeks, Osiris among the Egyptians, Mithra among the Babylonians and Persians, and Balder among the Scandinavians. These stories expressed ideals and longings that had their origin in the Creator. Mythmaking—what Tolkien called "mythopoeia"—was an imaginative way of reflecting God's attributes. The great myths, Tolkien explained, offered a glimpse of God's redemptive purpose in the death and resurrection of Jesus, "a splintered fragment of the true light."

It was a staggering, transformational moment: Perhaps no other individual in the world could have spoken so decisively into Lewis's mind and shattered his misconceptions about Christianity and its relationship to mythic literature.[76]

If there was one author who had prepared Lewis for this moment, it was George MacDonald. He was the silent traveler with them on Addison's Walk that night. "I found that I was still with MacDonald and that he had accompanied me all the way," Lewis later recalled, "and that I was now at last ready to hear from him much that he could not have told me at that first meeting."[77]

Even during his years as an atheist, Lewis could not resist MacDonald's charm. As he recorded in a journal entry dated January 11, 1923, "After this I read Macdonald's *Phantastes* over my tea, which I have read many times and which I really believe fills for me the place of a devotional book." His attachment to the author never waned. In the months leading up to his conversation with Tolkien and Dyson, Lewis was reading more works from MacDonald. In a letter to Arthur Greeves dated August 31, 1930, Lewis thanked him profusely for "the arrival of the Macdonalds"—his friend had sent him three of the author's novels. "Thanks, Arthur, again and again. I know nothing that gives me such a feeling of spiritual healing, of being washed, as to read G. Macdonald."[78]

On January 17, 1931, Lewis wrote to Arthur to express his enthusiasm over his latest MacDonald discovery, *What's Mine's Mine*. Considered MacDonald's finest novel, its portrait of the Scottish Highlands is awash in the experience of God's presence in nature. Its characters are richly drawn, earthy and yet possessing qualities that suggest something deeper. "An old-fashioned easy chair stood by the chimney; one sat in it whom to see was to forget her surroundings," writes MacDonald. "In middle age she is still beautiful, with the rare beauty that shines from the root of the being."[79]

Biblical concepts—the danger of pride, for example—are also laced throughout the story. "It . . . quite frankly subordinates story to doctrine," Lewis observed. "But such doctrine. Some of the conversations in this book I hope to re-read many times."[80] Lewis wrote Arthur again on February 23, "almost relieved" to hear that his friend shared his views of the book. "Yes, you are right in saying that it is good not despite, but because of, its preaching—or rather (preaching is a bad word) its spiritual knowledge. So many cleverer writers strike one as quite *childish* after MacDonald: they seem not even to have begun to understand so many things."[81]

What was it that George MacDonald achieved through his imaginative works that so impressed Lewis, who still did not share his bedrock Christian beliefs? Among other qualities, it was MacDonald's ability to convey the deepest truths about the human story through myth:

> It arouses in us sensations we have never had before, never anticipated having. . . . It gets under our skin, hits us at a level deeper than our thoughts or even our passions, troubles oldest certainties till all questions are reopened, and in general shocks us more fully awake than we are for most of our lives. It was in this mythopoeic art that MacDonald excelled.[82]

As they walked and spoke, Tolkien helped Lewis to understand why he admired the ancient myths and, thus, why he loved the works of MacDonald. They embodied actions and events that seemed to be an intimation of a larger, redemptive story. "What really delights and nourishes me is a particular pattern of events," Lewis later explained, "which would equally delight and nourish if it had reached me by some medium which involved no words at all—say by a mime, or a film. And I find this to be true of all such stories."[83]

If the story of the death and resurrection of Jesus was dimly echoed in the old myths of the dying god who comes to life, Tolkien explained, Christianity was the *true* myth—the myth that became fact.

Now, for the first time, Lewis could fully reconcile the two spheres of his mind: reason and imagination.[84] Tolkien and Dyson helped Lewis to grasp how the death and resurrection of Jesus, as historical realities, nonetheless embodied this mythic pattern.

Other friends and authors had played their part in making plausible the claims of Christianity. Nevill Coghill astonished Lewis when he met him during his student days at Oxford. "I soon had the shock of discovering that he—clearly the most intelligent and best-informed man in that class—was a Christian and a thoroughgoing supernaturalist."[85] Owen Barfield cured Lewis of his "chronological snobbery," making him more receptive to older ideas about morality. Even hard-boiled atheists like William Kirkpatrick, who taught Lewis how to think critically, must be added to the list.

Like so many others of his generation, Lewis came of age when religious belief was considered naive and irrelevant to modern life. He was like the doubters in John Bunyan's *The Pilgrim's Progress*: "The shame that attends Religion, lies also as a block in their way; they are proud and haughty, and Religion in their eye is low and contemptible." Over the course of many years, the authors and friends whom Lewis loved and admired the most finally shattered this prejudice against the Christian faith. "I had hoped that the heart of reality might be of such a kind that we can best symbolize it as a place," Lewis recalled. "Instead, I found it to be a Person."[86]

After returning to Lewis's rooms at Magdalen, the three men spoke until 2 a.m. Lewis had crossed another great frontier. Nine days later, during a motorcycle ride to the Whipsnade Zoo with his brother, he put his faith in Jesus Christ. "How deep I am just now beginning to see," he wrote to Arthur, "for I have just passed on from believing in God to definitely believing in Christ—in Christianity. . . . My long night talk with Dyson and Tolkien had a good deal to do with it."[87]

THE ACIDS OF MODERNITY

A new stronghold of traditional biblical faith was being established at one of the premier universities in the West at a moment when much of the world was at war with the ancient faith of the martyrs. And it was happening among the intellectual set—men of letters—who refused to accommodate Modernism's storm of disbelief.

To be sure, the Church of England maintained a strong visible presence at Oxford University. Nevertheless, the liberalizing trends in the arts, philosophy, and history had rendered the faith irrelevant; modern science made its supernatural claims appear wholly ridiculous.

Modernism in literature thus had its counterpart in religion—especially in the Anglican Church—and it had no stomach for miracles. A spokesman at the 1921 conference of the Modern Churchmen's Union declared that "the distinction between Creator and creature . . . seems to us to be a minor distinction."[88] Historian Adrian Hastings concludes that "the modern churchmen had been affected, profoundly affected, by the intellectual culture of their age."[89] The results were disastrous for the Church of England. As *Oxford Magazine* observed during this period, there was a widespread "vague and undefined" sense that "Christianity is intellectually effete and therefore, as a moral sanction, a spent force."[90]

By the late 1920s, skepticism was all the rage. American journalist Walter Lippmann, though not a person of faith, lamented the decline of traditional religious beliefs and the moral order they provided.

"The acids of modernity have dissolved that order for many of us," he wrote in *A Preface to Morals* (1928), "and there are some in consequence who think that the needs which religion fulfilled have also been dissolved." Lippmann disagreed. Men and women could not live well without an inspiring vision for human life. The collapse of certainty about the most fundamental questions had created a crisis. "But however self-sufficient the eugenic and perfectly educated man of the distant future may be . . . it is plain that we have succeeded only in substituting trivial illusions for majestic faiths."[91]

In *The Conquest of Happiness* (1930), English philosopher Bertrand Russell compared humanity to the sad expression on the faces of apes in a zoo: Though on the road to evolution, they quietly realize they have lost their way. "Something of the same strain and anguish seems to have entered the soul of civilized man," he wrote. "He knows there is something better than himself almost within his grasp, yet he does not know where to seek it or how to find it." One of the leading atheists of his day, Russell took no solace in religion; mankind must look elsewhere for the resources to overcome despair. "He must learn to enlarge his heart as he has enlarged his mind. He must learn to transcend self, and so doing to acquire the freedom of the universe."[92]

Other thinkers, such as American author and naturalist Joseph Wood Krutch, concluded that "the certitudes of science" had destroyed any rational basis for ethics, beauty, or religion. In a 1927 essay for *The Atlantic,* Krutch explained that the comforting worlds of poetry, mythology, and religion could not stand up to the raw facts about human biology. Echoing Freud, Krutch compared men and women to children in the nursery who are spoon-fed an assortment of myths to shield them from the bitter realities of life. "Illusions have been lost one by one. God, instead of disappearing in an instant, has retreated step by step and surrendered gradually his control of the universe."

The minds behind the great works of art in the Western tradition were of no use in the modern age, Krutch claimed, because "each presupposed a sense of human dignity which science nowhere supports." Many artists and poets, he said, have finally awakened to this fact:

> The romantic ideal of a world well lost for love and the classic ideal of austere dignity seem equally ridiculous, equally meaningless when referred, not to the temper of the past, but to the temper of the present. The passions which swept through the once major poets no longer awaken any profound response.[93]

It was precisely the romantic epic, inspired by the "austere dignity" of every person—a dignity rooted in the character and purposes of the Creator—that Tolkien and Lewis sought to reintroduce into the modern mind. "They were very concerned about the materialist view, in which nature is all there is, and they knew how debilitating that would be on human society," explains biographer Colin Duriez. "Even though they seemed to be in a backwater, in fact they were very much in the center of the cultural changes that were taking place, the conflict over what it means to be human."[94]

SITTING ON A VOLCANO

Thus, by the early 1930s the intellectual class—the scientists, psychologists, writers, philosophers, poets, and artists—had effectively stripped the West of its moral and spiritual foundations. Their materialistic outlook offered no solid basis for ethics, freedom, beauty, or hope. The cultural elites became, in the words of philosopher Russell Kirk, "enemies of the permanent things."[95]

The result was the rapid decline of what might be called *civilizational confidence.* The sense of foreboding that had arisen in the aftermath of the Great War was spreading across the cultural landscape.

In *Modern Civilization on Trial* (1931), C. D. Burns, a leading British atheist and lecturer, argued that modern trends were rendering all forms of traditional authority obsolete. "The creeds, theological or ethical, which contain 'final' summaries of acquired truth, have no place in the modern mind," he wrote. "Neither science nor philosophy can supply the kinds of certainty which believers felt for their creeds; and if anyone cannot live without such certainty, he cannot live in the modern world but must build himself a shelter in the ruins of temples."[96]

William Ralph Inge, the dean of St. Paul's Cathedral in London, concluded that the period of the 1920s and '30s brought with it "the fall of the idols" that had once captivated the Western mind: progress, democracy, capitalism, humanism, and religion. "For unquestionably the young are in revolt against all the traditions of their elders," he wrote. "They will not always be revolutionary; but the bands of authority have been loosened as never before, and every tradition must now justify itself before a skeptical and impatient tribunal."[97]

The tragic irony is that at the very moment when Western thinkers seemed crippled by a tribunal of self-doubt, the forces of totalitarianism—supremely self-confident—were on the move.

In 1929, Joseph Stalin launched a new policy of forced collectivization: the seizure and consolidation of individual peasant landholdings into collective farms, called the kolkhoz. Under this scheme, workers received no salaries; they would be given a share of what the kolkhoz produced, but only for the needs of themselves and their families—nothing more. The aim was to hasten the pace of national industrialization. The kulaks, the more prosperous farmers, resisted the policies, sometimes refusing to sell their crops as a form of political protest. Stalin blamed them for food shortages, ordered the seizure of their farms, and vowed to destroy them as a class.

Although the policies proved to be an economic and humanitarian disaster for the Soviet Union—it sparked a man-made famine of epic proportions—its communist architects were undeterred. "Today, we have an adequate material base for us to strike at the kulaks," Stalin proclaimed, "to break their resistance, to eliminate them as a class, and to *replace* their output by the output of the collective farms and state farms."

Opponents of collectivization were murdered or sent into labor camps by the thousands. Angry farmers killed their livestock and destroyed their farm machinery rather than turn them over to the state. A virtual civil war developed between the Russian military and the peasants. By 1931, millions of peasants had died unnatural deaths—either from political violence or starvation and disease because of famine.

Nevertheless, Stalin was unflinching in his determination to realize his communist vison for the country. In a 1931 speech to a group of industrial managers, he warned of the apocalyptic consequences of failure:

> Do you want our socialist fatherland to be beaten and to lose its independence? If you do not want this, you must put an end to its backwardness in the shortest possible time and develop a genuine Bolshevik tempo in building up its socialist system of economy. There is no other way. That is why Lenin said on the eve of the October Revolution: "Either perish or overtake and outstrip the advanced capitalist countries." We are fifty or a hundred years behind the advanced countries. We must make good this distance in ten years. Either we do it, or we shall be crushed.[98]

Western visitors to the Soviet Union returned with stories of economic abundance, industrial efficiency, and happy citizens. Even at the height of the famine, British notables such as Julian Huxley found the "general health [of the average Soviet citizen] rather above that to be seen in England." George Bernard Shaw, dining in Moscow, gushed that "Stalin has delivered the goods to an extent that seemed impossible ten years ago, and I take off my hat to him accordingly." *The New York Times* correspondent in Moscow, Walter Duranty, effectively functioned as a propagandist for the regime. "Compared with other countries," he wrote, "the Soviet Union has the advantage of complete internal peace."[99] Duranty was awarded the Pulitzer Prize for his reporting.

How do we explain such moral myopia? The secular outlook of Western elites offers a partial explanation. It seems likely, in the words of Paul Johnson, that "the evaporation of religious faith among the educated created a vacuum easily filled by secular superstitions." Intellectuals, journalists, and others swallowed the crudest Stalinist propaganda at face value. "They needed to believe; they wanted to be duped."[100]

The militant atheism of Soviet communism did not trouble these observers. It should have. Karl Marx viewed Christianity, and religion in general, as a great obstacle to his communist vision. "The first requisite for the happiness of the people," he wrote, "is the abolition of religion." Stalin took him at his word. Beginning in 1928 and continuing through the Second World War, the Soviet leader shut down and demolished churches, synagogues, and mosques and ordered the imprisonment or execution of thousands of religious leaders. No Soviet leader was more ruthless in his attempts to purge every vestige of religion from the "worker's paradise."

Despite all of this, many Oxford intellectuals and authors openly embraced socialism. A leading voice was that of G. D. H. Cole, who used his faculty post as an economist to promote the transformation of English society along socialist lines. Like-minded activists launched the Socialist Dons' Luncheon Club in 1932, attracting dozens of members. Writers of all kinds became infatuated with the communist ideal. "The typical literary man ceases to be a cultured expatriate with a leaning towards the church," observed George Orwell, "and becomes an eager-minded schoolboy with a leaning towards Communism."[101]

THE IDOLIZATION OF THE STATE

Meanwhile, in less than a decade Benito Mussolini had transformed Italy's constitutional monarchy into Europe's first fascist totalitarian state. Like Stalin, his apparent success in rejuvenating the national economy won him admirers at home and abroad. He was Il Duce, the leader, the "new man" of the early twentieth century, as beloved and feared as any Caesar of the Roman Empire. "His powers were limitless," writes Luigi Barzini in *The Italians*. "Where his legal prerogatives ended, his undisputed authority and immense personal prestige began."

The radical utopian schemes of the political left had fueled a cultural backlash. The communist contempt for capitalism, private property, traditional values, patriotism, Italy's cultural inheritance: All of it made Mussolini's political vision plausible, even attractive.

Thus, in June 1929, Mussolini's regime and Pope Pius XI signed the Lateran Treaty, making Vatican City an independent state and mandating the teaching of the Catholic faith in the public schools. In an elaborate ceremony marking the event, the pope entered St. Peter's Square before a crowd of 250,000 people. In praising the protocols, the papal paper, *L'Osservatore Romano*, declared that "Italy has been given back to God and God to Italy." Yet Mussolini also got what he wanted: a way for the Italian people to retain spiritual inspiration from Catholicism while directing their most important loyalties to the regime.

The object of veneration became the nation-state, embodied in a singular individual, a benevolent superman. The idolization of the state was complete, and fascism—with its militant nationalism—was the new creed. As Mussolini summarized it, "Fascism is not only a party, it is a regime; it is not only a regime, but a faith; it is not only a faith, but a religion that is conquering the laboring masses of the Italian people."

It was a short step from the idolization of the regime to the deification of its supreme leader. "The real novelty of his ambition," writes R. J. B. Bosworth in *Mussolini*, "lay in his pretensions to enter the hearts and minds of his subjects, and so install Fascism as a political religion."

Adolf Hitler would execute a similar strategy in Germany once he became chancellor. Thanks to the nation's social and economic woes, the Nazi Party's membership grew from 25,000 in 1925 to about 180,000 in 1929. But it was the stock market crash in 1929 and the ensuing Great Depression that catapulted the party to national prominence. Millions of jobless and unhappy voters joined the ranks of party membership. Its electoral strength in the Reichstag (the German parliament) skyrocketed from 800,000 votes in 1928 to about 14,000,000 votes in 1932.

The charismatic Hitler stood at the center of the Nazi Party, and racial eugenics was central to his political outlook. "If Germany was to get a million children a year and was to remove 700–800,000 of the weakest people, then the final result might even be an increase in strength," he told supporters at a 1929 rally in Nuremberg. He praised ancient Sparta for implementing racial laws systematically. "As a result of our modern sentimental humanitarianism, we are trying to maintain the weak at the expense of the healthy."[102] By 1933, the Nazi Party was the largest voting bloc in the Reichstag.

Just as the "acids of modernity" were dissolving the bonds of biblical religion, new menacing political religions had arisen in the West: The ideologies of nationalism, fascism, Nazism, and communism had established themselves in the heart of Europe.

Writing in the late 1920s, Walter Lippmann saw clearly how the decline in traditional religious belief made room for secular creeds:

> The modern man has ceased to believe in it, but he has not ceased to be credulous, and the need to believe haunts him. It is no wonder that his impulse is to turn back from his freedom, and to find someone who says he knows the truth and can tell him what to do, to find the shrine of some new god, of any cult however newfangled, where he can kneel and be comforted.[103]

As these political faiths advanced on the world stage, Tolkien and Lewis sensed something of the demonic at work. The new ideologies all promised to transform the world, to deliver a future that would fulfill mankind's desire for freedom, dignity, and prosperity. Both authors would confront them in their fictional works.

Thus, in *The Lord of the Rings*, Gandalf warns Frodo Baggins that, despite the serenity of the Shire, all is not well in Middle-earth. Sauron the Great, the Dark Lord, has arisen from the depths and taken up residence in Mordor. "Always after a defeat and a respite, the Shadow takes another shape and grows again."[104] In Lewis's satire, *The Screwtape Letters*, a senior demon, Screwtape, instructs a junior demon, Wormwood, in their strategy for leading people astray: "Hence the encouragement we have given to all those schemes of thought as Creative Evolution, Scientific Humanism, or Communism," he explains, "which fix men's affections on the Future, on the very core of temporality."

Biblical religion, in its most prophetic and morally serious expression, might have held back the forces of terror and totalitarianism—if it had not become so marginalized from the centers of political and cultural life. Likewise, the democracies of the West could have prevented the totalitarian impulse from finding fertile soil in their own backyard—had they not engaged in the industrialized slaughter of the Great War.

Instead, a new age of faith had begun: the arrival of secular creeds that could trace their lineage to an ancient story of rebellion. "For God knows that when you eat of it your eyes shall be opened, and you will be like God."[105]

CHAPTER 3

WHEN DRAGONS ROAM THE EARTH

Now at a stroke make young men thirst for weapons,
demand them, grasp them—now!
—Virgil, *The Aeneid*

It does not do to leave a live dragon out of your
calculations, if you live near him.
—J. R. R. Tolkien, *The Hobbit*

He is breeding and training them for a descent on this country. . . .
His theory seemed to be that fighting was an end in itself.
—C. S. Lewis, *The Pilgrim's Regress*

The debate hall at the Oxford Union Society was thick with the voices of young people disavowing any obligations to serve their country in wartime. Beneath the surface, however, was another argument over something more profound. What is demanded of us, as morally responsible people, when we face an all-devouring force of evil?

This was the subtext of the debate held on February 9, 1933, when the motion was put forward for a vote: "This House will in no circumstances fight for its King and Country." The motion, known as the Oxford Oath, was approved by a vote of 275 to 153. Never in the long history of Great Britain had a generation of future leaders—among the best educated in the Western world—publicly renounced any obligation to defend their nation from attack. "The debate received worldwide publicity," according to one historian, "and created a lasting impression of Oxford as a nursery of pacifist and Communist youth."[1] Winston Churchill denounced it as an "abject, squalid, shameless avowal."[2]

THE YEAR OF THE DEVILS

Their timing could not have been worse.

It could be argued that 1933 was the year in which the liberal democratic project of the West began to unravel. It was the year when Woodrow Wilson's dream of a new world order based upon "the brotherhood of man" started to dissolve, when naked aggression went unchallenged, when mass murder was committed with impunity. It was the year when much of the democratic West, including the United States, turned its back on the truth.[3]

The year began hopefully enough, with the ascension of the buoyant Franklin D. Roosevelt to the American presidency. FDR had served as Assistant Secretary of the Navy during the First World War, however, and he adopted the same isolationist temper that dominated the American mind in the postwar years.

With regards to the League of Nations, for example, Roosevelt was emphatic. "We are not members," he said in a 1933 speech, "and we do not contemplate membership." FDR would soon sign into law the first of a series of Neutrality Acts, legislation banning US arms sales and loans to countries at war, regardless of the circumstances. The aim was to remove any potential reason for the United States to enter another European conflict. As Paul Johnson has summarized it, the Roosevelt administration "was infected by the spirit of isolationism as much as any other element in American society during the 1930s decade."[4]

When FDR arrived in office, the United States was in the throes of the Great Depression, when the savings of millions of people were wiped out and at least a quarter of the population was unable to find work. He promised to solve the nation's economic woes, proclaiming that "the only thing we have to fear is fear itself."

There were other things to fear, however. There was militarism in Asia. Japan was led by an emperor, Hirohito, who, through an elaborate ritual, was "formally reborn as a living god" on November 14, 1928.[5] With his absolute command of the military, a new era had begun. It was known as *Shōwa*, "shining peace," and it proved to be anything but that.

In violation of naval treaties signed in 1922 and 1930, Japan expanded and modernized its fleet. Tokyo's chief foreign policy goal was to convert Japan into a vast colonial empire. The island nation required natural resources and living space, and China was the obvious source. The first strike came in 1931, when Japan invaded Manchuria on the pretext of restoring "law and order." On January 1, 1933, Japan launched a fresh attack along the Great Wall in the Rehe Province. The Japanese proceeded to bomb civilian populations in virtually every major city in China. Two months later, Japan quit the League of Nations when the League refused to recognize the puppet regime in Manchuria.

There was mass starvation and political violence in the Soviet Union. Under the dictatorship of Joseph Stalin, the communist regime was engaged in what appeared to be a systematic campaign of extermination against its peasant population.

Deliberate or not, Stalin's policy of collectivization created a famine of biblical proportions. By the spring of 1933, between 5 and 7 million people were dead, millions more on the brink of starvation. In Ukraine, once the breadbasket of the Soviet Union, the famine was killing 25,000 people a day; the death toll was about 3.5 million out of a population of 33 million. Opponents of Stalin's polices were sent to concentration camps. Polish philosopher Leszek Kolakowski has called this episode "probably the most massive warlike operation ever conducted by a state against its own citizens." Yet in the outside world, the magnitude of the famine—the worst in Russian history—and Stalin's responsibility for it, were either not understood or not reported.

There was Benito Mussolini, the fascist dictator determined to restore Italian greatness on the world stage. In June 1933, Mussolini received international applause for his role in negotiating the Four-Power Pact, a new peace agreement between Italy, England, France, and Germany. *The New York Times* announced that the plan would "assure European peace" for a decade.[6] Meanwhile, Mussolini was secretly drawing up plans to invade Abyssinia (now Ethiopia), making it a colonial possession. His aim, he later declared, was to give Italy an empire: "a Fascist empire, a peaceful empire, an empire of civilization and humanity."[7] Most Italians seemed to be on board.

And then there was Nazi Germany. On January 30, 1933—barely ten days before the Oxford Union Society vote—Adolf Hitler was elevated to chancellor, making him the second-most powerful person in the country. Two days later he dissolved the parliament. The German government was now led by a man who had announced his intention to tear up the Versailles Treaty, rebuild the military, and pursue a policy of territorial expansion.

More effectively than any other politician, Hitler told the German people exactly what they wanted to hear. As he described it in his first radio broadcast as the German chancellor:

> The National Government will therefore regard it as its first and supreme task to restore to the German people unity of mind and will. It will preserve and defend the foundations on which the strength of our nation rests. It will take under its firm protection Christianity as the basis of our morality, and the family as the nucleus of our nation and our state. . . . It wishes to base the education of German youth on respect for our great past and pride in our old traditions. . . . Germany must not and will not sink into Communist anarchy.

The anti-Semitism of Hitler's *Mein Kampf*—which appeared in an abridged English translation in 1933—immediately took political form. The regime launched a boycott of Jewish businesses; banned Jews as judges, teachers, professors, and other civil service positions; and passed a mandatory sterilization law affecting the disabled and those deemed mentally ill.

Jews began to leave Germany. In September, the most famous scientist in the world, Albert Einstein, renounced his German citizenship and fled to England, settling into a country hut in the coastal town of Cromer.

On October 3, just before he left for his permanent home in America, Einstein delivered a speech to an international audience at the Royal Albert Hall in London. "If we want to resist the powers which threaten to suppress the intellectual and individual freedom," he said, "we must keep clearly before us what is at stake and what we owe to that freedom which our ancestors have won for us after hard struggles." It was a ringing defense of the Western political and literary tradition.

The Nazi hatred of the Jews was making international news. In a letter to Arthur Greeves, dated November 5, 1933, C. S. Lewis excoriated Hitler for his anti-Semitic statements in *Mein Kampf*:

> Nothing can fully excuse the iniquity of Hitler's persecution of the Jews, or the absurdity of his theoretical position. Did you see that he said, "The Jews have made no contribution to human culture and in crushing them I am doing the will of the Lord." Now as the whole idea of the "Will of the Lord" is precisely what the world owes to the Jews, the blaspheming tyrant has just fixed his absurdity for all to see in a single sentence, and shown that he is as contemptible for his stupidity as he is detestable for his cruelty.[8]

Knowledge of the will of God is what the world owes to the Jews. Lewis's conversion to Christianity altered his outlook at many levels and none more important than this: He now understood that one of the great gifts of the Jews to Western civilization was the belief that there existed a good and righteous God who had a moral agenda for mankind. Lewis had traveled a long distance from his poetry of 1919, when he declared that "the good is dead. Let us curse God most High."

THE NAZIFICATION OF CULTURE

Meanwhile, the Nazi leadership sought to co-opt Germany's Christian churches. They found many ready collaborators in the Protestant community, who viewed Hitler's rise to power as the portent of a national spiritual awakening. As one Lutheran scholar declared: "Our Protestant churches have greeted the turning point of 1933 as a gift and miracle of

God."[9] Hitler, after all, had presented himself as a defender of Christian morals and a fierce opponent of atheistic communism.

Moreover, thanks to Europe's long history of anti-Semitism, many churchmen agreed that Germany had a "Jewish problem" that must be addressed. The Protestant "Confessing Church," led by individuals such as Karl Barth and Dietrich Bonhoeffer, openly denounced the Nazi regime. But they were vastly outnumbered by the Protestant German Christian movement, which had elevated anti-Semitism into a religious creed. Otto Dibelius, a Protestant bishop who had preached at Hitler's inauguration, openly considered himself an anti-Semite. "One cannot ignore," he wrote, "that Jewry has played a leading role in all the destructive manifestations of modern civilization."[10]

The leadership of the Catholic Church shared similar prejudices and fears—fear of communism as well as anxiety that the Nazi regime would wage a culture war against the church. Thus, the Vatican sought an agreement, or concordat, with the state. The aim of Pope Pius XI was to secure the church's independence and protect its civil liberties. Hitler's goal was to gain public acceptance of National Socialism from the most important international religious community in the world.

As word of the talks spread, a Jewish convert to Catholicism, Edith Stein, wrote an urgent letter to the pope. Stein had become a nun and a respected Catholic educator. In her letter, sent in April 1933, she appealed to the pope to change course:

> For weeks not only Jews but also thousands of fearful Catholics in Germany, and, I believe, all over the world have been waiting and hoping for the Church of Christ [the Roman Catholic Church] to raise its voice to put a stop to this abuse of Christ's name. Is not this idolization of race and governmental power which is being pounded into the public consciousness by the radio open heresy?

On July 20, 1933, the Vatican's secretary of state, Cardinal Eugenio Pacelli, and Germany's vice chancellor, Franz von Papen, formally signed a concordat between the Holy See and the German Reich. The pope did not respond to Stein's letter; she would perish in the death camps.

Any serious challenge to the authority of the Nazi Party would have to come from the German churches of both confessions: a massive, unified act of civil disobedience. It never arrived. Quite the opposite: Many priests and pastors swore an oath of allegiance to Hitler. As historian Michael Burleigh observes in *The Third Reich: A New History*, many German Christians found that they had much in common with the Nazis: anti-Bolshevism, anti-Semitism, and the sense that the nation had gone to the dogs.[11] Desperate measures were required to save it. Thus, the Christian faith was effectively abandoned for a political creed. "Nazi attacks on Christianity hardly encountered a resilient citadel," Burleigh writes, "and were facilitated by Trojan horses constructed, rather than dispatched within."[12]

The Nazification of German life extended into virtually all sectors of society, perhaps most importantly in education. In *The Treason of the Intellectuals* (1927), French philosopher Julien Benda observed how Europe's intellectual class had fully embraced extreme nationalism and racism. The vast majority of academics, philosophers, artists, and theologians, he wrote, "share in the chorus of hatreds among races and political factions."[13]

Germany led the chorus: On May 10, 1933, a scene occurred in Berlin that had not been witnessed in the life of Europe since the Middle Ages.[14] Beginning at midnight, thousands of university students formed a torchlight parade that culminated in a square opposite the University of Berlin. The torches were applied to a stack of more than twenty thousand books, all deemed incompatible with the values of the Reich. "These flames not only illuminate the final end of an old era," announced Joseph Goebbels, Germany's propaganda minister, "they also light up the new."[15]

Thus, from 1933 on, totalitarian regimes—the emperor-cult of Japan, fascism in Italy, Nazism in Germany, and communism in the Soviet Union—threatened the peace and security of the world.[16] All of these governments preached, practiced, and embodied the "Will to Power." German philosopher Friedrich Nietzsche had introduced this phrase in the late nineteenth century, arguing that the desire to exert complete control over oneself and one's environment is both primal and insatiable. The totalitarian states made this impulse an asset: All had become militarized societies, with grand visions of territorial and racial conquest. None had any use for the God of the Bible. Western democracy, with its historic commitment to the freedom and dignity of the individual, was the only force that stood in their way.

THE YEAR OF THE HOBBIT

It was at this precise moment in 1933, at the start of an unprecedented assault on the moral norms of Western civilization, that J. R. R. Tolkien and C. S. Lewis engaged their literary talents in new and powerful ways to try to hold the line. Whether acutely conscious or not of the tectonic political and ideological developments in Asia and Europe—forces of disintegration—they dedicated themselves to defending the Western tradition, especially its moral and religious foundations.

How did this come about? During the 1920s and '30s, according to Humphrey Carpenter, Tolkien's imagination was running along two distinct lines that did not intersect. On one side were the stories composed for his own pleasure or for entertaining his children. On the other side were the larger and more sober themes, like those found in *Beowulf* or in Thomas Malory and the tales of King Arthur.[17]

Aside from a few poems in the *Oxford Magazine*, however, Tolkien hadn't published anything. But something happened that began to bring the two strands of his imaginative life together. "It was on a summer's day," writes Carpenter, "and he was sitting by the window in the study at Northmoor Road, laboriously marking School Certificate exam papers." Tolkien recalled the moment thus:

> One of the candidates had mercifully left one of the pages with no writing on it (which is the best thing that can possibly happen to an examiner) and I wrote on it: "In a hole in the ground there lived a hobbit." Names always generate a story in my mind. Eventually I thought I'd better find out what hobbits were like.[18]

Tolkien's son Christopher remembered, when he was about four or five years old, "the evenings when my father would stand with his back to the fire in his small study of the house in North Oxford . . . and tell stories to my brothers and me." One night the hobbit appeared seemingly from nowhere.

Christopher's older brother Michael "remembered with perfect clarity" the moment when their father announced that he was going to tell them "a long story about a small being with furry feet, and asked us what he should be called—then answering himself, said, 'I think we'll call him a "Hobbit."'"[19]

We don't know exactly when Tolkien started writing *The Hobbit*, but he completed the first draft in early 1933. He lent it to Lewis. Once again, his friend's response was pivotal. He praised Tolkien's achievement and shared his enthusiasm in a letter to Arthur Greeves:

> Since term began, I have had a delightful time reading a children's story which Tolkien has just written. I have told of him before: the one man absolutely fitted, if fate had allowed, to be a third in our friendship in the old days, for he also grew up on William Morris and George MacDonald. Reading his fairy tale has been uncanny—it is so exactly like what we would both have longed to write (or read) in 1916: so that one feels he is not making it up but merely describing the same world which all three of us have the entry. Whether it is really *good* (I think it is until the end) is of course another question: still more, whether it will succeed with modern children.[20]

Tolkien's story would succeed well enough with modern children. Today *The Hobbit* is ranked one of the most popular fiction books of all time, with more than 100 million copies sold. His tale introduced the world to a race called hobbits, small people about half the height of men. They tend to be "fat in the stomach," "dress in bright colors," and wear no shoes "because their feet grow natural leathery soles and thick brown hair." They have "good-natured faces" and "laugh deep fruity laughs."[21]

The story's protagonist, Bilbo Baggins, lives in Bag End, a luxurious home built into the side of The Hill in the village of Hobbiton. Bilbo likes to mind his own business. One day he is visited by a wizard named Gandalf and thirteen Dwarves, who explain that they were driven out of their homes in the Lonely Mountain by a dragon named Smaug. The dragon sleeps on a mound of stolen treasure, and Gandalf has chosen Bilbo to travel with them as a burglar to retrieve it. Reluctantly, Bilbo is thrust into a dangerous adventure. Along the way, he acquires a ring that allows him to become invisible.

In a review for *The London Times* after the book was published, Lewis declared that in *The Hobbit* several good things were brought together for the first time: "a fund of humor, an understanding of children, and a happy fusion of the scholar's with the poet's grasp of mythology."[22] He praised the "deep sources in our blood and tradition" that supply the bedrock of Tolkien's story. Those sources, of course, include ancient and medieval myths, epic poetry, and centuries of English history and Christian culture.

A distinguishing trait of Bilbo Baggins is courage, but not the sort of courage one finds in classical or medieval epics. Bilbo seems incapable of fighting trolls or defeating dragons. His battles are usually internal: Should he risk exposing himself to danger to help the company? After escaping the goblins, he finds himself cut off from his companions and without his hood, cloak, food, and pony.

> He wondered whether he ought not, now that he had the magic ring, to go back into the horrible, horrible tunnels and look for his friends. He had just made up his mind that it was his duty, that he must turn back—and very miserable he felt about it—when he heard voices.[23]

Tolkien scholar Tom Shippey observes that Bilbo's courage is "distinctively modern" in that there is nothing like it in *Beowulf* or the Norse sagas.[24] Bilbo's bravery unfolds, usually reluctantly, as part of a coming-of-age story. His growth occurs "in scenes of solitude, always in the dark."[25] He turns a moral corner in his encounter with a giant spider. Just as he is "deep in thoughts of bacon and eggs and toast and butter," something touches him. What follows is a ferocious struggle with a hideous enemy:

> Somehow the killing of the giant spider, all alone by himself in the dark without the help of the wizard or the dwarves or of anyone else, made a great difference to Mr. Baggins. He felt a different person, and much fiercer and bolder in spite of an empty stomach, as he wiped his sword on the grass and put it back into its sheath.[26]

Is this not the recollection of a soldier in the Great War? Though Tolkien always described himself as a man who lacked physical courage, he fought honorably and endured the "animal horror" of modern warfare.[27] It would be surprising if bits of this horror did not appear in Tolkien's fiction, and it can be discerned even in a children's story.

Thus, we read that Bilbo and the company of Dwarves approach the end of their quest across the "desolation of Smaug," a land that was once green but now with "neither bush nor tree, and only broken and blackened stumps to speak of ones long vanished."[28] That's a fair description of no-man's-land amid the trenches. Consider Tolkien's equally graphic description of the goblins:

> Now goblins are cruel, wicked, and bad-hearted. They make no beautiful things, but they make many clever ones. . . . Hammers, axes, swords, daggers, pickaxes, tongs, and also instruments of torture, they make very well. . . . It is not unlikely that they invented some of the machines that have since troubled the world, especially the ingenious devices for killing large numbers of people at once, for wheels and engines and explosions always delighted them.[29]

Much later in the story, when Bilbo and his companions confront the goblins in battle, we read thus:

> "It will not be long now," thought Bilbo, "before the goblins win the Gate, and we are all slaughtered or driven down and captured. Really it is enough to make one weep, after all one has gone through. . . . Misery me! I have heard songs of many battles, and I have always understood that defeat may be glorious. It seems very uncomfortable, not to say distressing. I wish I was well out of it."[30]

A desolate land of blackened stumps; wheels and engines and explosions; the desire not for glory, but to simply get out of harm's way: Here is something more than a fertile imagination.

No soldier in the 1914–18 war could forget the irrepressible images of mechanized slaughter, or his first encounter with the prospect of a violent death far from home. "It would be misleading to suggest that *The Hobbit* is Tolkien's wartime experience in disguise," writes John Garth. "Yet it is easy to see how some of his memories must have invigorated this tale of an ennobling rite of passage past the fearful jaws of death."[31]

In *The Hobbit,* Tolkien is addressing children—originally, his own children—and limits his field of vision to themes appropriate to them. It has been described as a book "about entering and grasping and taking forth symbols of manhood."[32] Perhaps, in the end, it is about much more than that. The hero in this story does not carry the fate of civilizations on his shoulders, as he does in *The Lord of the Rings.* But he leaves the safety of his hobbit hole and confronts forces of genuine evil. He must even put his own life at risk to help his friends, resisting the powerful temptation to slip away to safety and return home. These are not ignoble themes.

The Great War produced a flood of writers disenchanted with notions of courage and sacrifice; many were consumed by the idea of lost innocence. *The Hobbit* is the beginning of Tolkien's reply: They shall not have the last word.

THE YEAR OF THE PILGRIM

About a year after C. S. Lewis's conversion to Christianity, in August 1932, he traveled to Belfast, Northern Ireland, to visit Arthur Greeves. Unexpectedly, Lewis began writing his spiritual autobiography.

Lewis first read *The Pilgrim's Progress* (1678), John Bunyan's classic allegorical story of Christian conversion, when he was a young atheist. He had admired Bunyan's imagination, even as he had rejected his religion. He now chose the work as his literary model. In Bunyan's story the protagonist, named Christian, travels from the City of Destruction to the Celestial City. At every step of the journey he encounters characters intent on diverting him from his goal: Mr. Worldly Wiseman in the Slough of Despond, Giant Despair, and the townspeople at Vanity Fair.

Lewis will call his book *The Pilgrim's Regress* because the protagonist, John, must *unlearn* many of the things he was taught to believe if he is to reach his goal. Born in Puritania, a country under the control of an unseen Landlord, John has visions of an Island that stirs a deep sense of longing, or "Joy." He sets out to find it. Along the way, he meets a host of characters who personify the various outlooks of the age.

Published in 1933, the full title of the book suggests something of the intellectual trends of the 1920s and '30s: *The Pilgrim's Regress: An Allegorical Apology for Christianity, Reason, and Romanticism.*[33] Lewis takes the reader through a labyrinth of ideologies: Modernism, occultism, pantheism, rationalism, and materialism. "The different intellectual movements of that time were hostile to one another," he wrote later, "but the one thing that seemed to unite them all was their common enmity to 'immortal longings.'"[34]

In a chapter entitled "Freedom of Thought," Lewis skewers the intellectual and artistic set of the postwar years—the Clevers—for their cynicism. Their conversation bitingly captures the Modernist outlook: "You have got to realize that satire is the moving force in modern music. . . . It is the expression of a savage disillusionment. . . . Our art must be brutal. . . . Reality has broken down." Explains a very young Clever, "We lost our ideals when there was a war in this country. . . . They were ground out of us in the mud and the flood and the blood."[35]

We lost our ideals. . . . They were ground out of us in the mud and the flood and the blood. No line better describes the Modernist mood, something like a T. S. Eliot salon.[36] As Lewis explained, "T. S. Eliot is the single man who sums up the thing I am fighting against."[37]

Sigmund Freud also gets rough treatment. Freudian psychology and Freud's sharp rejection of the validity of religious belief became immensely popular in educated circles in the 1920s and '30s.[38] As we've seen, Freud regarded the religious impulse as an illusion, a conceit, a lie, a psychosis. "The whole thing is so patently infantile, so foreign to reality," he wrote, "that to anyone with a friendly attitude to humanity it is painful to think that the great majority of mortals will never be able to rise above this view of life."[39]

Writing in 1933, W. R. Matthews, the dean of Exeter College, lamented the capacity of Freudian thinking to undermine any firm basis for ethics or Christian morality. "There can be no doubt that this type of psychology has had a far-reaching effect on the attitude of the educated classes of Europe and America to morals."[40] While in his twenties, Lewis counted himself among their number. "The new Psychology was at that time sweeping through us all," Lewis recalled. "We did not swallow it whole (few people then did) but we were all influenced."[41]

Lewis now viewed Freud as the offspring of nineteenth-century rationalism, which also had rejected the supernatural claims of traditional religion. Thus, the pilgrim, desperate to travel to the island that he had glimpsed through the woods, meets old Mr. Enlightenment and his son, Sigismund Enlightenment (Sigismund was Freud's given name):

> Then [Mr. Enlightenment] spoke again.
>
> "It may save trouble if I tell you at once the best reason for not trying to escape: namely, that there is no place to escape to."
>
> "How do you know there is no such place as my island?"
>
> "Do you wish very much that there was?"
>
> "I do."
>
> "Have you never before imagined anything to be true because you greatly wished for it?"
>
> John thought for a little, and then he said, "Yes."
>
> "And your island is like an imagination—isn't it?"
>
> "I suppose so."
>
> "It is just the sort of thing you *would* imagine merely through wanting it—the whole thing is very suspicious."[42]

Lewis's pathway to faith had convinced him that Freud had it exactly backwards. Man's universal sense of longing, quite often stirred by experiences of beauty, was not an illusion. Rather, it was a signpost to another world, to the God of heaven and earth, what the psalmists called "the beauty of holiness."

In a chapter entitled "Furthest North," John meets several species of dwarfs, some wearing black shirts (a nod to the black shirts worn by fascist paramilitary groups) and "a red kind" who call themselves Marxomanni (red flags were a symbol of Marxism-Leninism). "They are all very fierce and apparently quarrel a good deal," Lewis writes, "but they all acknowledge some kind of vassalage to this man Savage."[43] Dressed in a Viking's helmet and seated on a high chair, Savage quotes from Nietzsche and expounds the Nietzschean philosophy of life's futility and the Will to Power. "If I am to live in a world of destruction," he says, "let me be its agent and not its patient."[44] Many intellectuals in the West either idealized communism for its supposed egalitarianism or fascism for its economic efficiency and reassertion of national pride.

Lewis was prescient in realizing that the ideologies of the left and the right were fundamentally authoritarian, political manifestations of the Will to Power. They both functioned as "forces of mass violence waiting to be unleashed."[45]

Although Lewis adapted some of the characters from Bunyan's tale, the emotive force of his story departs dramatically from that of Bunyan. In *The Pilgrim's Progress*, it is *fear* that launches Christian on his journey: to escape the City of Destruction and the flames of hell.[46] "I do believe," Hopeful says to the pilgrim, "as you say, that fear tends much to men's good, and to make them right at their beginning to go on pilgrimage."[47] In *The Pilgrim's Regress*, by contrast, it is the sensation of *Joy* that compels John to begin his quest. He is captivated by a desire for what might lie ahead—not a sense of dread of what lies behind.

The Pilgrim's Regress was Lewis's first attempt to bring his vast knowledge of classical, medieval, and Renaissance literature to bear upon modern ideologies. There are nearly three hundred references and allusions in half a dozen languages in the book: from classical poets; from Dante, Shakespeare, and Milton; and from contemporary philosophers. Lewis responded to one admiring reader who was having trouble deciphering his message:

> I don't wonder that you got fogged in Pilgrim's Regress. It was my first religious book and I didn't then know how to make things easy. I was not even trying to very *much*, because in those days I never dreamed I would become a "popular" author, and [I] hoped for no readers outside of a small "highbrow" circle.[48]

Nevertheless, *The Pilgrim's Regress* offers insight into the spiritual journey of every modern pilgrim. It touches upon the deepest motivations of the human heart: for meaning, beauty, and love. It upholds what Lewis would call "the Moral Law," a clue to the meaning of the universe. It explores the relationship between reason and imagination. Just as Lewis himself struggled in his journey to faith, the pilgrim must navigate between two extremes: excessive rationalism and excessive sensualism. Lewis developed all these themes in his later works.

Walter Hooper once remarked that probably no book written so quickly ever had such a long shelf life (it is still in print). Lewis produced his allegorical tale in about two weeks—it poured out of him.[49]

Arthur played no small role in the event. He was Lewis's first close friend and intellectual sparring partner, the man with whom he shared his deepest doubts and secret longings, a faithful correspondent over many years. Thus, after he found a publisher, Lewis dedicated the book to his friend: "I suppose you will have no objection to my dedicating my book to you? It is yours by every right—written in your house, read to you as it was written, and celebrating (at least in the most important parts) an experience which I have more in common with you than anyone else."[50]

The experience Lewis had in mind was something he had tasted from childhood, when he and his brother were playing in their garden and his brother brought him a little model garden in the lid of a biscuit tin, which he had made out of bits of moss. "And there was something about the poignancy of this little garden as they were in the big garden," explains Malcolm Guite, author of *Faith, Hope, and Poetry*. "It's a garden within a garden. That's very important. It's that sense that hidden inside this thing is *another* thing."[51]

The emotion—stabbing and undeniable—created in Lewis a sense of exile, as if he were cut off from the real source of Beauty. As Guite summarizes it: "He realized then that sense of exile and the longing to journey forward, the person as pilgrim who has not completed their pilgrimage, was absolutely at the core of all the literature that he loved."[52] This experience—the desire for "the far-off country"—forms the narrative thread of Lewis's story.

> While he strained to grasp it, there came to him from beyond the wood a sweetness and a pang so piercing that instantly he forgot his father's house, and his mother, and the fear of the Landlord, and the burden of the rules. All the furniture of his mind was taken away. A moment later he found that he was sobbing.[53]

Against a literary establishment awash in cynicism and despair, *The Pilgrim's Regress* is about the human longing for Joy—a desire that must not be despised. As Lewis explained, "the central story of my life is about nothing else."[54]

THE INKLINGS: WRITERS AND REBELS

The intellectual and spiritual transformation that began in the life of Lewis when he converted to Christianity also had a catalytic effect on his friends. Chief among them was Tolkien.

A devout Catholic, Tolkien found his relationship with Lewis immediately enriched by their common Christian faith. His friendship with Lewis, he wrote in his diary in October 1933, "besides giving constant pleasure and comfort, has done me much good from the contact with a man at once honest, brave, intellectual—a scholar, a poet, a philosopher—and a lover, at least after a long pilgrimage, of Our Lord."[55]

The two made a point of meeting together on Monday mornings, often concluding their conversation with a pint of beer at the Eastgate Hotel. "This is one of the pleasantest spots in the week," Lewis wrote. "Sometimes we talk English School politics; sometimes we criticize one another's poems; other days we drift into theology or 'the state of the nation.'"[56] Among other works, Tolkien read parts of *The Hobbit* to Lewis; Lewis shared parts of *The Pilgrim's Regress* with Tolkien.

Their tiny nucleus was bound to expand. They both placed a high value on friendship, had launched their own literary clubs, and sought criticism for their works in progress.

Beginning around 1933, the two men, in Tolkien's words, drew around them an "unelected circle of friends" to read aloud their compositions.[57] They called themselves the Inklings, picking up the name of a recently defunct Oxford reading group. They began meeting on Thursday evenings in Lewis's rooms at Magdalen College, with their host as the center of gravity for the group. "C. S. L. had a passion for hearing things read aloud, a power of memory for things received in that way," recalled Tolkien, "and also a facility in extempore criticism, none of which was shared (especially the last) in anything like the same degree by his friends."[58]

War veterans dominated their ranks: Lewis's brother Warnie, who served with the British Expeditionary Force in France during the Great

War; Hugo Dyson, a first lieutenant who was seriously wounded at Passchendaele; Nevill Coghill, a second lieutenant who saw action with the Royal Artillery; R. E. Havard, a Royal Navy officer and physician; and Owen Barfield, who served with the Royal Engineers. Lewis was nearly killed by a mortar shell that obliterated his sergeant standing nearby, and Tolkien narrowly survived the Battle of the Somme.

There were no strict rules for membership, though all of the participants shared a Christian faith, broadly defined, and a love of literature. Warnie Lewis recalled their meetings thus:

> When half a dozen or so had arrived, tea would be produced, and then when pipes were well alight Jack would say, "Well, has nobody got anything to read us?" Out would come a manuscript, and we would settle down to sit in judgment upon it—real unbiased judgment, too, since we were no mutual admiration society: praise for good work was unstinted, but censure for bad work—or even not-so-good work—was often brutally frank. To read to the Inklings was a formidable ordeal.[59]

Tolkien read sections of *The Hobbit* and would share much of *The Lord of the Rings*; Lewis would read to the group his first science fiction novel—*Out of the Silent Planet*, as well as *The Screwtape Letters*, *The Great Divorce*, and other works. Yet the first member of the Inklings to write a fantasy novel was Owen Barfield. Published in 1925, *The Silver Trumpet* was a children's book that nonetheless addressed very adult themes. Lewis read it when he was still an atheist and recorded his enthusiasm in his journal: "Nothing of its kind can be imagined better."

After his conversion, Lewis evidently gained a deeper appreciation for the story, giving the book to Tolkien, who read it to his children. It made a huge impression on the Tolkien family. In a letter to Barfield, dated June 28, 1936, Lewis summarized its impact:

> I lent The Silver Trumpet to Tolkien and hear that it is the greatest success among his children that they have ever known. His own fairy-tales, which are excellent, have now no market: and its first reading—children are so practical!—led to a universal wail "You're not going to give it back to Mr. Lewis, are you?" All the things which the wiseacres on child

> psychology in our circle said when you wrote it turn out to be nonsense. "They liked the sad parts," said Tolkien, "because they were sad and the puzzling parts because they were puzzling, as children always do."[60]

Tolkien, Lewis, Barfield, and the other members of the Inklings believed that there are truths and concepts that children really ought to know, but which must be introduced indirectly—not through didactic preaching, but rather through their imagination.

The Silver Trumpet has the features of a children's story: kings, princesses, a dwarf, a toad, and a miraculous trumpet. But it teaches children that there are real dangers in this world—temptations to pride, greed, and envy—that can be overcome only by people who hold fast to a set of principles regardless of the dangers. "Yet, amid all her terror," Barfield writes, "Princess Lily knew what she must do."

Part fable, fairy tale, and parable, *The Silver Trumpet* offered Tolkien and Lewis a template for how serious ideas could be transmitted to children to help them meet hardship with courage and fortitude.[61] "It created a sort of 'proof-of-concept' for all three of them, that a valid way of communicating a philosophy is through fairytales," explains Barfield's grandson, Owen Barfield. "Barfield felt that imagination was a valid route to truth. If you imagine a fairytale world, you're going to reach a truth through that fairytale world, and you'd better be careful what you're imagining."[62]

The appropriation of myth and fantasy to deliver universal moral truth: Here was an approach to storytelling completely at odds with the spirit of their age. Warnie Lewis once described Oxford of the 1930s as a "hard-boiled materialistic, scientific university."[63] That's not far off the mark.

"The Inklings were attracted to the fantasy genre at a time when it was despised by the academics," says Colin Duriez, author of *Tolkien and C. S. Lewis: The Gift of Friendship*. "They were very concerned about the materialistic view in which nature is all there is, and they knew how debilitating that would be on human society. They wanted people to become undeceived. They wanted their stories to be subversive, like all good stories are."[64]

Alan Jacobs, author of *The Narnian: The Life and Imagination of C. S. Lewis*, also emphasizes the subversive intent of the Inklings. "They constituted a kind of tiny counterculture, an ongoing reminder to each member that there were possibilities for the human mind, heart, and spirit beyond what one might read in the newspapers, or in the intellectual journals, or in the textbooks."[65] Novelist John Wain, another Inklings participant, remembers them as "a circle of instigators, almost of incendiaries, meeting to urge one another on in the task of redirecting the whole current of contemporary art and life."[66]

THE MONSTERS AND THE CRITICS

If that assessment sounds grandiose, consider the impact of the academic scholarship produced by Tolkien and Lewis.

John Lawlor, a professor of English literature who studied under both men, believed that they possessed "an unsleeping sense of the practical relevance" of their scholarship.[67] As Lawlor put it, the question that seemed to lie behind much of their academic writing was this: "What is the worth of scholarly work unless it can be shown to bear on modern values?"[68]

There can be no doubt that Tolkien viewed works such as *Beowulf* as containing enduring insights into the human predicament, as important in the twentieth century as they were in the Middle Ages. Thus, in the early 1930s, when Christopher Tolkien was seven or eight years old, his father introduced him to the story of *Beowulf* by singing him a ballad of his own invention called the *Lay of Beowulf.*

> Grendel came forth in the dead of night;
> the moon in his eyes shone glassy bright,
> as over the moors he strode in might,
>   until he came to Heorot.[69]

Tolkien had translated all of *Beowulf* into modern English prose by 1926, though he made changes throughout the years as he prepared and delivered weekly lectures on the poem. He committed much of *Beowulf* to memory, usually beginning his lectures by reciting the opening lines of the poem. Tolkien concluded that the literary critics had fundamentally misunderstood the work: They mined it for its history but neglected it as poetry, overlooked its transcendent elements, and failed to grasp the moral significance of the monsters that Beowulf defeats. Tolkien was determined to set them straight.

The prestigious British Academy in London gave him the opportunity. His lecture, delivered on November 25, 1936, would overturn the entire scholarly approach to *Beowulf* studies. Writing at the time, R. W. Chambers described Tolkien's contribution as "the finest appreciation which has yet been written of our finest Old English poem."[70] Literary scholar Michael D. C. Drout has described the lecture as possibly "the single most influential essay in the history of literary studies in the twentieth century."[71]

Before Tolkien's address, the accepted view of the poem was that its author had squandered his talents on an unworthy theme: the slaying of monsters. *Beowulf* put fanciful distractions at the center of the story, said the critics, and left the serious matters on the periphery.

With a combination of wit, scholarship, and poetic sensibility, Tolkien argued that the critics got it exactly backwards. The monsters are not a conceptual blunder; they are essential to the narrative.

Rather than cheapening the story, Tolkien insisted, the monsters lend it a unique seriousness and nobility: a glimpse of pure evil, an enemy of God and humankind. Against such a foe, no hero has any hope of victory. Nevertheless, "the worth of defeated valor in this world is deeply felt."[72] Scholar Randal Helms, author of *Tolkien's World*, does not overstate Tolkien's achievement. "Here is a distinctly striking moment in the history of modern imagination," he writes, "the resurgence of a critical grasp of the mythological perception of radical evil."[73]

Such is the nature of the real world, Tolkien implies: It is threatened by malevolent forces that demand a response. Thus, Beowulf is a leader who does not wait for danger to arrive at his doorstep; he goes out to meet it. He is a man "at war with a hostile world," a man who makes commitments and keeps them, regardless of the cost. "We do not deny the worth of the hero by accepting Grendel and the dragon," Tolkien explained. "Let us by all means esteem the old heroes: men caught in the chains of circumstance or of their own character, torn between duties equally sacred, dying with their backs to the wall."[74]

One of Tolkien's objectives in his lecture was to reintroduce to the world "a theory of courage," which he called the "great contribution" to humanity of the old literature of the North. "Something more significant than a standard hero, a man faced with a foe more evil than any human enemy of house or realm, is before us," he said, "and yet incarnate in time, walking in heroic history, and treading the named lands of the North." Like no other interpreter of the story, Tolkien cast the struggle of Beowulf in epic and existential terms, almost anticipating the force of evil that would threaten European civilization before the decade was out.

Tolkien was intent on reviving the concept of courage, in part because it was being discarded by the *literati* of his day. And he had witnessed acts of bravery up close: in the killing fields in France. "Even today (despite the critics) you may find men not ignorant of tragic legend and history, who have heard of heroes, *and indeed seen them.*"[75] Tolkien almost certainly had his war experience in mind. He surely knew that his own regiment, the Lancashire Fusiliers, earned more Victoria Crosses (seventeen) during the First World War than any other.[76]

Another stock criticism of *Beowulf* was that the author clumsily mixed pagan and Christian elements, making a muddle of both. Yet Tolkien again turned the argument on its head. The *Beowulf* poet, he reminded his audience, was a Christian believer living at a moment of immense cultural change: looking back in time at a society touched by the gospel yet still animated by pagan virtues. Herein lies the source of much of the poem's grandeur and moral vigor:

> The whole must have succeeded admirably in creating in the minds of the poet's contemporaries the illusion of surveying a past, pagan but noble and fraught with a deep significance—a past that itself had depth and reached backward into a dark antiquity of sorrow.[77]

Perhaps only a scholar-storyteller such as Tolkien could have discerned the deeper significance of the poem. Tolkien's explanation of the poet's achievement—creating a world with a distant and morally complex past—describes precisely his own objective in *The Lord of the Rings.* His 1936 lecture was a signal to himself—and to his future audience—of how he would approach his greatest imaginative work. Like the author of *Beowulf,* Tolkien would become "a learned man writing of old times, who looking back on the heroism and sorrow feels in them something permanent and something symbolical."

THE ALLEGORY OF LOVE

Just as Tolkien was establishing himself as a brilliant and innovative scholar, Lewis took the literary establishment by storm.

William Kirkpatrick, Lewis's tutor before he left home to study at Oxford, had announced to Albert Lewis: "You may make a writer or a scholar of him, but you'll not make anything else. You may make up your mind to *that*."[78] Kirkpatrick's judgment proved prophetic. By the late 1930s, many of his contemporaries already had come to regard Lewis as "possibly the best of modern critics and certainly one of the best of modern writers."[79]

The chief reason was the publication in 1936 of his first work of literary criticism, *The Allegory of Love.* In his review in *The London Observer,* Ifor Evans gave it the highest praise: "Out of the multitude of volumes on literary history there arises once or twice in a generation a truly great work. Such I believe is this study by Mr. C. S. Lewis."[80] Kathleen Tillotson, in *The Review of English Studies,* lauded Lewis for tracing "a widespread moral revolution" in the medieval approach to love. "It is rarely that we meet with a work of literary criticism of such manifest and general importance as this," she wrote. "No one could read it without seeing all literature a little differently ever after."[81] Surveying the scholarship of the twentieth century, Norman F. Cantor called it a "bold, original, seminal" book that "rocked the transatlantic Anglophone world of medieval studies and did a great deal of good."[82] Alan Jacobs is surely correct to argue that this single book established Lewis as a rising star in the British intellectual world.[83]

What *The Allegory of Love* achieved was something no other scholar had ever attempted: to trace the development of two powerful currents of the human mind—romantic love and allegory—until they converged in medieval French and English literature.[84] It was a vast undertaking, beginning in pre-Christian antiquity, and exploring themes such as the origins of romantic love, the concept of chivalry, and the moral psychology of the medieval virtues.

The driving ambition of Lewis's work is "rehabilitation"—to recover a "long-lost state of mind" that made possible the triumph of romantic love, embodied supremely in the state of marriage. In the modern world, Lewis writes, we take it for granted that romantic love "should be regarded as a noble and ennobling passion." On the contrary, he insists, "love," in our sense of the word, was as absent from the literature of the early "Christian" Middle Ages as from that of ancient Greece and Rome. "Their favorite stories were not, like ours, stories of how a man married, or failed to marry, a woman. They preferred to hear how a holy man went to heaven or how a brave man went to battle."[85]

The concept of romantic love emerged—seemingly out of nowhere—in the poetic and allegorical literature of the later Middle Ages. Its authors drew upon both pagan and Christian sources for inspiration. "They effected a change which has left no corner of our ethics, our imagination, or our daily life untouched."[86]

To appreciate this seismic shift in outlook, Lewis enters deeply and sympathetically into the medieval world of courtly love, which involved a code of ethics that placed a high value on courtesy, honor, humility, and chivalry. At the same time, marriage in medieval Europe was a cold transaction of property and inheritance, not a thing of the heart. This arrangement regarded women as mere possessions, easily disposable. For the men—particularly the noble knights—romantic love most often led to adultery.

The literary revolution that transformed courtly love into something truly ennobling for both sexes found its greatest expression for Lewis in the writings of the Christian poet Edmund Spenser. His allegorical masterpiece, *The Faerie Queene*, had a singular effect. Its author became "the great mediator" between the Middle Ages and the modern poets. According to Lewis, Spenser was the man "who saved us from the catastrophe of too thorough a renaissance"—meaning a complete secularization and debasement of the concept of romantic love.

"His work is one, like a growing thing, a tree; like the world-ash-tree itself, with branches reaching to heaven and roots to hell," Lewis writes. "To read him is to grow in mental health."[87]

The salutary effects of this revolution, pioneered by Spenser and a handful of other medieval writers, became deeply embedded in Western culture. Without it, Lewis implies, our modern lives would be immeasurably poorer: characterized by a degraded view of marriage, a breakdown of family life, a brutalization of girls and women, and a devolution of male-female relationships into a zero-sum game. If this describes the state of love and sexual relations in the modern world, we cannot blame the medievalists.

In fact, argue scholars Philip and Carol Zaleski, Lewis was "the last of the romantic medievalists," a man determined to retrieve from an older tradition a more humane and uplifting approach to our familial and social lives. Lewis believed that *it was the creative literature of this period*, not its politics or formal theology, that ultimately moved the heart and mind of Western culture. Thus, his entire scholarly project "was nothing less than to give an account, at once historical and spiritual, of Europe's Christian literary imagination."[88]

A BRAVE–AND BRUTAL–NEW WORLD

It is hard to conceive of a more important task in light of the cultural crisis that was engulfing the West. Beliefs and ideals that for generations had been taken for granted—and considered essential for sustaining liberal democratic societies—were under assault.

The Modernist Movement in literature and the arts viewed human personality as hopelessly fractured and meaningless. Freudian psychology had disrupted the family by validating nearly all forms of sexual expression and placing hatred of the father at the center of its doctrines. The theory of evolution regarded belief in a Creator as irrelevant and irrational. Social Darwinism reduced political and social relations to a frantic "survival of the fittest." The eugenics movement sought to redesign human nature itself, weeding out the "unfit" in the process. The new discoveries in physics and astronomy mocked the idea of man as the center of divine love. The academic establishment treated the Bible as a collection of myths and forgeries, hardly above the level of *Aesop's Fables*.

Writing in the 1930s, W. R. Matthews described the "decay of institutional religion" across much of the Western world. He spoke for many when he lamented the "incoherence of the Christian message" and its "apparent contradiction with modern knowledge." The result was a crisis of meaning. "The new knowledge will not fit into the old framework," he wrote. "We are really living in a new world."[89]

Tolkien and Lewis were living in the shadow of this "brave new world," as Aldous Huxley famously titled his futuristic novel about a dystopian World State. Published in 1932, Huxley's book anticipated how totalitarian societies would use science and technology to enslave entire populations. In Huxley's story, humans are genetically engineered, indoctrinated, and anesthetized to passively submit to an authoritarian regime. Traditional religious belief is replaced by the State and the soothing communion of the drug soma.

Art was again imitating life. As Michael Burleigh has observed, Nazism did not merely hijack the externals of religion. "It sank a drill head into a deep-seated reservoir of existential anxiety," he writes, offering "salvation" from a societal crisis of meaning.[90]

The weakness of traditional religious belief, and the relative strength of its intellectual rivals, invited the rise of political ideologies that were threatening the entire Western political project. Societies cannot thrive under conditions of disorder, disorientation, and degeneration. The human soul craves meaning and purpose: The new political religions of the twentieth century promised to deliver the goods.

In their pursuit of the ideal society, however, the dictators did not confine their acts of repression and violence to their own populations. They launched a series of military operations throughout the 1930s that raised the specter of another world war.

The first shock was Italy's invasion of Ethiopia on October 2, 1935. For Mussolini, the absorption of Ethiopia would be a stepping stone to constructing a modernized version of the Roman Empire. The new Italian empire would depend upon Italy's dominance of the Mediterranean, the Adriatic, Greece, the Aegean, and North and East Africa. More than five hundred thousand Italian troops poured into the tiny African country.

It was a barbaric war. Italian bombers dropped poison gas to terrorize the population, and soldiers and civilians alike were mowed down by machine-gun fire. On May 5, 1936, after the Ethiopian emperor, Haile Selassie, fled for his life, Italian troops entered Addis Ababa, the Ethiopian capital. "At last, Italy has her empire," Mussolini told a crowd in Rome.

"The Italian people have created an empire with their blood. They will fertilize it with their work. They will defend it against anyone with their weapons. Will you be worthy of it?"

Mussolini's unprovoked attack on a member state in the League of Nations created an international crisis. The British government feared that punishing Italy too severely would drive Mussolini into Hitler's arms. News leaked that British Foreign Secretary Samuel Hoare and French Premier Pierre Laval had secretly agreed to appease Mussolini's aggression by giving him a large chunk of Ethiopia. As the British ambassador in Berlin put it, Italian colonialism was "mere child's play compared with the German problem."[91]

The result was that Mussolini achieved a godlike status among ordinary Italians. "He had defied the world, and he had triumphed," writes biographer Christopher Hibbert, "and to most Italians his triumph was a just reward and defiance a proud and honorable attitude; for they did not recognize in his determination to build an empire in Africa either cruelty or rapacity."[92]

Quite the contrary, in fact. Mussolini was hailed in the Italian press as a "genius," a "titan," "infallible," and likened to the gods of ancient Rome.

"He is always alone like every founder of a religion," gushed one propagandist. "The name of this religion is Italy."[93] The leading newspaper, *Corriere della Sera*, asked: "When you are looking around and don't know who to turn to anymore, you remember that He is there. Who, but He, can help you?"[94] The editors were referring not to God, Jesus, or the Holy Spirit, but to Mussolini. Italian bishops gave the invasion their blessing, saying it would "open the door of Ethiopia to the Catholic faith and Roman civilization."[95] Pope Pius XI, who once called Mussolini a man "sent by Providence" to save Italy, kept silent.[96]

Italy's invasion provoked widespread condemnation in the League of Nations. A 1935 Peace Ballot, however, had revealed that more than ten million of the eleven million respondents rejected military action against an aggressor state. Sanctions were imposed but were limited and ineffective. Thus, the League appeared helpless and feckless. "Following Ethiopia, the League was reduced to idealistic irrelevance," writes Ian Kershaw. "As an instrument intended to uphold and secure the peace of Europe, it was dead."[97]

The lesson was not lost on the dictator in Berlin. In *Mein Kampf*, two major themes dominated Hitler's political vision. One was the removal of the Jews from German society; the other was a militarily revitalized Germany.

The Nazis had accelerated their anti-Jewish agenda in 1935, when the regime announced passage of the Citizenship Law and the Law for the Protection of German Blood and German Honor, collectively known as the Nuremberg Laws. Jews were stripped of their German citizenship, becoming "state subjects." Marriage and sexual intercourse between Aryans and Jews were prohibited. German lawyers and judges were mobilized to convert the racial hatreds of the Nazi leadership into an elaborate system of shame and discrimination.[98]

With the manifest weakness of the Western powers exposed, the second pillar of Nazism took center stage. Hitler had repudiated the disarmament clauses in the Treaty of Versailles the moment he became chancellor. For the next two years Germany was secretly rebuilding its military. By 1935, there were 2,500 planes in the *Luftwaffe* and an army of 300,000 men. Now, after Italy's cost-free adventurism in Ethiopia, Hitler knew the moment was ripe. He publicly announced the creation of his air force and ordered mandatory military conscription, with the goal of an army of 550,000—bald violations of the Versailles Treaty. Western leaders protested but took no action.

A reinvigorated Germany would require expanded lebensraum for a growing Aryan community. The obvious place to start was the Rhineland, a portion of western Germany that bordered France and was demilitarized under Versailles. The Treaty stipulated no fortifications, no military forces, no maneuvers, no mobilizations. Any violation of any of the provisions was considered an act punishable by war.

On March 7, 1936, three battalions of the *Wehrmacht*, about twenty-four thousand troops, crossed the Rhine River and reoccupied the demilitarized zone. Crowds lined the streets cheering their arrival.

The Nazi reoccupation of the Rhineland created another crisis of legitimacy for the Western powers. In his address to the Reichstag that day, Hitler declared: "The struggle for German equal rights can be regarded as closed . . . we have no territorial demands to make in Europe."[99] British leaders were inclined to go along with him. Lord Lothian remarked that the reoccupation was "no more than the Germans walking into their own backyard."

In the end, neither Britain nor France nor the League of Nations took any action against Germany. The United States, for its part, was still in the grip of isolationism. Congress had overwhelmingly reaffirmed the 1935 Neutrality Act, and 1936 was an election year. "We shun political commitments which might entangle us in foreign wars; we avoid connection with the political activities of the League of Nations," proclaimed Franklin Roosevelt on the campaign trail. "We are not isolationists except in so far as we seek to isolate ourselves completely from war."[100]

Thus, Hitler's gamble paid off and his prestige soared. "Even bitter opponents of the regime had to resign themselves to depressed acceptance of the widespread adulation for Hitler," writes Ian Kershaw. "The march into the Rhineland took his virtual deification to new heights."[101]

AN AXIS OF EVIL

Prior to the events of 1936, Mussolini and Hitler eyed each other as potential rivals for influence in Europe. But their mutual victories in the face of Western criticism drew them together.

Nazi officials began making trips to Rome. In September 1937, Mussolini made his first visit to Germany and was met by jubilant crowds. Hitler praised him as "the leading statesman in the world, to whom none may remotely compare himself." That clinched it for Il Duce: The two dictators agreed to a military alliance, forming the Berlin–Rome Axis. Three weeks later, Germany entered into a military alliance with Japan. Italy joined the alliance and quit the League of Nations.

Meanwhile, a full-blown war between Japan and China was raging. By November 1937, Japan had captured Beijing and Shanghai. In a radio broadcast at the height of the battle for Shanghai, the wife of Chiang Kai-shek, the Chinese nationalist leader resisting the Japanese invasion, delivered a radio address pleading for international help.

> Japan is acting on a preconceived plan to conquer China. Curiously, no other nation seems to care. She seems to have secured their spell-bound

> silence. . . . All treaties and structures to outlaw war to regularize the conduct of war appear to have crumbled, and we have a reversion to the day of the savage.[102]

It was not hyperbole. The conduct of the Japanese army at Nanking, the capital of Nationalist China, was beyond description. It became known as the Rape of Nanking. Beginning in December 1937, over a six-week period, Japanese soldiers engaged in a campaign of rape and sadistic violence against Chinese civilians and POWs. It is estimated that between 250,000 and 300,000 people were killed. Based on eyewitness accounts, between 20,000 and 80,000 women—young girls and elderly women—were raped and tortured. Many were then mutilated and killed. Nanking was left in ruins.

The atrocities at Nanking represented not only a war crime but also an act of racist rage almost unprecedented in the history of warfare. Once again, members of the League of Nations expressed outrage but took no action. With Japan as an important US trading partner, President Roosevelt declared that sanctions "are out of the window."

Japanese imperialism—and barbarism—makes the significance of its alliance with Germany and Italy hard to overstate. Japan saw itself as a righteous hegemonic power; other states in the region, including China, were viewed as culturally inferior and ripe for subjugation. After all, wasn't colonialism the accepted behavior of the "liberal" regimes of the West? They had penetrated China and treated it like a vassal state. "If the rule of force was the law of nations in China, why should Japan alone be refused to follow it?" asks Paul Johnson. "Japan could not accept that the Great War had ended the era of colonialism. For her, it was just the beginning. China was Japan's manifest destiny."[103]

Like Germany, the Japanese leadership considered its two great enemies to be international communism (the Soviet Union) and international liberalism (Great Britain and the United States). Like the fascist regimes in Rome and Berlin, Tokyo's political leadership was animated by a vision of ethnic and racial purity. Japan, too, had created a militarized state that was unashamedly authoritarian. Like Mussolini and Hitler, the emperor took on godlike qualities among the population. As in the European dictatorships, any dissent was met with intimidation, imprisonment, exile, or death.

Thus the 1937 pact between Rome, Berlin, and Tokyo was as potent symbolically as it was politically. The three most militaristic and expansionist powers in the world—all rooted in racist theologies, all totalitarian in outlook—had found their way to one another. They represented an axis of evil with no historical parallel. Another global conflict was just around the corner.

THE FINAL TEST OF HEROES

It was during this period of geopolitical turmoil—probably at the end of 1936—that Tolkien and Lewis made a pact between themselves that signified a new resolve to resist the gathering Dark. "Tollers, there's too little of what we really like in stories," Lewis said. "I am afraid we shall have to try and write some ourselves." It was agreed: Tolkien would write a story on time travel, and Lewis would write a thriller based on space travel. Both their stories would point the way to the great Myth.

On the face of it, their pledge might seem frivolous and utterly irrelevant to the geopolitical situation. These were Oxford dons, not political figures. Neither author had published any popular fiction. Although they were building an academic reputation among their peers, they were virtually unknown outside of Oxford. What did they hope to accomplish?

Whatever their objectives, we must not forget that Tolkien and Lewis were Englishmen who cared deeply about their country and its civilization. They knew there were threats all around. They knew that England could not insulate itself from the machinations of the aggressor states: They knew this from their personal horror of the First World War, as well as from Britian's historic connection to the European continent. They resented the confused and cynical outlook that was in vogue, and they surely concluded that the literary establishment could not be counted on to pierce through the moral fog.

Yet Britain's national life—its culture and politics—desperately needed moral clarity. The two friends decided to do something about it. "They were challenging each other to write popular fiction that would have an impact on a lot of people," explains Colin Duriez. "It turned out that some of what they wrote would impact the whole world."[104]

Published in 1937, *The Hobbit* was an instant success. The British Library Association nominated it for the Carnegie Medal, an annual award that recognizes an outstanding new English-language book for children or young adults. A reviewer for *The New York Times* called it "a glorious account of a magnificent adventure, filled with suspense and seasoned with a quiet humor that is irresistible."[105] In his review for the *Times Literary Supplement*, Lewis offered a prediction about the book's impact:

> For it must be understood that this is a children's book only in the sense that the first of many readings can be undertaken in the nursery. *Alice* is read gravely by children and with laughter by grown-ups; *The Hobbit*, on the other hand, will be funnier to its youngest readers, and only years later, at a tenth or a twentieth reading, will they begin to realize what deft scholarship and profound reflection have gone to make everything in it so ripe, so friendly, and in its own way so true. Prediction is dangerous: but *The Hobbit* may well prove a classic.[106]

Lewis also noted a "curious shift" in the story, from a matter-of-fact beginning with descriptions of hobbits and Dwarves, to a "saga-like tone" in the latter chapters. Might the pressure of world events have had something to do with it?

Perhaps a clue can be found in a lecture that Tolkien delivered a few months after the book was published. For its 1937–38 Christmas Lectures for Children, the Ashmolean Natural History Society of Oxfordshire announced forthcoming talks on coral reefs, birds, whales, horses—and dragons. The Society invited Tolkien to take up the latter topic. His talk, delivered on January 1, 1938—before an audience of children of all ages—tackled a decidedly adult subject: the problem of evil in the world and the heroism required to combat it.

Tolkien began, disarmingly, with a slideshow of prehistoric reptiles, including a Pteranodon in flight, to remind his listeners that "science also fills this past with dreadful monsters—many of the largest and most horrible being of a distinctly lizard-like or dragonish kind." These ancient creatures, he said, embodied legendary qualities found in dragon mythology. The dragons with whom he had an acquaintance "loved to possess beautiful things." Greed and hatred motivated them. "And how can you withstand a dragon's flame, and his venom, and his terrible will and malice, and his great strength?"[107]

Tolkien's analysis went deeper still. Drawing on his favorite English poem, *Beowulf,* he said that the English people had a special insight into the moral significance of dragons. In the poem Beowulf defeats the demon Grendel, Grendel's mother, and a fearsome dragon—but at the cost of his own life. "One might say that the chief morals that such stories teach, or rather awake in one's mind, are all shining in this story," Tolkien told his audience.

In the perpetual fight against dragons, Tolkien suggested, modern weapons would not be decisive; something else was required. "Dragons can only be defeated by brave men—usually alone," he said. "Sometimes a faithful friend may help, but it's rare: Friends have a way of deserting you when a dragon comes."

The theme of betrayal would loom large in *The Lord of the Rings,* as the inhabitants of Middle-earth quarrel among themselves about their responsibility to resist the forces of Mordor. Politically speaking, Tolkien's warning would become something of a prophecy: After Hitler invaded Poland in 1939, triggering World War II, Britain's chief military ally—France—abandoned its treaty obligations and signed a peace agreement with Germany.

Just as Tolkien insisted upon the moral significance of the monsters in his *Beowulf* lecture, he emphasized the symbolic importance of dragons in ancient and medieval literature. "For the dragon bears witness to the power and danger and malice that men find in the world," he said. "And he bears witness also to the wit and the courage and finally to the luck (or grace) that men have shown in their adventures—not all men, and only a few men greatly." His reference point was not on a distant past, but rather on *the malice that men find in the world*—in *our* world as we encounter it.

The message would have been blindingly clear to an audience in the late 1930s: Radical evil exists and is likely to confront us with fearsome choices and profound opportunities for growth. As Tolkien neatly summarized it: "Dragons are the final test of heroes."[108]

It is stunning to consider that Tolkien felt compelled to share such adult concepts with an audience of young people. As we'll see, his friend took on the same task in *The Chronicles of Narnia,* stories written for children and yet awash in morally serious themes. "Since it is so likely that they will meet cruel enemies," Lewis explained, "let them at least have heard of brave knights and heroic courage."[109]

TWO LETTERS, A LION, AND A NEW FRIEND

The immediate success of Tolkien's hobbit story validated the literary pledge the two men had made. Yet another work of fantasy, unabashedly Christian, made an even deeper impression. It was *The Place of the Lion* by Charles Williams, an editor at Oxford University Press in London. Lewis probably read it in January 1936 and immediately wrote about it to Arthur Greeves:

> It is not only a most exciting fantasy, but a deeply religious and (unobtrusively) a profoundly learned book. The reading of it has been a good preparation for Lent as far as I am concerned: for it shows me (through the heroine) the special sin of abuse of intellect to which all in my profession are liable, more clearly than I ever saw it before. I have learned more than I ever knew yet about humility. . . . It isn't often now-a-days you get a *Christian* fantasy.[110]

Lewis made a bold move and wrote directly to the author himself. His letter to Williams, dated March 11, 1936, reveals much about the cultural isolation that Lewis experienced at Oxford in the 1930s: a medieval scholar with a deep sympathy for the medieval mind; a lover of fantasy novels imbued with a religious imagination; a Christian believer committed to the historic faith. For Lewis (and Tolkien), living in modern England often felt like living in a foreign land:

> A book sometimes crosses one's path which is so like the sound of one's native language in a strange country that it feels almost uncivil not to wave some kind of flag in answer. I have just read your *Place of the Lion* and it is to me one of the major literary events of my life—comparable to my first discovery of George MacDonald, G.K. Chesterton, or Wm. Morris.[111]

It is hard to imagine a greater compliment, given the influence of these Christian authors on Lewis's literary and spiritual formation. He went on to praise the work for delivering good fantasy, meaty philosophy and theology, compelling characters, and "substantial edification." It all caught Lewis off guard. "Honestly, I didn't think there was anyone now alive in England who could do it."[112]

On the surface, *The Place of the Lion* is a story about large, supernatural animals—a lion, snake, unicorn, lamb, eagle, and others—marauding the English countryside and "absorbing" smaller animals of their own kinds. But underneath is a supernatural thriller: a fantastic tale of "angelicals," creatures drawn from Plato's theory of forms, in which ideas are seen as timeless and unchangeable and, in this sense, more real than the physical world. The Platonic Forms, or archetypes, embody virtues that expose and do battle with their evil counterparts.

All of this appealed to Lewis's love of fantasy, his training in philosophy, and his moral code. The story's attention to the value of friendship, where individuals come together in a common quest for truth and virtue, must have struck a chord. "No mind was so good that it did not need another mind to counter and equal it," writes Williams, "and to save it from conceit and blindness and bigotry and folly."[113] Just as Owen Barfield's *The Silver Trumpet* had confirmed his belief in the appeal of evocative fantasy, *The Place of the Lion* must have persuaded Lewis that mythopoeic literature, rooted in a Christian outlook, could speak powerfully into the modern mind. This discovery surely emboldened Lewis as he set out to fulfill his part of the Tolkien-Lewis literary agreement.

A few words of praise would not be enough, however. Lewis instantly decided that Charles Williams belonged among the Inklings, and he concluded his letter by describing the group to him and inviting him to travel from his London office to Oxford and join one of their meetings. "Can you come down some day next term . . . spend the night as my guest in the College, eat with us at a chop house, and talk with us till the small hours. Meantime, a thousand thanks."

As fate—or Providence—would have it, Williams had just finished reading the page proofs of *The Allegory of Love*, which was published later that year by Oxford University Press. He was preparing to send Lewis a letter praising the work just as Lewis's letter arrived. "My dear Mr. Lewis. If you had delayed writing another 24 hours our letters would have crossed," he wrote. "It has never before happened to me to be admiring an author of a book while he at the same time was admiring me. My admiration for the staff work of the Omnipotence rises every day."[114] The onset of the Second World War would bring Williams to Oxford, where he would become an important member of the Inklings and one of Lewis's closest friends.

NO SAFETY IN FAIRY TALES

The outbreak of political repression and militarism across the globe that began in 1933 occurred simultaneously with a massive international effort to secure the peace. Representatives from fifty-nine countries—including the United States, Great Britain, France, Italy, and Germany—met in Geneva for the World Disarmament Conference. Millions of people from all over the world had signed pro-peace petitions in support of the conference. In England, *The Sunday Times* declared that "disarmament is the thing."

The goal of "the complete elimination" of all offensive weapons, however, was exposed as a fool's errand.[115] On October 23, failing to achieve what he called "real equality" with the militaries of other nations, Hitler pulled Germany out of the conference and out of the League of Nations. By the late 1930s, every attempt to realize Woodrow Wilson's dream of a new international system based upon "collective security" and shared democratic norms had ended in failure.

If, as suggested, the year 1933 was a hinge in the history of the twentieth century, the beginning of the gathering storm, then perhaps this moment made itself felt upon the imaginative lives of Tolkien and Lewis in ways largely unappreciated.

In 1920, soon after the birth of his first child, John, Tolkien began writing colorful Christmas letters to his children signed by Father Christmas. They arrived every year through the childhoods of his three other children, Michael, Christopher, and Priscilla. The letters were filled with the escapades of the Polar Bear, Father Christmas's chief assistant and the cause of comical adventures and disasters affecting the annual Christmas stock.

The 1933 letter from Father Christmas, however, took on a more menacing tone. A new character entered the scene: goblins.

"The worst attack we have had for centuries," explained Father Christmas. "They have been fearfully wild and angry ever since we took all their stolen toys off them last year and dosed them with green smoke." The goblins went on a rampage, burning the stores, capturing gnomes, scattering reindeer. It took the combined efforts of the Polar Bear and the gnomes to overcome them—killing at least one thousand—and drive the rest away, he reported. "They must have gathered their nasty friends from mountains all over the world and been busy all the summer while we were at our sleepiest."[116]

Here are themes of courage and struggle and unexpected peril that Tolkien cannot keep out of his mind for long.

In a way he could not have anticipated, the publication and success of *The Hobbit* in 1937 was a transformative event in Tolkien's life and literary career. His publisher, Stanley Unwin, immediately implored him to produce a sequel. "A large public," he predicted, would be "clamoring next year to hear more from you about Hobbits!" Tolkien at first demurred. "I cannot think of anything more to say about *hobbits*."

Unwin's enthusiasm, however, planted a thought in Tolkien's mind that apparently had not occurred to him, namely, that his "mad hobby" might become a source of income and thus lift a burden off his back:

> I mean, I begin to wonder whether duty and desire may not (perhaps) in future go more closely together. I have spent nearly all the vacation-times of seventeen years examining, and doing things of that sort, driven by immediate financial necessity (mainly medical and educational). Writing stories in prose or verse has been stolen, often guiltily, from time already mortgaged, and has been broken and ineffective. I may perhaps now do what I much desire to do, and not fail of financial duty. Perhaps![117]

In fact, by the end of the year, Tolkien started writing the first chapter of "a new story about Hobbits." Thus began the long incubation of Tolkien's masterpiece, a tale that "grew in the telling, until it became a history of the Great War."[118]

It's important to remember the practical realities of the personal and professional lives of Tolkien and Lewis. They carried heavy academic workloads and were expected to produce works of scholarship, a labor-intensive task. They attended countless college committee meetings. They had responsibilities at home, people who depended upon them emotionally and financially. Yet neither enjoyed an income that provided a margin of safety when unexpected expenses appeared. Both men supplemented their salaries by grading student examination papers.

Thomas Shippey observes that university instructors, like everyone else, are marked by their work. "Biographers of Tolkien and Lewis write as if the two men didn't spend eight hours a day, five days a week, and a lot more time besides, thinking about work."[119] This truism makes it all the more remarkable that they each found time to think about other things. They were moved—compelled, it seems—to invest enormous energy into composing mythic tales of the struggle between light and darkness. And yet this imaginative work was *stolen, often guiltily, from time already mortgaged.*

They did not pursue and cultivate their vocations in a political void: New forces of evil were loose in the world. "A dragon is no idle fancy," Tolkien remarked, because it represents "a personification of malice, greed, destruction."

By 1938, the real-life dragons roaming the earth—the totalitarian regimes threatening the peace of the world—were becoming impossible to ignore. Other novelists, such as Aldous Huxley and George Orwell, began taking them on directly. "It seems to me nonsense, in a period like ours, to think that one can avoid writing of such subjects," Orwell declared. "Everyone writes of them in one guise or another. It is simply a question of which side one takes and what approach one follows."[120]

The moment for choosing was fast approaching. As Lewis expressed in *The Pilgrim's Regress,* "We have been on a fool's errand, then," said John, "ever since we left the main road."[121] As Winston Churchill warned at the time: "We seem to be moving, drifting, steadily, against our will, against the will of every race and every people and every class, towards some hideous catastrophe."[122] Most people in the West were completely unprepared for it. Their leaders were unwilling to contemplate the burgeoning threats to human freedom and persuade their nations, morally and militarily, to meet them head-on.

Perhaps a fellowship of Christian authors could stand in the gap. One admirer of *The Hobbit* worried that parents would consider certain parts of it "too terrifying for bedside reading." Tolkien replied that the presence of the terrible gave his work a vital sense of realism: "A safe fairyland is untrue to all worlds."[123]

CHAPTER 4

THE INKLINGS GO TO WAR

Peace is despaired,
For who can think submission?
War then, war
Open or understood, must be resolved!
—John Milton, *Paradise Lost*

But everywhere he looked he saw the signs of war.
—J. R. R. Tolkien, *The Lord of the Rings*

We are a little land. And little lands on the borders of a great empire were always hateful to the lords of the great empire. He longs to blot them out, gobble them up.
—C. S. Lewis, *Prince Caspian*

I have been in considerable trouble over the present danger of war," wrote C. S. Lewis to Dom Bede Griffiths in April 1938. "Twice in one life—and then to find how little I have grown in fortitude despite my conversion."[1]

More letters like this followed. Lewis worried about the prospect of war again in September, in a note to Owen Barfield. "I have a lot more to say on this . . . when we meet. That is, if we meet, for of course our whole joint world may be blown up before the end of the week. I can't feel in my bones that it will, but my bones know dam' all about it. If we are separated, God bless you, and thanks for a hundred good things I owe to you, more than I can count or weigh." On October 5, Lewis wrote again to Griffiths: "I was terrified to find how terrified I was by the crisis. Pray for me for courage."[2]

Writing to his publisher on October 13, J. R. R. Tolkien also had the prospect of war on his mind. He said that his new story about Middle-earth "was becoming more terrifying than the Hobbit." He worried that it "may prove quite unsuitable" for young people because it carried more of an "adult" tone. "The darkness of the present days has had some effect on it."[3]

The "crisis" and the "darkness" of which Lewis and Tolkien spoke—the fear of another European war—arrived like a thunderbolt in the spring of 1938. The Treaty of Versailles had left 3.5 million Germans within the borders of the newly created Czechoslovakia. Adolf Hitler began complaining about the treatment of these ethnic Germans, located mostly in the Sudetenland, the northern and western portions of the country bordering Germany. Hitler demanded that they be incorporated into the Third Reich.

British Prime Minister Neville Chamberlain flew to Germany on September 15 to meet with Hitler at his mountain retreat, the Berghof, in the Bavarian Alps, and make a personal appeal to avoid war. "The thing has got to be settled at once," Hitler said. "I do not care whether there is a world war or not."

A few days later, in a broadcast to the British people, Chamberlain's mood was somber. "How horrible—fantastic—incredible it is that we should be digging trenches and trying on gasmasks here because of a quarrel in a far-away country between people of whom we know nothing."[4]

Hitler invited Chamberlain to return to Munich on September 29 to negotiate an end to the crisis. The House of Commons gave him a standing ovation before he left.

The leaders of Britain, France, and Italy arrived in Munich to cheering crowds as they made their way to the *Führerbau*, the Führer's house, where Hitler liked to conduct business. The negotiations, concluded in the early-morning hours of September 30, sealed the fate of Czechoslovakia: The Sudetenland was to be turned over to Germany.

Without firing a shot, Hitler acquired Czechoslovakia's frontier defenses—1.5 million rifles, 750 aircraft, 6,000 tanks, and 2,000 field guns—along with hundreds of thousands of ethnic Czechs.[5] Without a plebiscite, without even the presence of the Czechs at the negotiating table—they were not invited—the borders of Czechoslovakia were redrawn. "If you have sacrificed my nation to preserve the peace of the world, I will be the first to applaud you," warned Jan Masaryk, son of the founding father of the Czechoslovak Republic. "But if not, gentlemen, God help your souls!"[6]

Upon his return to England, Chamberlain waved in the air his paper agreement with Hitler that their two nations would "never go to war again." It represented, he declared, "peace in our time." All of Britain, it seemed, was in a state of euphoria, such was the intense desire to avoid another war. An editorial in *The Times* captured the mood: "No conqueror returning from a victory on the battlefield has come home adorned with nobler laurels than Mr. Chamberlain from Munich yesterday." In the days following, more than twenty thousand letters and telegrams praising the prime minister's diplomacy arrived at 10 Downing Street.

But not everyone was celebrating. In a speech before the House of Commons a few days later, Winston Churchill denounced the Munich Pact as "a disaster of the first magnitude." He made a fearsome prediction. "And do not suppose this is the end," he said. "This is only the beginning of the reckoning. This is only the first sip, the first foretaste of a bitter cup which will be proffered to us year by year unless, by a supreme recovery of moral health and martial vigor, we arise again and take our stand for freedom as in the olden time."[7] Britain's act of appeasement, he warned, invited another European war.

THE CULTURAL TASK

After Churchill became prime minister in 1940, he played an indispensable political role in mobilizing the British people for war and sustaining their war spirit over the next five years. Yet the reconstitution of "moral health" and "martial vigor" was also a cultural task. Tolkien and Lewis took on this obligation—not as wartime propagandists, but as authors and academics who believed that their scholarship, teaching, and imaginative literature could help shake a generation loose from its moral cynicism and spiritual lethargy. In this endeavor they drew from deep wells: the collective wisdom of the literary canon of Western civilization.

In her World War I memoir, *Testament of Youth*, Vera Brittain chided her generation for regarding classical literature as irrelevant to the bitter realities of the modern world. "I cannot yet feel as near to Light and Truth as I did when I was 'wasting my time' on Plato and Homer," she wrote. "I can't help feeling that the despised classics taught me the finest parts of it better."[8] Daisy Dunn argues that there is a timeless quality to this literature that Tolkien and Lewis were determined to retrieve. "They're seeing the destruction of history in the news every day," she says. "There's a sense, as a scholar, that by writing about the past you are doing something to preserve it against the forces all around you that you can't control. You're doing something to preserve civilization as it's being swept away."[9]

Many of the young people who studied under Tolkien and Lewis during the war years later recalled the sense of living through a singular moment in their intellectual development.

"We made our way weekly through the blackouts to hear this extraordinary man," recalls Rachel Trickett, a student of Lewis. "Pupils who survived the combat of his tutorials learned to love and rely on his humanity and loyalty and his stealthy generosity."[10] Rosamund Cowan, among the first of Lewis's female students, remembers students from disciplines outside of literature—including politics, medicine, and science—flocking to hear him speak. "If Lewis was known to be lecturing, the big hall in Magdalen was absolutely full," she said. "They were even sitting on the windowsills."[11]

Helen Tyrrell Wheeler attended lectures by Tolkien and was a pupil of Lewis during the war, when "fire-watching, or other war work, was part of every student's week." War news, often wrenching, was unavoidable. "But at few times can there have been such splendidly exciting lectures and such overflowing lecture halls," she recalled. "What it meant for my generation of English Language and Literature undergraduates was that what happened in the great books was of equal significance to what happened in life, indeed, that they were the same, and that to this importance, time could make no difference if you read the text as it should be read."[12]

What happened in the great books was of equal significance to what happened in life. Here is a remarkable insight from a young woman who came under the influence of these two scholars. Like no one else, Tolkien and Lewis helped a generation to understand that the truths and ideals expressed in the great works of the ancient and medieval worlds bore upon the events of the modern world—a world at war.

Every age has its own outlook on the world, a mixture of clarity and blindness. Yet the moral blindness of the twentieth century represented something entirely novel: ideologies that threatened to destroy the foundations of civilized life. Tolkien and Lewis believed that only an outlook rooted in the ancient truths could resist it. "The only palliative is to keep the clean sea breeze of the centuries blowing through our minds," Lewis wrote, "and this can be done only by reading old books."[13] Malcolm Guite argues that their mastery of the classic texts of the Western tradition accounts for the enduring power of their fictional works. "I think they saw in the ancient resources they had, in the older books they were reading, not an irrelevant world into which you could escape," he explains, "but curiously enough exactly the diagnostic tool they needed to critique the world they were in. And they did so to devasting effect."[14]

The themes that inspired their imaginary worlds, embedded in these "ancient resources," also defined everyday life for the British people during the nightmare years of 1939–45.

Tolkien began writing *The Lord of the Rings* in December 1937 and, despite the ongoing anxieties and terrors of wartime, nearly finished it before the Allied victory in 1945. Its length—over half a million words—allows for a rich mix of compelling personalities, evocative landscapes, invented languages, poetry, ancient histories, all supporting an epic story of moral complexity.

In one of Tolkien's summaries of the book's plot, he identified themes that were obviously important to him. "Rumors of troubles in the great world outside reach the Hobbits," he wrote, "especially the rise again of the Enemy." There is "the breaking up of the Company" and the reappearance of the Black Riders "in still more terrible form." There are the "politics of the defense of the West" and the machinations of the wizard Saruman, "who has turned himself to evil and seeks for domination." There is the "apparent disaster" of Frodo being struck down by the monstrous spider, yet there remains the figure of Sam and "his supreme plain dogged common-sense heroism in aid of his master."[15]

The contagion of war, the lust for power, the existence of radical evil, and the courage required to resist it: The catastrophic events of war brought all of these concepts into focus.

For his part, Lewis entered a season of astonishing literary creativity. Throughout the war, he labored seemingly nonstop to produce works of both prose and fiction that explained and defended historic Christianity for the modern mind.

With a speech from Hitler ringing in his head, he set out to write a diabolical fantasy about the stratagems of the devil to corrupt the human soul. Outraged by a modern grammar book that effectively annihilated the concept of truth, he produced a defense of the Moral Law as a check against nihilism. Stunned by the humanistic appeal of pseudoscience from authors such as H. G. Wells, he wrote a science fiction thriller that recast the biblical concepts of the Fall, divine grace, and redemption. With Great Britain still enduring bombing raids by the Nazis, he traveled to London to deliver radio talks expounding the core doctrines of the faith. And, after taking into his home English children displaced by the Blitz, he conceived of a children's story involving a magical wardrobe, a White Witch, and a fearsome Lion.

PREPARATIONS FOR WAR

The year 1939 began ominously enough. On January 30, Hitler delivered a major speech to the German Reichstag in which he declared that if there was another world war, he would hold the Jews responsible. The result of such a conflict, he warned, would be "the annihilation of the Jewish race in Europe." The hall, overflowing with Nazi Party officials, erupted into frenzied applause.

On the eve of the Second World War, the concept of government by consent, the political jewel of the West since the eighteenth century, was in crisis. Sixteen European states were dominated by repressive and authoritarian governments. Of the democracies created in Europe after the First World War, in the breakup of the Austro-Hungarian Empire, only Czechoslovakia remained. And its future was bleak.

In February 1939, Sir Nevile Henderson, Britain's ambassador in Berlin, reported that "the Germans are not contemplating any immediate wild adventure" and that "their compass is pointing towards peace."[16] Many in England desperately wanted to believe it was true. As an island nation it sought to preserve a sense of "splendid isolation" from the intrigues on the European continent. Britain's parliamentary democracy was the oldest in the world, their society relatively unscathed by the social and political revolutions that had wracked other European states. Tolkien captured the English outlook perfectly in his description of the Shire: "And there in that pleasant corner of the world they plied their well-ordered business of living, and they heeded less and less the world outside where dark things moved, until they came to think that peace and plenty were the rule in Middle-earth and the right of sensible folk."[17]

Nevertheless, within a few weeks of the British ambassador's cheery report—barely six months after the Munich Pact—German tanks rolled into Prague, absorbing the rest of Czechoslovakia.

The entire geopolitical landscape shifted overnight. All the rationalizing talk about Hitler only wanting to reincorporate ethnic Germans into the Third Reich was finally exposed as fairy dust. The age of appeasement was over.

On March 31, the British prime minister offered Poland a guarantee of military support, despite the fact that neither Poland nor Britain was prepared for war with Germany. Meanwhile, on April 7, news arrived that Mussolini had invaded Albania. In response, Britain and France guaranteed military aid to Romania and Greece. Proposals were made in the House of Commons for the reintroduction of conscription.

Isolationist attitudes no longer seemed tenable. An opinion poll in July revealed that about three-quarters of the respondents thought Britain should fulfill its promise to defend Poland in the event of war.[18] At Oxford University, students debated "whether they would have to fight this year or next." Unlike at the Oxford Union debate in 1933, a student recalled, "rearmament was no longer a dirty word."[19]

Even before these latest acts of aggression, war anxiety in Britain was mounting. Government ministers were reaching out to Oxford dons who possessed expertise that might be useful if hostilities broke out.

Tolkien's reputation as a philologist got their attention: They needed codebreakers. In January 1939, they asked Tolkien if he would work in the cryptological department of the Foreign Office in the event of war. "I shall have . . . some work in preparation for a possible 'National Emergency,'" he wrote his publisher in February.[20] Tolkien received four days of training in cryptography at the office in London, known then as the Government Code and Cipher School. In August, with the prospect of aerial bombings in view, it was moved to Bletchley Park.

In January 1939, Lewis wrote to his friend Daphne Harwood to wish her a happy new year and closed the letter with this: "I hope it will be less exciting than the last but not with much confidence . . . the prospect of leaving this planet gets daily less terrible."[21] A few days later, he wrote to A. K. Hamilton Jenkin, a friend from his undergraduate days. After describing a wintry walking tour with Warnie, he admitted to being tired of the winter, among other things. "The truth is I am tired of so many things—of weather, of work, of reading, of writing, above all of News," he wrote.

> As to News and "the state of the nation" what worries me sometimes more than the dangers is our reaction to them, beginning, of course, with my own reaction. To be faced with wars and ruins is I suppose the normal state of humanity: did any people before lie shivering under it as we do?[22]

In March, the government announced that Britain's Territorial Army—part-time soldiers supplementing the regular army—would be increased to 170,000 and then doubled. Lewis's friend Dom Bede Griffiths wrote to him, asking if he planned to join the Territorials. Lewis replied that he was too old and confessed that he didn't regret the fact.

> My memories of the last war haunted my dreams for years. Military service, to be plain, includes the threat of every temporal evil: pain and death, which is what we fear from sickness: isolation from those we love, which is what we fear from exile: toil under arbitrary masters, injustice and humiliation, which is what we fear from slavery: hunger, thirst, cold and exposure, which is what we fear from poverty. I'm not a pacifist. If

> it's got to be, it's got to be. But the flesh is weak and selfish and I think death would be much better than to live through another war.[23]

Death would be better than to live through another war. So much for the stereotype of dreamy Oxford dons detached from the realities of the modern world. Another sign of looming disaster arrived on August 23, 1939, when the Soviet Union and Nazi Germany announced the Nazi-Soviet Non-Aggression Pact.[24] Given the decades of hatred between communists and fascists in Europe—including assassinations, mob violence, and attempted coups—the agreement sent shock waves around the world.

The two nations formally pledged not to go to war with each other. That was the paper agreement. There was also a secret protocol in which the two totalitarian states would carve up spheres of influence in Europe. Hitler would get most of Western Europe and half of Poland; Stalin would receive the other half of Poland, Finland, and the Baltic states.[25] With the pact in hand, the Soviet Union bought time to strengthen its military, while Germany had sealed its eastern front from attack.

Nothing now prevented the German invasion of Poland. "Our enemies are little worms," Hitler remarked two days before the treaty was signed. "I saw them at Munich."[26]

THE MYTHIC IMAGINATION

Although Tolkien was making headway on *The Lord of the Rings*, his efforts were often interrupted for weeks at a time—from illness, family and financial obligations, his teaching load, or a combination of all the above. "It is now flowing along, and getting quite out of hand . . . and progresses toward quite unforeseen goals," he wrote his publisher. "But it is no bedtime story."[27] By February 1939, he seemed to have stalled again. "The writing of *The Lord of the Rings* is laborious, because I have been doing it as well as I know how, and considering every word," he wrote. "The story too has (I fondly imagine) some significance."[28]

By suggesting that his story had a special "significance," was Tolkien hinting that its themes might illuminate the present world crisis? We cannot be sure, but it seems likely.

The same could be said of Tolkien's academic scholarship. His work was not nourished by an idiosyncratic obsession but rather by things much deeper, matters that touched the roots of his moral and spiritual life. Thus, although his choice of research topics reflected his own personal interests, he wrote about them in a way that exposed their universal importance to our mortal lives. No topic was closer to the heart of his entire literary project than that of the fairy tale: fantastic stories found in nearly every society; tales of wonder, adventure, and danger that address the most basic human desires.

As we have seen, when Tolkien was a student at Oxford, the need to deliver a literary talk before his peers—the story of *The Fall of Gondolin*—swung open a window into his imagination. Twenty years later, another lecture, for a more prestigious peer group, may have had a similar effect.

On March 1, 1939, Tolkien wrote to his son Michael about a lecture he was scheduled to give at the University of St. Andrews. "I am going off to Scotland on Monday night or Tuesday morning, & have not written the infernal lecture yet."[29] Tolkien was asked to deliver the annual Andrew Lang Lecture, named after the nineteenth-century English author and scholar famous for his fairy tales and interest in mythology. Although Tolkien had been researching the topic, he had little time to prepare and labored on it until the eleventh hour.[30]

His talk, "On Fairy-Stories," which he later expanded into an essay, is a profound meditation on the meaning and significance of mythic literature in the human experience. "The realm of fairy-story," he said, "is wide and deep and high and filled with many things: all manner of beasts and birds are found there; shoreless seas and stars uncounted; beauty that is an enchantment, and ever-present peril; both joy and sorrow as sharp as swords."[31]

Modern prejudices against the fairy tale—that it's fit only for children, for example—come under attack. As Tolkien described it, faerie is the realm of enchantment. It may contain creatures such as elves, witches, giants, or dragons because they represent an old desire—"as ancient as the Fall"—to converse with other living things. Yet the land of faerie also holds the seas, the sky, the earth, "and all things that are in it: tree and bird, water and stone, wine and bread, and ourselves, mortal men, when we are enchanted."[32]

Good fairy-stories, he explained, are about the adventures that men and women have in "the Perilous Realm," where decisions of real consequence must be made. The fantastical agents of this realm present its visitors with all manner of dangers and temptations. "At least part of the magic that they wield for the good or evil of man is power to play on the desires of his body and his heart."[33] There is nothing whimsical or juvenile about a first-rate fairy tale. "If fairy-story as a kind is worth reading at all," Tolkien said, "it is worthy to be written for and read by adults."

What are fairy-stories good for? In answering, Tolkien anticipated the narrative arc of *The Lord of the Rings* years before he completed it. Like no other mode of literature, fairy-stories offer *Fantasy*, *Recovery*, *Escape*, and *Consolation*. The modern mind, in its cynicism and unbelief, had rejected these concepts and thus cut itself off from the resources required to live a fully human life.

The inventor of *Fantasy* seeks to create a world that seems real or plausible—but also strange, wonderful, magical. Though it may contain all sorts of imaginary creatures, it embodies truths about the human story.

Tolkien quoted from a letter he wrote to an unnamed friend, a religious skeptic, to argue that creating fantasy was natural to human beings and suggestive of our true nature: "Although now long estranged, Man is not wholly lost nor wholly changed, Dis-graced he may be, yet is not dethroned, and keeps the rags of lordship once he owned."[34] The existence of fantasy was a hint of the dignity that man possessed as a "sub-creator" in God's world. "We make in our measure . . . because we are made; and not only made, but made in the image and likeness of a Maker."[35]

The friend in question, of course, was C. S. Lewis in the days before his conversion to Christianity. Lewis was drawn to these stories for the same reasons and came to believe, like Tolkien, that myths awakened a longing for something beyond our mortal lives. "Myth is the mountain whence all the different streams arise," Lewis wrote, "which become truths down here in the valley."[36]

The enchanted world is the setting for the trilogy of themes that form the crux of Tolkien's imaginative mind. Implicit in the theme of *Recovery* is man's need to retrieve something of value that has been lost. The modern outlook, he suggests, has given us a distorted, dark, and violent vision of the world. We need to see the natural world around us with fresh eyes: like an ancient shepherd saw sheep, dogs, horses—and wolves.

Landscapes could move Tolkien deeply in this regard. If, as he confessed, the Shire was "more or less a Warwickshire village," it seems likely that his vision of Rivendell, the land of the Elves, was inspired by his trip to the Swiss Alps in the summer of 1911. A hiking adventure in the Lauterbrunnen—a valley of sublime beauty, as this author recently discovered—evidently left its mark. As Tolkien writes in *The Lord of the Rings*, the hobbits discover that even after a short stay in Rivendell, "all fear and anxiety was lifted from their minds." It is a sanctuary for those who need it. "The future, good or ill, was not forgotten, but ceased to have any power over the present. Health and hope grew strong in them, and they were content with each good day as it came, taking pleasure in every meal, and in every word and song."[37]

In Tolkien's story, Rivendell itself is an enchantment, a haven of beauty and wisdom and joy. It is ageless and innocent—and unforgettable. If, as Tolkien believed, modern man had entered an age of disenchantment, fairy tales could help him become *reenchanted* with the creatures and beauty of the world.

Tolkien described *Escape* as one of the main purposes of fairy-stories. But he rejected the charge of escapism—that fantasy writers sought to evade life's struggles—by turning the argument around. The writers of fantasy are "acutely conscious of the ugliness of our works, and of their evil." They look at the "progressive things" of twentieth-century European society—like factories, machine guns, and bombs—and properly reject them. They discern the patterns of the world that conspire to enslave us—and they point us toward freedom. Prisoners should not be scorned for trying to go home, he said, or for talking about topics other than jailers and prison walls.

Worse still, the critics of fairy tales—like modern propagandists—are abusing language: "Just so a Party-spokesman might have labelled departure from the misery of the Fuhrer's or any other Reich and even criticism as treachery." By heaping contempt on the writers of fantasy, these critics demean the qualities necessary to combat the Darkness. The result: something like the moral cowardice that had overtaken European leaders in the face of Nazi aggression. "Not only do they confound the escape of the prisoner with the flight of the deserter," Tolkien said, "but they would seem to prefer the acquiescence of the 'quisling' to the resistance of the patriot."[38]

The oldest and deepest desire of mankind, Tolkien explained, is the Great Escape: to escape from death.[39] Herein lies perhaps the greatest gift of a good fairy tale, the *Consolation* of the happy ending, what Tolkien called the *eucatastrophe.* It involves the undoing of a catastrophe, the reversal of a great evil. It is "a sudden and miraculous grace" that brings about deliverance, restoration, and renewal.

The universal human response to this deliverance is joy. It has a special quality, Tolkien believed, pointing us toward a reality outside of ourselves: "joy beyond the walls of the world, poignant as grief." Tolkien was almost prepared to say that all complete fairy-stories must have it.[40]

However, the fairy story, he admitted, could be put to evil purposes. It could delude the minds of its creators.

> But of what human thing in this fallen world is that not true? Men have conceived not only of elves, but they have imagined gods, and worshipped them, even worshipped those most deformed by their authors' own evil. But they have made false gods out of other materials: their nations, their banners, their monies; even their sciences and their social and economic theories have demanded human sacrifice.[41]

The meaning of Tolkien's reference to the false gods of his age would have been starkly obvious to his audience. Militant nationalism, materialism, eugenics, fascism, communism: These were the ideological idols of his day, to which millions of people had sworn allegiance.

It is surely significant that Tolkien expressed his defense of the fairy tale—redefined and reinvigorated—on the eve of Europe's calamity in 1939. Nations such as Italy, Germany, and Russia, the source of some of the most compelling cultural achievements in history, had become morally degraded and culturally vacuous dictatorships. Even in liberal societies such as Great Britain, the mechanistic wheels of modernity were crushing the soul of creative man underfoot. Tolkien watched with dismay as the civilization of the West fell under a shadow of ignorance: a darkening of the imaginative life no less consequential than the degradation of political life.

Uniquely and powerfully, Tolkien's lecture validated the careful study and deep appreciation of mythological literature. For in this literature, he insisted, society might preserve "an oasis of sanity in a desert of unreason."[42]

THE RANSOM TRILOGY

These themes were taken up by Lewis at this crisis moment in the West, most importantly in *The Ransom Trilogy*: a series of science fiction novels in which he exposes the catastrophic combination of human pride, scientific technique, and the Will to Power.

In a letter to Ruth Penelope Lawson (Sister Penelope) dated August 9, 1939, Lewis explained why he began writing the series. It was "the discovery that a pupil of mine took all that dream of interplanetary colonization quite seriously" and that there were many others just like him. For these believers, "the whole meaning of the universe" was based on "some hope of perpetuating and improving the human species."[43]

It stunned Lewis to realize that a pseudoscientific hope of defeating death "is a real rival to Christianity."[44] He decided to do battle with it. "I like the whole interplanetary idea as a *mythology*," he explained, "and simply wished to conquer for my own (Christian) point of view what has always hitherto been used by the opposite side."[45] In other words, he intended to use the genre of science fiction to reintroduce biblical concepts into the cultural mainstream, to reach an audience that neither Christian ministers nor educators seemed to be reaching.

In *Out of the Silent Planet*, the first book in the series, Lewis revealed his talents as poet, philosopher, satirist, novelist—and mythmaker. It is a deeply Christian story involving a trio of earthlings who travel to another planet, Malacandra (Mars), where they encounter three different species of rational creatures living in perfect harmony and social peace. In this sense, Malacandra appears as a rebuke to the race-based hatreds that, at the moment of Lewis's writing, were threatening to destroy civilization on earth.

The story's protagonist is Elwin Ransom, a Cambridge professor and a humble philologist modeled, in fact, on Tolkien. He represents the rehabilitation of modern man: a man of faith obedient to the Good.

Ransom must battle two other travelers: Dick Devine, a profiteer, and Dr. Weston, a mad physicist hell-bent on planting the human species on other planets. They meet the planet's ruling intelligence, the Oyarsa, who reveal to Ransom a terrifying secret. His beloved home planet of Thulcandra (Earth) has become a cautionary tale throughout the universe: a "silent planet" alienated from the joy of heaven because of the schemes of a fallen angel and the race of men and women ensnared by their own rebellion.

Although Lewis loved the science fiction novels of H. G. Wells as a boy, by the late 1930s he had rejected what Wells represented: an apostle of human progress. The "myth of progress," as Lewis called it, did not die in the embers of the First World War. Rather, it took new forms: fueled by science and technology, guided only by reason, and managed by a gifted race of technocrats. Wells's philosophy of life was Lewis's chief target in the series.

A staunch evolutionist, Wells nevertheless did not believe that human progress would come easily. Quite the opposite: He expected another global catastrophe, either natural or manmade. Out of its ruins, however, mankind would lift himself to new plateaus of technological, moral, and political achievement. By the 1930s, Wells was one of the most influential popular speakers and authors in the English-speaking world, and he used his platform to propound this vision in lectures, essays, interviews, and books. The key to its fulfillment, he argued, was the creation of a World State, an idea he first introduced in the aftermath of World War I. Wells's unified, global government quickly took on the trappings of a totalitarian regime.

In his influential book *The Shape of Things to Come* (1933), Wells blends science fiction and historical speculation to imagine a world governed by a select group of "scientific samurai" who ensure peace and plenty. Through "education," "social discipline," and "eugenic effort," mankind will transform itself into a new species.[46] With Wells as screenwriter, the book was made into the 1936 film *Things to Come*, starring Raymond Massey and Sir Cedric Hardwicke. The film closes with the prospect of a reconstituted human race expanding into the cosmos as it populated—conquered—other planets.

Wells's political vision was as fanciful as his science fiction. He took up the theme again in *The New World Order* (1940), a polemical defense of his World State in which only the "comprehensive collectivization of human affairs"—an international dictatorship—could prevent mankind's self-destruction.[47] Science would pave the way. "Can one doubt that the 'scientific world' will break out in this way when the revolution is achieved, and that the development of man's power over nature and over his own nature . . . will undergo a continual acceleration as the years pass?" he asked rhetorically. "No man can guess beforehand what doors will open then nor upon what wonderlands."[48]

Lewis believed he knew exactly what doors would open if Wells's vision was pursued successfully. First, it would be used to validate one of the besetting sins of powerful nations: the desire to dominate the weak. When considering the possibility of an encounter between humans and members of another life-form from outer space, Lewis was unflinchingly honest:

> I observe how the white man has hitherto treated the black, and how, even among civilized men, the stronger have treated the weaker. If we encounter in the depth of space a race, however innocent and amiable, which is technologically weaker than ourselves, I do not doubt that the same revolting story will be repeated. We shall enslave, deceive, exploit or exterminate. . . . We are not yet fit to visit other worlds.[49]

The personalities of Devine and Weston in *Out of the Silent Planet* embody the race-based imperialism that characterized much of modern European history. As Lewis saw it, Wells was giving colonialism a new scientific rationale. Thus, Devine is pilloried in the story for having absorbed Wells's outlook. "His mind, like so many minds of his generation, was richly furnished with bogies," Lewis writes. "He had read his H. G. Wells and others. His universe was peopled with horrors such as ancient and medieval mythology could hardly rival."[50]

Unhinged from a traditional moral code, the lust to dominate opened the door to mass atrocities. Lewis drives this point home in a climactic exchange between Weston, Ransom, and the Oyarsa, in which they discuss why Ransom and his companions came to Malacandra. Devine is motivated by greed, but Weston by a darker force: an obsession with the survival and flourishing of the human race that overwhelms all other considerations.

"There are laws that all *hnau* [rational creatures] know, of pity and straight dealing and shame and the like, and one of these is love of kindred," explains the Oyarsa. "This one he has bent it till it becomes folly and has set it up, thus bent, to be a little blind Oyarsa [ruler] in your brain."[51] Thus, Weston is known as "the Bent One" in the story. "I think he would destroy all your people to make room for our people; and then he would do the same with other worlds again," says Ransom. "He wants our race to last for always, I think, and hopes they will leap from world to world."[52]

Weston would destroy one race to make room for his own. Lewis did not need to invent this apocalyptic possibility through fiction. Nor did he need to look back on European history to discover this disturbing fact about our civilization. It was occurring on Britain's doorstep. William Shirer, working as a journalist in Berlin in the 1930s, witnessed for himself the impact of this ideology on the German people. "It is this primitive racial instinct of 'blood and soil' which the Nazis have reawakened in the German soul more successfully than any of their modern predecessors," he wrote, "and which has shown that the influence of Christianity and Western civilization on German life and culture was only a thin veneer."[53]

In Hitler's *Mein Kampf*, the elimination of the Jewish people from Europe was a prerequisite for Germany's attainment of lebensraum for the Aryan race. By the time Lewis began composing the Ransom series in 1937, this goal was already the focus of Hitler's domestic policy. Before Lewis completed the trilogy in 1945, it had become the most important cause of Nazi Germany's wars of aggression. "For the Nazis, the destruction of the Jews was itself a war aim of the highest priority," writes John Weiss in *Ideology of Death*. "In a war to secure the future of the Germanic race, the Jews, symbol of all the humane values the Nazis opposed, could not be allowed to live."[54]

Second, Wells's philosophy would reinforce the "scientific" view that considered religious belief an obstacle to human progress. Discoveries in astronomy, such as those by Sir Arthur Stanley Eddington in *The Expanding Universe* (1933), seemed to reduce earth to infinitesimal importance in the cosmos.[55] Philosophers and others touted this as evidence against the core doctrines of the Bible, namely, that man was God's special creation, the object of divine love, and yet alienated from the Creator through disobedience.

Next to Tolkien, probably no Christian author of this period did more to make plausible a biblical view of man's dignity and man's shame. Against the scientific materialists, the reintroduction of the Genesis story of Creation and the Fall became for Lewis almost a literary obsession.

The concept throbs throughout *The Ransom Trilogy.* In *Out of the Silent Planet,* the travelers from earth are "the bent men" in a virtuous and unfallen world. In *Perelandra,* Ransom battles Weston, the Un-Man, a demonic figure who tries to persuade a prototypical Eve to disobey her Creator.

> The forces which had begun, perhaps years ago, to eat away his humanity had now completed their work. The intoxicated will which had been slowly poisoning the intelligence and the affections had now at last poisoned itself and the whole psychic organism had fallen to pieces. Only a ghost was left—an everlasting unrest, a crumpling, a ruin, an odor of decay.[56]

In *That Hideous Strength,* a cosmic struggle between good and evil occurs, surprisingly enough, among the faculty and administrators at a university campus. This is because, as Lewis explained, the diabolical "had to be shown touching the life of some ordinary and respectable profession."[57]

A third result of Wells's outlook would be the creation of a totalitarian society under the cloak of scientific planning and egalitarian motives. The theme appears in all three of the Ransom stories and forms the main plot in *That Hideous Strength.* The chief protagonist, Mark Studdock, naively announces that "this time we're going to get science applied to social problems and backed by the whole force of the state." Meanwhile, the scientific elite, in support of the "progressive" vision of the National Institute of Coordinated Experiments (the N.I.C.E.), has dispensed with religious ideas about truth and morality.

> The physical sciences, good and innocent in themselves, had already, even in Ransom's own time, begun to be warped, had been subtly maneuvered in a certain direction. Despair of objective truth had been increasingly insinuated into the scientists; indifference to it, and a concentration upon mere power, had been the result.[58]

As Lewis was writing his trilogy, experiments by Nazi scientists to support the Third Reich—from eugenics to radar to rockets—were becoming well known. Between 1933 and 1945, for example, Nazi doctors carried out 400,000 forced sterilizations of those considered "unfit" or enemies of the Reich. Like no other modern state in history, the scientific and medical communities of Germany had willingly put themselves in the service of a criminal regime. Winston Churchill, in one of his most famous speeches as prime minister, warned that the triumph of Nazism would usher in "a new Dark Age made more sinister, and perhaps more protracted, by the lights of perverted science."[59]

Throughout his Ransom series, Lewis's ideological nemesis is not the scientific profession but what he called "scientism." It is the belief that science—not religion—provided the answers to man's most profound questions and aspirations. As such, the material world was the only reality; man's mortality was the final fact about him. The supreme moral vision of scientism, Lewis argued, was "the perpetuation of our own species." This goal was to be pursued "even if, in the process of being fitted for survival, our species has to be stripped of all those things for which we value it—of pity, of happiness, and of freedom."[60]

A STARTLING DISCOVERY

In all this, Lewis assailed one of the tacit assumptions of the science fiction genre, namely, that science could solve all of mankind's most desperate problems—even the scourge of death itself—and perfect human existence. To achieve his aim, Lewis imbued his stories with a mythic quality: They retell the biblical account of the Fall, expose the futility of human pride by echoing the story of the tower of Babel, and recount a cosmic struggle between the forces of light and the forces of darkness.

It came as something of a shock to Lewis that most of the reviewers of the first book in the series failed to discern the biblical motif at the center of the story. As Lewis put it in a letter to Sister Penelope:

> You will be both grieved and amused to learn that out of about sixty reviews, only two showed any knowledge that my idea of the Bent One

> was anything but a private invention of my own! But if only there were someone with a richer talent and more leisure, I believe this great ignorance might be a help to the evangelization of England: any amount of theology can now be smuggled into people's minds under cover of romance without their knowing it.[61]

It is hard to overstate the significance of Lewis's discovery. He not only became more fully aware of the biblical illiteracy and rampant secularism of English society. He began, for the first time, to grasp the potential of imaginative literature to tell a compelling story about the human condition: to recover and articulate the teachings of the Bible for an unbelieving generation.

A reviewer for *The New York Times* compared Lewis's story to that of Huxley's *Brave New World*, noting their common assault on the "slavish scientific materialism" in vogue. Yet the reviewer discerned a different quality to the Ransom story. "But when Mr. Huxley wrote his bitter books his mood was one of cynical despair. Mr. Lewis, on the contrary, sounds a militant call to battle."[62] Perhaps a well-told tale—a modern story wrapped in mythic language and washed with Christian imagery—could lead some souls to the threshold of God's kingdom.

HITLER STRIKES

In February 1939, Tolkien got a letter from his publisher telling him that the German publisher of *The Hobbit* planned to release his book in the fall and promised to let him see a proof of the German translation. Tolkien was ambivalent. In a previous letter from the same publishing house, he had gotten a taste of the anti-Semitic bigotry that was overwhelming nearly all aspects of German life.

Tolkien was asked if he was of Aryan extraction. He wrote first to his publisher, wondering if Germany's "lunatic laws" required a certificate of Aryan origin from every person doing business with the Reich. He was inclined to "let a German translation go hang." He mentioned his many Jewish friends and that he "should regret giving any color to that notion that I subscribed to the wholly pernicious and unscientific race-doctrine."[63]

Tolkien then wrote directly to Rütten & Loening, replying that he was not of Aryan origin and cautioning them:

> But if I am to understand that you are enquiring whether I am of Jewish origin, I can only reply that I regret that I appear to have no ancestors of that gifted people. My great-great-grandfather came to England in the eighteenth century from Germany: the main part of my descent is therefore purely English, and I am an English subject—which should be sufficient. I have been accustomed, nonetheless, to regard my German name with pride, and continued to do so throughout the period of the late regrettable war, in which I served in the English army. I cannot, however, forbear to comment that if impertinent and irrelevant inquiries of this sort are to become the rule in matters of literature, then the time is not far distant when a German name will no longer be a source of pride.[64]

Throughout the spring and summer, Tolkien continued with his academic duties: attending English faculty meetings, delivering several lectures each week, serving as an examiner for students seeking degrees in philology. Progress on his sequel to *The Hobbit*, however, had stalled.

Tolkien was "at a halt, even at a loss, to the point of a lack of confidence in radical components of the narrative structure that had been built up with such pains."[65] He had taken the story up to the fateful Council of Elrond, where Gandalf, Aragorn, the hobbits, Dwarves, Elves, and men gather to decide what to do about the Ring and the looming war with Sauron.[66] "And it is not our part here to take thought only for a season, or for a few lives of Men, or for a passing age of the world," says the Wizard. "We should seek a final end of this menace, even if we do not hope to make one."[67]

In August 1939, on the eve of Hitler's invasion of Poland, however, no council of this kind was being contemplated by the democracies of the West. Everyone, it seemed, was planning to go on vacation.

In France, no preparations were being made to fortify its defenses past the Maginot Line to the coast of Dunkirk. In Great Britain, Parliament announced that it would adjourn from August 4 until October 3. The prime minister headed for Scotland on a fishing trip.

In an angry parliamentary debate on August 2, Churchill denounced their actions as shameful and disastrous. "This is an odd moment for the

House to declare that it will go on a two month's holiday . . . when the powers of evil are at their strongest."[68] A week later, in a radio broadcast to the United States, Churchill warned that all over Europe was "a hush of fear" because of the actions and ambitions of the Nazi regime. "In Germany, on a mountain peak, there sits one man who in a single day can release the world from the fear which now oppresses it; or in a single day can plunge all that we have and are into a volcano of smoke and flame."

The day of smoke and flame arrived at 4:45 a.m. on September 1, when German troops crossed the border into western Poland: 1.8 million soldiers, more than three thousand tanks, and hundreds of armored cars and personnel carriers, all supported by devastating bombardment from the air. German warplanes made no distinction between military and civilian targets. Thus, the Polish people became the first in military history to experience sudden death and destruction from the skies: the first of many victims of the Nazi blitzkrieg, or "lightning war."[69] Historian William Shirer, who visited the battlefield a few days after the collapse of Poland, summarized the German military thus: "This was a monstrous mechanized juggernaut such as the earth had never seen."[70]

Later that same day, Lewis was returning from a walking tour of the English countryside with some of his friends from the Inklings, Hugo Dyson and R. E. Havard. This trip involved a boat—a two-berth cabin cruiser, the *Bosphorus*—which belonged to Warnie and which he kept moored on the Thames in Oxford. They met at Folly Bridge in Oxford—without Warnie, who was on reserve with the Royal Army Service Corps and called back into service—where they boarded the boat and followed the river through meadows and riverside pubs. The Nazi-Soviet Pact had just been signed, and there was much anxiety in the air. Yet their spirits were buoyed by the thought of escaping the news for a while by going on a little adventure.[71]

When they returned to Godstow on September 1, they learned of the German invasion of Poland. As Havard recalled: "We knew then that war was imminent . . . and the return to Oxford was in an unnatural silence." They dined at the Clarendon Hotel. Lewis tried to lighten the gloom: "Well, at any rate, we now have less chance of dying of cancer."[72]

Two days later, Chamberlain sent an ultimatum that Germany immediately withdraw its troops. Hitler was given two hours to respond. The deadline came and went unanswered.

At 11:15 a.m. on Sunday, September 3, Neville Chamberlain announced to the nation that Britain was at war with Germany. Winston Churchill was invited to join the government as Secretary of the Navy. Air raid sirens sounded over London, and Londoners quickly became accustomed to seeking safety in shelters and subway stations. "We made our way to the shelter assigned to us," Churchill said, "armed with a bottle of brandy and other appropriate medical comforts."[73]

Unlike in August 1914, when many young men celebrated the opportunity to fight for king and country, the prime minister's declaration of war was met with grim resignation. "I had gone to Mass with my father and Christopher at St. Gregory's Church in the Woodstock Road," recalled Priscilla Tolkien. The parish priest offered to let people remain at church to hear Chamberlain's announcement on his radio. "But my father, visibly upset to be at war, said we should go home to my mother, who was listening to the wireless in the kitchen."[74]

Two weeks after Britain's declaration of war, Tolkien wrote to his publisher to explain why he didn't expect to make much progress on his new story about hobbits. "Any far-reaching work of my own is out of the question, for I am liable to be summoned to a job undertaken last Spring at any moment, and have no idea what time, if any, outside it I shall have." The job, as we learned, was that of codebreaker for the British Foreign Office. (In the end, his skills would not be required.) Tolkien also apologized for his long silence about his story. "I do not suppose this any longer interests you greatly," he wrote, "though I still hope to finish it eventually."[75]

Too old to enlist in the army, Tolkien signed up as an air raid warden and was expected to investigate reports of unexploded bombs, deliver first aid, and put out small fires. As in London, Oxford homes were ordered to be blackened at night. Usually with a companion, Tolkien patrolled his neighborhood in the evening and early-morning hours, sometimes sleeping in a hut near his home that served as a headquarters. "Number 27, dowse that glim!" might come the cry.[76] After the first air raid warning sounded in Oxford, Priscilla Tolkien watched "the chaos this caused quite early in the morning with traffic at its height and police stopping the traffic with the Air Raid Wardens out in the streets"—with her father presumably among them. "If there had been a raid it would have been catastrophic."[77]

Lewis dreaded the possibility that he might be called back into active service. He joined the Home Guard, Britain's "last line of defense" against a German invasion. Drawing on volunteers from seventeen to sixty-five years of age, the Home Guard would deploy a well-trained army of 1.7 million men. "We had our first air raid warning at 7:45 the other morning when I expect you had yours too," Lewis wrote to his brother. With the help of his gardener, Lewis built a concrete shelter buried underground near his house. It would get plenty of use.

In September 1939, preparing for invasion on the home front was the least of Britain's problems. Despite its declaration of war, it would be eight months before British troops engaged the Germans on the continent. Despite a promise to the Polish government that "His Majesty's Government would at once lend them all the support in their power," none was forthcoming. Great Britain was simply unprepared for an all-out war against Germany.

So was France. Having lost 1.3 million soldiers during the First World War, the French were horrified at the prospect of their nation again becoming a vast killing field. Poland expected France to begin its offensive on the Western Front by September 17, as promised. Instead, the Soviet Union launched its own remorseless assault, invading Poland across its eastern border.

The Poles fought courageously but were outgunned and outnumbered. Before the end of September, the *Wehrmacht* entered Warsaw. The Nazis immediately began to decapitate Polish society. Over the next month, from the Polish surrender on September 28 until October 25, between sixteen and twenty thousand Poles were executed without trial. Jews who had not already fled were immediately rounded up and sent into ghettos. Meanwhile, the Russians began the eviction of 1.5 million Poles from their homes. During the months that followed, hundreds of thousands died in a nightmare of captivity and starvation at the hands of their Soviet masters.

INTO THE BREACH

The failure of Britain and France to prevent the disintegration of Poland, though predictable, nevertheless darkened the mood in England, especially among those who, like Tolkien and Lewis, had lived through the First World War.

"The next few years will be ghastly, but though my *nerves* are often staggered, my faith and reason are alright," Lewis wrote to Arthur Greeves. "I have no doubt that all this suffering will be for our ultimate good if we use it rightly . . . but I can't help wishing one could *hibernate* till it's all over!"[78] After learning that Tolkien's son Michael would probably be called into active service, Lewis wrote to Warnie: "Of course, it is only one of countless such tragedies."[79] Writing again to his brother: "Today is a bad day because we have just heard the news about Russia, and poor Minto, for the moment regards this as sealing the fate of the allies—and even talked of buying a revolver!"[80]

Russia's invasion of Poland was only the beginning of the butchery committed by Stalin's military. On November 30, 1939, the Soviet Union sent an attack force of 120,000 men and 600 tanks into Finland. "We go into Finland not as conquerors," Soviet officials proclaimed to their troops, "but as friends and liberators of the Finnish people from the yoke of the landowners and capitalists."[81] A nation of barely 3.6 million, Finland had no hope of resisting the Red Army.

Yet, for a time, they did so, to the astonishment of the world. Fiercely nationalistic, the Finns joked: "There are so many and our country is so small, where shall we find room to bury them all?"[82] Using ski patrols, booby traps, snipers, and Molotov cocktails, the Finns held out for over three months against the Soviets, revealing a fighting spirit that inspired the free world.

On the night of the Soviet invasion of Finland, Tolkien was at his home, sharing a glass of gin and lime juice with Lewis and reading him a chapter from his new story about hobbits.

Finland would have been on Tolkien's mind, and not only because of the international situation. The nineteenth-century Finnish epic, *The Kalevala*, had made a deep impression on Tolkien as a young man. A collection of ancient songs and myths, *The Kalevala* had given the Finnish people a history and a cultural tradition—a national identity—of their own. It is credited with helping the Finns to break away from Russian rule during World War I.[83]

Tolkien first discovered *The Kalevala*, in English translation, at King

Edward's School. But he wanted to read it in its original language. In 1911, during his first term at Oxford, he found a Finnish grammar book at the Exeter College library. It not only altered his course of studies: It changed the direction of his professional life.

"It was like discovering a complete wine-cellar filled with bottles of an amazing wine of a kind and flavor never tasted before," he recalled. "It quite intoxicated me."[84] Joanna Bowring, the Exeter College librarian, retrieved for this author the Finnish grammar book from a shelf and described its likely impact on Tolkien: "We think that *Quenya*, the language of the Elves in *The Lord of the Rings*, was based on Finnish grammar and, indeed, this little book."[85] Bowring pointed out Tolkien's annotations in the margins: Apparently, he couldn't resist breaking the library's rules and writing in its pages. "Well, as we know," she said with a smile, "I think he was quite keen on breaking the rules."[86]

Before he left for the front lines in 1916, Tolkien wrote a paper about the story, "On 'The Kalevala' or Land of Heroes," which he read to various Oxford societies.[87] The title of his paper is worth emphasizing: *The Land of Heroes.* It is in wartime, when a nation is fighting for its life, that heroes are most needed.

By absorbing works such as *The Kalevala,* Tolkien cultivated a lifelong ambition: to give England an epic story of its origins. "I was from early days grieved by the poverty of my own beloved country," he explained. "It had no stories of its own (bound up with its tongue and soil), not of the quality that I sought, and found (as an ingredient) in legends of other lands." It seems likely that Finland's fierce resistance to Russian aggression ultimately worked its way into Tolkien's imagination. "The love the Elves have for their land and their works is deeper than the deeps of the Sea," says Lady Galadriel. "Yet they will cast all away rather than submit to Sauron."[88]

As they sipped their drinks, Lewis read his friend a chapter from his new book, a layman's attempt to explain the mystery of human evil. It was his first work of straight Christian apologetics, and it ultimately helped make him the best-known defender of historic Christianity in the English-speaking world.

As we learned, the problem of evil—on display in the suffering of the First World War—reinforced Lewis's atheism as a young man. In a letter to Arthur, he explained why he couldn't return to "the bondage" of believing in Christianity. "Strange as it may appear, I am quite content to live without believing in a bogey who is prepared to torture me for ever and ever if I should fail in coming up to an almost impossible ideal."[89] His war poetry mocked the "ancient hope" of there being "a just God that cares for earthly pain." As Walter Hooper summarized it to this author, "Lewis believed in 'good' before he believed in God. The problem for him was that God wasn't good."[90]

Lewis now believed that God and Goodness were inseparable. Yet, with the horrific realities of war once again front and center, pain and suffering demanded an explanation.

Though strongly attached to the Church of England, Lewis considered the answers being offered by Christian ministers woefully inadequate. The Christian tradition offered a compelling explanation for the problem of evil, he said, "but to bring this doctrine into real life in the minds of modern men, and even of modern Christians, is very hard." He took up the task.

The possibility of pain, Lewis argued, was inherent in a world in which men and women possessed free will: the capacity to abuse their freedom and turn away from God and his Moral Law. "When our souls become wicked," he writes, "they will certainly use this possibility to hurt one another." This fact accounts for most of the sufferings experienced in the world. "It is men, not God, who have produced racks, whips, prisons, slavery, guns, bayonets, and bombs."[91]

Nevertheless, Lewis writes, God intends to use the experience of pain to shatter man's self-absorption, his attempt to live his life without any reference to his Creator. Because pain is an "unmasked, unmistakable evil," it creates an opportunity for the sufferer to come to his senses. "It removes the veil. It plants the flag of truth within the fortress of a rebel soul."[92]

A BEWILDERED UNIVERSITY

Hardly anyone living in Britain in 1939 could have missed the point. During the First World War, Oxford University was effectively converted into a military camp, with colleges turned into barracks and military hospitals. The student population plummeted. Like Tolkien and Lewis, thousands of young men interrupted their academic careers to join the military; many perished in battle and many survivors never returned to complete their studies.

"The gloom of this place is terrible," Tolkien had written his wife from Exeter College shortly after England declared war on Germany in 1914. "It is like being on a sinking ship . . . everything I and my friends cared for or spent our time in running or establishing here has crashed to the ground."[93] Just before leaving for France in 1917, when German submarines were terrorizing Britain's coast, Lewis wrote to his father: "Of course it would be absurd to complain at present but it looks very black for the future, if this submarine business goes on."[94]

The Second World War also threatened to completely upend university life. At the start of the Michaelmas term in 1939, 2,761 men and 750 women were in residence. If the age of conscription were set at eighteen, about 80 percent of the undergraduate population would vanish. The War Office decided to set the call-up age at twenty, though most undergraduates would be forced to leave before completing their degrees. Faculty were asked to develop "short courses" for students to gain credits that could lead to a full degree if they returned.

George Gordon, the president of Magdalen College—where Lewis taught as an instructor in English Language and Literature—became Oxford's vice-chancellor and negotiator with the British government to determine the wartime uses of the university. Science departments were redirected to support the war effort. College buildings were requisitioned and converted to other war-related uses. Balliol College, for example, housed the political intelligence department of the Foreign Office. The secretarial staff from MI5 was given space at Keble College. Most of Merton College—where Tolkien taught from 1945 until his retirement—was taken over by the Ministry of Transport. Government mapmakers occupied the Bodleian Library, where scholars like Tolkien and Lewis spent many hours conducting research.[95]

Nearly everyone, whether in government or civilian life, understood that the war against Nazi Germany would involve weapons exponentially more destructive than anything deployed in the 1914–18 war.

Unlike in the previous conflict, civilians would become the target of these weapons. In addition to the exodus of students and faculty, Oxford now faced the possibility of massive bombing raids; food shortages as the waters off England's coast became death zones; an enormous influx of evacuees; and the likelihood of a land invasion. Bomb shelters were constructed, rationing of petrol and food was enforced, and students were recruited as firewatchers. Oxford became, in Tolkien's words, "a bewildered university."

LEARNING IN WARTIME

It was at this moment in October 1939, in the days immediately after the outbreak of war, that the leadership at the University Church of St. Mary the Virgin asked Lewis to deliver a talk to the congregation. Nearly a thousand years old, the church stood near the spiritual center of university life. The war in Europe already had touched the congregation. Earlier in the year, Canon Dick Milford had welcomed a group of German Jewish converts to Christianity who had escaped Nazi Germany. With a community composed mostly of university students, the war was creating a climate of fear and frustration for many congregants.

Lewis was invited to speak not only because of his growing reputation as a Christian scholar but also because, as a student at Oxford in 1917, his own academic life was violently disrupted by his service in the Great War. His sermon, "Learning in War-Time," forged in the fires of two global conflicts, must rank as one of the most thought-provoking reflections on the nature of Christian vocation ever delivered from a church pulpit. It also offers the key to understanding Lewis's acute sense of purpose and remarkable productivity during the war years.

> What is the use of beginning a task which we have so little chance of finishing? Or, even if we ourselves should happen not to be interrupted by death or military service, why should we—indeed how can we—continue to take an interest in these placid occupations when the lives of our friends and the liberties of Europe are in the balance? Is it not like fiddling while Rome burns?[96]

These surely were the questions on everyone's mind. Avoiding platitudes as well as abstract theological speculation, Lewis nonetheless set the war in a larger context. His first task was to explain why "the learned life" has always been vital to human flourishing and nearly always pursued under the shadow of some great event or difficulty or danger. "If men had postponed the search for knowledge and beauty until they were secure," he said, "the search would never have begun."[97]

Nevertheless, there was a danger in pursuing an academic career, especially in a place like Oxford. Echoing the Protestant reformer Martin Luther, Lewis undercut the temptation to intellectual pride by insisting that the work of the academic was no more "spiritual" than that of a house cleaner. All vocations would become pleasing to God on the same terms: by being offered to him in humility. "The intellectual life is not the only road to God, nor the safest, but we find it to be a road, and it may be the appointed road for us."[98] For some in the audience, he added, it might become their duty.

Next came a warning: The war created distinct enemies to the would-be scholar. The first enemy is the tendency to become constantly distracted by the events of the hour. Lewis reminded his listeners that there are always rivals to their work: anxieties over relationships, illness, employment. They must be put to one side. "The only people who achieve much are those who want knowledge so badly that they seek it while the conditions are still unfavorable," he said. "Favorable conditions never come."[99]

Another enemy is frustration—the feeling that there will not be enough time to finish the task at hand. Everyone in mid-life knows this feeling. A Christian approach to the future, though, would benefit the young as well as their elders. "Never, in peace or war, commit your virtue or your happiness to the future," he advised. "The present is the only time in which any duty can be done or any grace received."[100]

A final enemy to the scholar created by the war is fear. Lewis counseled his listeners to redirect it: to realize that the war forces them to take stock of their lives and to consider their own mortality, "and that would have been regarded as one of its blessings by most of the great Christians" in history.

The intellectual anchor in this storm of war, Lewis insisted, was found in the wisdom of the ages: the literary and philosophical inheritance of the Western tradition.

> Most of all, perhaps, we need intimate knowledge of the past. . . . A man who has lived in many places is not likely to be deceived by the local errors of his native village; the scholar has lived in many times and is therefore in some degree immune from the great cataract of nonsense that pours from the press and the microphone of his own age.[101]

Could it really be the case that the scholar, immersed in the outlook of his ancestors, might be best equipped to resist the political cant and propaganda of the modern world? The proof was in the pudding. Lewis and Tolkien remained undeceived by the most seductive lies of the twentieth century and helped a generation to do the same.

EVACUEES AND A GLIMPSE OF NARNIA

Among the British population, perhaps no group endured greater war anxieties—fears for loved ones, fears for the future—than the people forced to leave their homes to get out of harm's way. The evacuees.

Even before Britain declared war on Germany, the government had begun the voluntary evacuation of mothers and children from urban areas to the English countryside to escape the anticipated bombing campaign. Between 1.5 and 3 million people were evacuated during the first days of the exodus, called Operation Pied Piper, making it the largest population movement in British history. Many of the children wrote about their experience of being ripped from their homes and families.

Twelve-year-old Lilian Hansen, evacuated from London, captured the moment as eloquently as any journalist on the scene:

> A sadder day there was never before
> When all mothers both rich and poor
> Stood and wept when their children went away
> On the great evacuation day.[102]

Ten to fifteen thousand refugees soon arrived in Oxford. Thousands of working-class mothers and children, evacuees from the East End of London, were given accommodations in colleges or movie houses until being placed in private homes.[103] Entire schools from London were relocated to Oxfordshire; the women's colleges adopted them, supplying undergraduate students to spend weekends looking after the children.[104]

"I am a bachelor," Lewis told his friend Sister Penelope, "and never appreciated children till the war brought them to me."[105] Four children, all girls, appeared at the Kilns the day after the Nazi invasion of Poland. Lewis and Mrs. Moore welcomed them with open arms. He wrote to Warnie about them. "Our schoolgirls have arrived and all seem to me—and, what's more important, to Minto—to be very nice, unaffected creatures and all most flatteringly delighted with their new surroundings."[106]

The Lewis household took in evacuees throughout the war, almost always girls. "My first impression of C. S. Lewis was that of a shabbily clad, rather portly gentleman, whom I took to be the gardener, and told him so," recalled Patricia (Boshell) Heidelberger. "He roared—boomed!—with laughter!"[107] Heidelberger arrived with another girl, Marie Jose Bose. They were, admittedly, "extremely lively, noisy, and giggly." But Lewis was gracious. "He never reproached us . . . and during the next year, when both of us were preparing to take school-leaving certificates, he would invite us many an evening into his smoke-laden den, go through our homework with us and impart ideas."[108]

Walter Hooper, who edited four volumes of Lewis's personal letters, observes that Lewis wrote to his brother every week during this time, and that every letter contained news of the children. "There is not one sour note from Lewis about the children," he concludes. "In fact, one gets the impression that he enjoyed their company."[109]

When sixteen-year-old June Flewett arrived at the Kilns, she intended to stay for only a few months until heading off to drama school. But after Mrs. Moore became ill, she decided to stay on and help with the household. "We were always talking about books," she recalled. "And he [Lewis] told me to go to Blackwell's Bookshop in Oxford, anytime, and buy any book I wanted on his account." Lewis gave much more to June, however, than an open tab at Blackwell's bookstore:

> May I say I went to the Kilns with no opinion whatever of my intellectual ability. Lewis was the first person who made me believe I was an

> intelligent human being and the whole of the time I was there he built up my confidence in myself and in my ability to think and understand. He never put me down. He never made me feel foolish, no matter how small my contribution towards any conversation might be. . . . If he had let me see how ignorant I was at that time, I would have suffered for it. But now I can look back and see what he did for me.[110]

If Lewis brought about something like an intellectual awakening in the young people who came into his home, their presence transformed him as well—from a confirmed bachelor who did not enjoy the company of children to the author of one of the most beloved series of children's books in modern fiction, *The Chronicles of Narnia*. "He had the gift of talking to children as though their opinions were as valuable and interesting as those of anybody else," recalls Mary Clare Havard, daughter of R. E. Havard, "which was all the more refreshing as it was very unusual in those days."[111] The Narnia books possess a warmth and empathy—and humor—that capture the emotional life of children like few works of its kind.

It was probably about this time, in 1939 after children evacuees had become a fixture at the Kilns, that Lewis scribbled the opening lines of the first book he would write in his celebrated series.

> This book is about four children whose names were Ann, Martin, Rose, and Peter. . . . They all had to go away from London suddenly because of the Air Raids, and because Father, who was in the army, had gone off to the war and Mother was doing some kind of war work. They were sent to stay with a relation of Mother's who was a very old Professor who lived by himself in the country.[112]

Lewis would rename three of the four children in the final version, but the catalyst for their adventure into Narnia was the same: the "great evacuation" from London at the start of the Second World War. In *The Lion, the Witch and the Wardrobe*, the Pevensie children flee the terrors of a world at war only to enter Narnia, where another war is being waged between Aslan and his allies and the forces of the White Witch.

WRITERS IN COMMUNITY

Meanwhile, university life carried on as best it could. The group that Tolkien and Lewis had launched to reform the syllabus, the Cave, had achieved many of its goals. But they continued to meet socially over dinners and other gatherings to discuss literature, even with Oxford on a wartime footing. Tolkien and Lewis attended a meeting in December 1939 that seemed especially lively. As Lewis described it: "Everyone remarked that it was more frolic and youthful than any we have had for years—quite one of the old caves in fact—a curious result, if it is a result, of war conditions."[113]

As in the previous conflict, the Second World War placed an immense emotional burden on the families whose loved ones were sent into battle. Yet the burden was intensified by the advances in communication; war news traveled quickly. The BBC was still in its infancy, but its daily radio broadcasts transformed everyday life for ordinary Britons.

Neville Chamberlain had taken to the airwaves to announce Britain's declaration of war on Nazi Germany. Recalled M. R. Spurgeon: "After that, although I was usually in bed, I was aware that the family was glued to the wireless every night at 9 pm to hear the BBC News preceded by the reassuring sound of Big Ben's chimes."[114] The British people learned almost immediately about events at sea, in the air, or on the continent.

In a letter to his brother in November 1939, Lewis mentioned, without comment, that "this morning we hear of the loss of the Dutch liner."[115] The Dutch passenger ship *Simon Bolivar* was bound from Holland to the West Indies when it struck a mine in the North Sea off the coast of Great Britain, killing 140 of the 400 passengers, including many women and children. Five more ships were struck by mines the next day. The British government immediately accused the Nazis of creating "a blockade of floating explosives" off its coast.[116]

A few weeks later, Lewis wrote to his brother again, after Britain initiated the first naval battle of the Second World War. Three Royal Navy cruisers intercepted a German battleship that had been terrorizing British merchant ships in the South Atlantic.

In what became known as the Battle of the River Plate, the Germans were forced to scuttle their vessel, the *Graf Spee*, in the Uruguayan port of Montevideo. "This battle off Montevideo has been an odd experience, hasn't it?" Lewis wrote. "I suppose there never has been a war till now in which people at home were getting news of distant naval actions only a few minutes after the event."[117] Lewis worried that constant war news could turn military victories into "disgusting" sporting events. He already was weary of the gloomy war updates and prognostications. "The Imperial News Bulletin asks me to renew my subscription," he wrote. "I think I shall not." What was the point, he asked, of paying "to be tormented by prophecies which if false are needless misery and if true can't be averted by us?"[118]

In the early months of the war, when his brother was stationed in France, Lewis's letters revealed much about their lifelong friendship: its warmth, joys, and sorrows.

"Why should quiet ruminants as you and I have been born in such a ghastly age?" he asked.[119] Reflecting on a brief visit from Warnie before he left for the continent, Lewis grew somber. "I too enjoyed our short time together in College enormously, until the shadow of the end began to fall over it: not that one has lost the art (our boyhood was well trained in it) of dealing with such shadows," he wrote, "but that one so resents having to start putting it into practice again after so many years. Pox on the whole business."[120]

Droll humor also found its way into his correspondence. Complaining about a malfunctioning furnace, he wrote,

> The study is smoking abominably while I write. . . . It's at the stage now when I don't notice it (visually) as long as I keep my eyes on the paper, but if I look up at the bookcase I perceive that I am sitting in the middle of a fog. It is also giving out practically no heat. . . . I shall be asphyxiated in a few minutes. I can hardly see out of the window now. Yours, Jack.[121]

Just as the war created fears for those on the home front, it also heightened the need to cordon them off: to make space for relationships that were meaningful, for conversations rich in wit and wisdom, and for creative work that could inspire and enchant. For Tolkien and Lewis, male friendship fulfilled all of these needs like nothing else.

Throughout the crisis years of 1939–45, the Inklings continued to meet on Tuesday mornings at the Eagle and Child pub (also known as the

Bird and Baby) and Thursday evenings in Lewis's rooms at Magdalen. "I know no more pleasant sound than arriving at the B. and B. and hearing a roar, and knowing that one can plunge in," Tolkien wrote.[122] "There is no sound I like better," Lewis said, "than adult male laughter." Owen Barfield's grandson explained to this author that, in addition to their "love of words" and "a love of truth," they shared something else. "What the Inklings really had in common was a great sense of humor."[123]

The war unexpectedly brought Charles Williams to Oxford and into their fellowship. Williams's employer, Oxford University Press, had moved its London staff to Oxford soon after Hitler invaded Poland. Though not an academic, Williams was a novelist and poet and greatly admired by Lewis and was welcomed into the group. The war created a shortage of English faculty, and Lewis was able to "smuggle him into the Oxford lecture list."[124] He sometimes found refuge in Lewis's rooms at Magdalen College. "I have fled to C. S. Lewis's rooms," Williams told his wife. "He is a great tea-drinker at any hour of the night or day, and left a tray for me with milk and tea, and an electric kettle at hand."[125] Williams soon became one of Lewis's most cherished friends.

In addition to Warnie, Williams, and Barfield, another important participant was Hugo Dyson, a lecturer in English at both the University of Reading and Oxford. Dyson (along with Nevill Coghill) was in the audience in 1919 when Tolkien first read his short story *The Fall of Gondolin* before an Oxford literary club. Lewis did not meet Dyson until 1930, when he entertained him and Coghill for dinner at Magdalen. They talked until 3 a.m., and both recognized in the other a kindred spirit.

"We sat up so late with the feeling that heaven knew when we might meet again," Lewis said, "and the new friendship had to be freed past its youth and into maturity in a single evening." Lewis was drawn to Dyson's intelligence, humor, and robust Christian faith. It was Dyson, along with Tolkien, whose articulation of the gospel played a key role in Lewis's breakthrough at Addison's Walk. As Lewis described him: "He is a man who really loves truth: a philosopher and a religious man: who makes his critical and literary activities depend on the former."[126] That's a good description of Lewis himself.

The purpose of the Inklings, as Lewis described it, was "theoretically to talk about literature, but in fact nearly always to talk about something better."[127] A mix of eccentric personalities and egos, they nonetheless consented to share their works in progress, reading them aloud and subjecting them to both high praise and stinging criticism. They were "writers in community" who decided they needed others to help them work out their stories.[128]

"I don't think writers by nature are team players," explains Daisy Dunn. "Writers like to have their own space. They have their own ideas fermenting in their heads. They want to lay it down in just the way that they see it, and they can't necessarily share their vision that easily until they've actually completed their work." The fact that Tolkien and Lewis spent much of their time in tutorials helping students craft their own compositions, Dunn suggests, probably played a role. Delivering constructive criticism was part of their daily experience. Nevertheless, the commitment of the Inklings to engage with their peers "shows the bravery and the boldness, and also the open mindedness of these writers."[129]

Another member of the Inklings was R. E. Havard, the physician who attended to Tolkien and Lewis and their families. Though not widely appreciated by biographers, Havard became a friend to both men and played a truly important role in their lives.

At the Inklings meetings, Havard observed in Tolkien the "depth of feeling behind his Roman Catholic religious convictions. . . . I was impressed by the breadth of his learning and the sharp edge of his wit, also by the way that neither was ever paraded or used to inflict pain."[130] Havard met Lewis in the early 1930s when he made a house call to treat him for influenza. "On my first visit we spent some five minutes discussing his influenza," Havard recalled, "and then half an hour or more in a discussion of ethics and philosophy."[131]

Because neither Tolkien nor Lewis liked to drive, they often enlisted Havard as their chauffeur. When he failed to arrive one evening to collect Warnie, he was given the name "the useless quack," which quickly became a term of endearment. "It certainly meant a lot to my father, the relationship, joining the Inklings," recalls Mary Clare Havard. "It was very much a man's club, and they loved it."[132]

When Lewis read aloud to the Inklings some chapters of his book exploring the nature of evil—published in 1940 as *The Problem of Pain*—he decided he needed a doctor's perspective on the function of pain.

Lewis turned to Havard, who was intensely interested in the relationship of medicine to the humanities. He asked him to write a paper on the clinical experience of pain. The doctor read his paper to the Inklings, and it so impressed Lewis that he included it in the appendix to his book. Addressing both physical and mental suffering, Havard observed that by acts of courage some people can overcome even chronic mental pain. "They often produce brilliant work and strengthen, harden, and sharpen their characters till they become like tempered steel," he wrote. "Pain provides an opportunity for heroism; the opportunity is seized with surprising frequency."[133]

NO CHRISTMAS TRUCE

The opportunity for heroism on a national scale would arrive in 1940, when the Royal Air Force took on the German *Luftwaffe* over the skies of Great Britain, and the citizens of London faced down a bombing campaign that killed thousands and reduced much of the city to a fiery ruin. Their slogan of defiance—"London can take it!"—would echo around the world.

But not in 1939. While Finland struggled for survival through the winter, the Allied armies were frozen in inactivity in snow-covered trenches and bunkers on the German border.

The British government wanted to mine the Rhine, thus disrupting a German supply route. But the French sought to avoid a direct military assault, fearing Nazi retaliation. Their paralysis on the continent became known as "the phony war," and it gave the German military time to regroup. Hitler maintained his psychological dominance. "His great advantage was that the Allies had made a principled commitment to confront and defeat Nazism," writes historian Max Hastings, "while lacking any appetite for the bloody initiatives and human sacrifice required to achieve this."[134]

Most of the other states in Europe were in the same frame of mind. Denmark, Norway, Sweden, Switzerland, Spain, Portugal, Ireland, the Netherlands, Luxembourg, and Belgium all declared their neutrality. By the spring of 1940, half of them would be overrun by the Nazis.

In the First World War, German and French troops famously stopped fighting on Christmas Eve of 1914. During the Christmas Truce, the armies on both sides of the Western Front laid down their weapons, sang hymns, and swapped drinks and tobacco. It was a spontaneous expression of decency and common humanity. But there would be no Christmas truce in 1939.

With totalitarian regimes dominating the continent, Europe plunged into a maelstrom of violence and inhumanity unrivaled in world history. "It was a descent into the abyss never previously encountered, the devastation of all the ideals of civilization that had arisen from the Enlightenment," writes Ian Kershaw. "It was a war of apocalyptic proportions, Europe's Armageddon."[135] Before it was all over, the conflict would claim the lives of more than forty-six million soldiers and civilians—more than four times the number that perished in the First World War. The extent of the losses would be incalculable: nothing less than "a heritage of work and joy, of struggle and creativity, of learning, hopes and happiness, which no one would ever inherit or pass on."[136] It touched nearly every aspect of everyday life for hundreds of millions of people.

Not even Father Christmas could ignore it. In his 1939 Christmas letter to Priscilla, Tolkien did not try to conceal from his daughter the bitter realities of a world at war. "I am very busy and things are very difficult this year owing to this horrible war," he wrote. "Many of my messengers have never come back."[137] Father Christmas offered no explanation for what had happened to them.

In fits and starts, Tolkien continued to work on his story. "I fear it is growing too large," he told his publisher. "I am not at all sure that it will please quite the same audience (except in so far as that has grown up too)."[138] By December 1939, his hobbits faced another moment of crisis in their attempt to destroy the Ring.

The Company found itself in the Mines of Moria, the tunnels under the Misty Mountains and the ancient home of the Dwarves now under the influence of a Balrog, a vision of hell itself. No matter what path the Fellowship chooses, dangers await them. Frodo longs to return to Bag End in the Shire, to Bilbo, to the life he once knew. "He wished with all his heart that he was back there, and in those days, mowing the lawn, or pottering among the flowers, and that he had never heard of Moria, or *mithril*—or the Ring."[139]

Many in England shared that wish in December 1939. A new shadow of evil had entered the world, and it loomed over the island nation just as Sauron's dark malevolence had crossed the borders of the Shire.

Niall Ferguson observes that, as in Tolkien's story, the living embodiment of evil—the architect of Nazism—had acquired a fortress in the mountains. Earlier in the year, Hitler's personal secretary, Martin Bormann, gave the Führer an astonishing gift for his fiftieth birthday. At the top of the Kehlstein mountains Bormann had built a magnificent granite lodge, the Eagle's Nest. A four-mile road meandered up the mountainside, followed by a torch-lit pedestrian tunnel. An elevator shaft, carved out of the mountain's core, took the Führer to his magnificent perch.[140] "From here it seemed as if the whole of Europe lay prostrate beneath his piercing gaze. If the Nazi empire was Mordor, then this was Sauron's Tower."[141]

CHAPTER 5

NO HOLIDAY FROM HISTORY

Because you have seen the reality of beauty, justice, and goodness, you will be able to know idols and shadows for what they are.
—Plato, *The Republic*

There is a seed of courage hidden (often deeply, it is true) in the heart of the fattest and most timid hobbit, waiting for some final and desperate danger to make it grow.
—J. R. R. Tolkien, *The Lord of the Rings*

We knew that one of the most dangerous attacks ever made upon the human race was coming very soon and in this island.
—C. S. Lewis, *That Hideous Strength*

At the Council of Elrond in *The Lord of the Rings*, Gandalf the Wizard describes to the Company his encounter with Saruman the White, who pressed upon him a scheme to make peace with the forces of Mordor. "A new Power is rising," warned Saruman. "Against it the old allies and policies will not avail us at all." The only sensible course, he announced, was to be on the right side of this overwhelming power, with the ultimate hope of directing it. "We can bide our time, we can keep our thoughts in our hearts, deploring maybe evils done by the way, but approving the high and ultimate purpose."[1]

In May 1940, when virtually all of Western Europe was under Nazi control, Britain's foreign secretary, Lord Halifax, took a page out of Saruman's book of diplomacy.

After a clandestine conversation with the Italian ambassador, Halifax approached Prime Minister Winston Churchill about an offer from Benito Mussolini to help Britain negotiate a settlement with Hitler's Germany. Neville Chamberlain, who had just resigned as prime minister and been brought into Churchill's War Cabinet, was "ready to consider decent terms" if they were offered. Two Labor members of the War Cabinet agreed with him.[2] French Premier Paul Reynaud, staying at his London embassy, also tried to prevail upon Churchill to engage with the Italians or allow France to make a separate peace with Germany.

Many ordinary Britons, if they had known about this possibility, might have opted to sue for peace. The international situation was desperate. On April 9, Germany had invaded and occupied Denmark and Norway. Warnie Lewis, now a major in the army, was with his unit in France, and his brother wanted to know when his scheduled home leave would be granted. "Is the invasion of Norway going to be made the pretext for permanently stopping *your* leave from *France*, and, if so, why? Oh, the absurdity of the whole damn affair."[3]

On May 10, the Netherlands, Belgium, and Luxembourg were overrun. Three days later, German tanks shattered the French line, racing westward.[4] On May 15, Reynaud was told by his generals that Paris might fall within two days; the French High Command had no counterattack in place. Panic swept over the country. Thousands fled the eastern cities of Rheims, Lille, and Chartres. Many refugees were gunned down by the advancing German army. Within weeks, eight million people abandoned their homes, the largest mass migration in Western European history.

Compared to the Allies, German military strength—roughly 3.5 million men, more than 5,500 aircraft, and 10 panzer divisions—was overwhelming. Churchill appealed to the American president for 50 destroyers, unused since the First World War and lying idle in US naval yards. Roosevelt refused, fearing they would fall into enemy hands.

Meanwhile, British and French forces were being driven north, toward the coast. Churchill ordered the British Royal Navy to take all possible measures to evacuate its troops from the continent. On May 27, 200,000 British soldiers were encircled at Dunkirk, together with 160,000 French and Belgian troops. Hitler's *Wehrmacht* was poised to annihilate them.

It was at this moment, while waiting for news from the beaches at Dunkirk, that Churchill listened to Halifax's plan for a negotiated peace.

Two days later he told his full Cabinet that he considered carefully whether he should enter into negotiations with Hitler. Any arrangement, he explained, would reduce Great Britain to a "slave state" with a puppet government. "I am convinced that every man of you would rise up and tear me down from my place if I were for one moment to contemplate parley or surrender," he said. "If this long island story of ours is to end at last, let it end only when each one of us lies choking in his own blood upon the ground."[5]

One of the soldiers trapped at Dunkirk was thirty-one-year-old Alan Rook, a former student of Tolkien's and an editor at *New Oxford Poetry*, the journal in which Tolkien had published the poem "Goblin Feet" during the First World War. Rook was now a lieutenant antiaircraft gunner with the Royal Artillery. He wrote a poem about his experience, "Evacuation," an expression of fear and longing that would have resonated with his teacher:

> day 1. By the patient sea
> and homesick sand-dunes
> by docks and quays
>   rank with the smell of blood.
> *rank with death and blood.*
> night. In the darkness life
> sings sadly in the sand-dunes;
> the army throws
> its wishes across the sea
> *across the hopeful sea.*
> day 2. Another day of wishes
> embraces the army
> on docks and quays
> scenting the acrid blood.
> *scenting the hopeful blood.*[6]

In what was considered a miracle of deliverance, the Royal Navy—aided by hundreds of small boats from volunteers—safely evacuated 338,000 British, French, and Belgian troops across the Channel and back to England. Nevertheless, there were mounting fears that Great Britain would ultimately succumb to a German onslaught. On June 18, 1940, Churchill addressed the House of Commons with words of defiance that will be remembered as long as the English language survives.

> Upon this battle depends the survival of Christian civilization. Upon it depends our own British life, and the long continuity of our institutions and our Empire. The whole fury and might of the enemy must very soon be turned on us. Hitler knows he will have to break us in this Island or lose the war. . . . Let us therefore brace ourselves to our duties, and so bear ourselves that, if the British Empire and its Commonwealth last for a thousand years, men will still say, "This was their finest hour."[7]

Churchill's speech—his determination to resist Nazism at all costs—proved decisive. "The prime minister's exalting leadership secured public support for his defiance of the logic of Hitlerian triumph," writes Max Hastings, "even when cities began to burn and civilians to die."[8] Echoes of Churchill's steely resolve can be discerned in Tolkien's story, especially in his description of the Battle of the Pelennor Fields. The armies of Mordor, Tolkien writes, were emboldened by their victories and "filled with a new lust and fury" to destroy the forces of Gondor and Rohan. But the leader of the armies of Rohan is unyielding:

> Stern now was Éomer's mood, and his mind clear again. He let blow the horns to rally all men to his banner that could come hither; for he thought to make a great shield-wall at the last, and stand, and fight there on foot till all fell, and do deeds of song on the fields of Pelennor.[9]

Despite the epic heroism of the Dunkirk deliverance, the military situation was grim. The British Expeditionary Force left behind all of their military hardware: 64,000 vehicles, 76,000 tons of ammunition, and 2,500 guns. The navy suffered grievously, including six destroyers lost and twenty-five damaged. During the nine days of the evacuation, the RAF lost 177 aircraft. Dunkirk was, in fact, "a colossal military disaster."[10]

More disaster awaited. On June 10, 1940, Italy declared war on Britain and France, cementing the military alliance of Europe's fascist regimes. Tolkien's son John, studying for the priesthood at the English College in Rome, barely managed to slip out of the country after a five-day train ride. On June 25, France surrendered to Germany, accepting a Nazi-installed regime in Paris. With the fall of France, Hitler accomplished in six weeks what Kaiser Wilhelm did not accomplish in four years.

Thus the political doctrines of isolationism and appeasement—the belief that granting the territorial demands of the dictators would ensure the peace—lay in ruins. "And we all remember what that state of mind was. We remember also what it led to; it led to Munich, and via Munich to Dunkirk," Lewis wrote. "All of us, with very few exceptions, shared the guilt, and all, in some measure, have paid for it."[11] The manifest failure of these doctrines transformed the outlook of the English people almost overnight.

The folly of these doctrines, though, also found its way into the writings of Tolkien and Lewis. Indeed, the temptation to disregard or compromise with evil, even for noble purposes, is a recurring theme. In *The Lord of the Rings*, early in the story, Frodo expresses surprise that the influence of Sauron, the Dark Lord, could penetrate the Shire. "The wide world is all about you," replies Gandalf. "You can fence yourselves in, but you cannot forever fence it out."[12] The decision to flirt with the forces of darkness corrupts the wizard Saruman beyond healing; in Boromir, it leads to his death and the breaking of the Fellowship. In *The Lion, the Witch and the Wardrobe*, Edmund's pact with the White Witch nearly destroys him. In *The Last Battle*, the final book in the Narnia series, the Dwarfs seek to isolate themselves from the struggle against the wicked Tash—to their undoing. "We're on our own now. No more Aslan, no more Kings, no more silly stories about other worlds. The Dwarfs are for the Dwarfs."[13]

A DIABOLICAL FANTASY

Everything Hitler promised the German people had come true. In less than a decade he had torn up the Treaty of Versailles, revived the economy, rebuilt the military, regained German lands seized after the First World War, reunited ethnic Germans under the Third Reich, neutralized the nation's enemies, and restored Germany's prestige on the world stage. After the defeat of France, the German people were ready to follow him anywhere.

Hitler's speech to the Reichstag on July 19, 1940, broadcast around the world, evoked the dynamism and triumphalism of his Nazi movement. C. S. Lewis was with R. E. Havard when the speech aired over the BBC and was simultaneously translated into English.

They listened to it together, and it had an almost hypnotic effect. "I don't know if I'm weaker than other people: but it is a positive revelation to me that *while the speech lasts* it is impossible not to waver just a little," Lewis confessed to his brother. "Statements which I *know* to be untrue all but convince me, at any rate for the moment, if only the man says them unflinchingly."[14]

Hitler claimed that "despite my persistent, sincere efforts" to achieve peace with Great Britain and France, he was rebuffed. The usual culprits, he said, included "the international Jewish poison" and "the big capitalist clique of war profiteers," always hungry for a conflict. "It is almost painful to me to have been chosen by Providence to give a shove to what these men have brought to the point of falling," Hitler complained. "It was not my ambition to wage wars, but to build up a new social state of the highest culture. And every year of war takes me away from my work."

Addressing Winston Churchill and the British people directly, he claimed the mantle of a prophet: "A great world empire will be destroyed. A world empire which I never had the ambition to destroy or as much as harm."

Two days later, while attending Holy Trinity Church in Headington Quarry, Lewis got the idea for a diabolical satire. It would consist of secret correspondence between a senior devil and a young novice attempting to thwart the plans of the Enemy (God) and secure the soul of their "patient" for their Father in hell (Satan). "The idea," wrote Lewis, "would be to give all the psychology of temptation from the *other* point of view." He called his book *The Screwtape Letters*, and it would achieve the status of "a spectacular and satisfactory nova in the bleak sky of satire."[15]

The story contains obvious allusions to the ideological hatreds of the day. "All extremes, except extreme devotion to the Enemy, are to be encouraged," counsels Screwtape. Some ages are complacent, but "other ages, of which the present is one, are unbalanced and prone to faction, and it is our business to inflame them." There are numerous references to the war that had enveloped Britain and Europe. "Pray do not fill your letters with rubbish about this European war," Screwtape admonishes Wormwood. "I am not in the least interested in knowing how many people in England have been killed by bombs."[16] The important thing, he emphasizes, is to bend the patient's impulses and emotions to their advantage.

Yet Lewis's purpose, paradoxically, was to direct the reader's attention away from the temporal war being waged on earthly battlefields. Greater dangers lay elsewhere: in the everyday emotional and spiritual struggle for the human heart. It is "the small sins" that can lead a soul "away from the Light and out into the Nothing."[17]

Like a spiritual surgeon, Lewis exposes the ways in which fear, avarice, and ambition fix men's minds on the future. This produces all sorts of schemes—political, economic, and scientific—to control it. "He [God] does not want men to give the Future their hearts, to place their treasure in it," explains Screwtape. "But we want a man hag-ridden by the Future—haunted by visions of an imminent heaven or hell upon earth—ready to break the Enemy's commands in the present if by so doing we make him think he can attain the one or avert the other."[18]

Thus, in a work of fiction, we find the roots of the totalitarian outlook. The eugenics movement, fearing the biological collapse of the human species, worked tirelessly to enlist the state to carry out its sterilization schemes. Soviet communism waged a war against its own population to achieve a utopian vision of a classless society, freed from the vices of envy, competition, and greed. Nazism identified "the Jewish menace" as the greatest threat to the German people, the "bacillus" of mankind that would trigger the disintegration of civilization itself.

"A metaphysic, held by the rulers with the force of a religion, is a bad sign," Lewis explained. "It forbids them, like the inquisitor, to admit any grain of truth or good in their opponents."[19] Though ideological rivals, the totalitarian states each relied on terror and violence to silence their critics and maintain their grip on power. Stalin had been at it longer, but

Hitler was a quick study. "Hitler increasingly resembled a kind of apprentice Stalin," writes Niall Ferguson, "rather like some sort of junior devil."[20]

The political religions of the twentieth century all claimed to be the solution to an approaching apocalypse. All of this, Lewis implied, emerged from the pit of hell.[21]

Speaking through Screwtape, Lewis identifies one of the remedies to the moral and spiritual crisis of his age: the reading of "old books." By this he meant the greatest works of the classical-Christian tradition. In the "intellectual climate" that Screwtape and his minions have produced, "only the learned read old books and we have now so dealt with the learned that they are of all men least likely to acquire wisdom by doing so." The devil's strategy, he writes, has been to introduce "the Historical Point of View," in which any statement from an ancient author is dissected, contextualized, relativized—and untethered from anything solid or enduring.

> Since we cannot deceive the whole human all the time, it is most important to cut every generation off from all others; for where learning makes a free commerce between the ages there is always the danger that the characteristic errors of one may be corrected by the characteristic truths of another. But thanks be to Our Father and the Historical Point of View, great scholars are now as little nourished by the past as the most ignorant mechanic who holds that "history is bunk."[22]

Here is an echo of the breakthrough in Lewis's thinking when he was a skeptic, which occurred with the help of Owen Barfield. It was during one of his arguments with Barfield that Lewis was cured of his "chronological snobbery," the impulse to disregard the values and ideals of the past as antiquated and irrelevant.

Aldous Huxley, in his futuristic satire, *Brave New World* (1932), had delivered a similar warning about the materialistic trends of modern life. In his story, Henry Ford, with his purely materialistic view of the world, has become a kind of global deity, worshipped as the supreme source of wisdom and virtue. Thus, the Residence World Controller for Western Europe explains why the old books—Shakespeare, the Bible, Pascal—have been banned. "You all remember, I suppose, that beautiful, inspired saying of Our Ford's: History is bunk."[23]

The publication of *The Screwtape Letters* removed any doubt about Lewis's religious beliefs. He effectively announced to the entire Oxford community that he was committed to the historic Christian teachings about heaven and hell, about a cosmic struggle between Light and Darkness.

In this he could not have been more out of step with the temper of the times. In *Religion Without Revelation*, Julian Huxley, a leading evolutionary biologist, probably represented the mainstream scientific and materialist view held by Lewis's peers. "It is obvious that any religion which lays primary emphasis on salvation in the next world will be something of an obstacle towards getting the best out of this world as speedily as possible," Huxley wrote in 1940. "Once we have rid ourselves of this doctrine of a Divine Power external to ourselves, we can get busy with the real task of dealing with our inner forces."[24]

As Lewis saw it, mankind's "inner forces" were the chief reason for the massive disorder and violence in the world. *The Screwtape Letters* resonated with many. A few years after it was published, *TIME* magazine chose Lewis for its cover story, with a portrait of him in the foreground and the depiction of a devil lurking in the background. The article was titled "Oxford's C. S. Lewis: His Heresy: Christianity." A reviewer in *The Guardian*, the religious weekly in which *The Screwtape Letters* were first published, observed that Lewis was "earnest with his belief in devils, and as anxious to unmask their strategy against souls as our intelligence department to detect the designs of Hitler."[25]

BRITAIN FIGHTS FOR ITS LIFE

After German tanks rolled into Paris, British intelligence believed that they knew fairly well what Hitler's plans were for their island nation: invasion. But before Hitler could invade England, he would have to destroy the Royal Air Force and cripple the Royal Navy. His generals assured him they could do it.

What the contest represented, as Churchill continually reminded the British people, was a struggle between civilization and barbarism. This point bears emphasis: A bottomless chasm separated the political vision of Great Britain from that of Nazi Germany. To be sure, Britain was a colonial empire, and all empires involved the use of force to maintain political and social stability. Nevertheless, the British people could rightly view their empire, for all its failings, as a civilizing force in the world. They could lay claim to advancing the concepts of political equality, the rule of law, inalienable rights, and government by consent of the governed. They found it hard to imagine that rational people would want to destroy this way of life.

"I looked down on the calm and peaceful English countryside, the smoke rising not from bombed villages, but lazily from cottage chimneys, and saw a game of cricket in progress on a village pitch," reported an RAF fighter pilot wounded in France and flown home in June. "With my mind still filled with the blast and flame that had shattered France, I was seized with utter disgust at the smug contentedness England enjoyed behind her sea barrier."[26] The idealized image of England as a haven of civility, an innocent backwater, was still strong.

"And there in that pleasant corner of the world they plied their well-ordered business of living," writes Tolkien in *The Lord of the Rings*, "and they heeded less and less the world outside where dark things moved, until they came to think that peace and plenty were the rule in Middle-earth and the right of sensible folk."

Niall Ferguson discerns this English viewpoint in Tolkien's story, especially in his description of the Shire and its homely inhabitants. "'The Shire,' with its thatched cottages, dappled sunlight and babbling brooks, was England precisely as she imagined herself in 1940," he writes in *The War of the World*. "Mordor was the totalitarian antithesis, a blasted industrial hell 'bored and tunneled by teeming broods of evil things,' spewing forth monstrous hordes and devilish weaponry; a realm of slaves and of camps."[27] Tolkien warned against allegorical readings of his story and denied that it represented a mythological version of the struggle unfolding in Europe. At the same time, he acknowledged that the Shire was based on the England of his youth: "I take my models like anyone else—from such 'life' as I know," he said, meaning the village of Warwickshire.[28]

Nevertheless, the age of contented innocence had drawn to a close. On July 10, 1940, the German *Luftwaffe* crossed the English Channel, setting off the Battle of Britain. It began with attacks on coastal convoys and quickly shifted to factories, dockyards, and airfields. Tolkien's son Michael, stationed with his regiment near the Oxfordshire village of Thame, was training as an antiaircraft gunner. He soon went into action.

"This is a desperately serious war," Tolkien wrote to him. In his letters to his sons during the Second World War, Tolkien often reflected on his own military service. "I was not even able to get to your mother for days when John was born, and she was at death's door—just about the time of the Battle of Cambrai." Like his father, Michael interrupted his studies at Oxford to enlist. "War is a grim, hard, ugly business. But it is as good a master as Oxford, or better," Tolkien wrote. "You three boys all seem to have a decent share of courage and guts. You owe that to your *mother*."[29]

The attacks intensified throughout August, as the *Luftwaffe* deployed a daily average of about 1,000 bombers and 750 fighters. It was an armada that no nation had ever confronted: a war fought from the skies. Yet the daring and determination of the RAF pilots made the Germans bleed. When the battle was over, the Nazis lost 2,698 highly skilled airmen; the British lost 1,345. Although the RAF could not destroy the *Luftwaffe*, it denied them dominance over the Channel and southern England.[30]

In this existential moment for Great Britain, everything hinged on the youngest of men. Unlike any other form of combat, aerial warfare involved men in their teens or a little older; only they possessed the reflexes for duels at speeds approaching six hundred miles an hour.[31]

The RAF pilots knew the fearsome attrition rate—about one in five perished—and yet each day, sometimes several times a day, they climbed into their Spitfires to defend their nation from destruction or occupation and servitude. At the height of the battle, Churchill told guests at his home at Chequers that the life of Great Britain depended upon the spirit of the airmen. "What a slender thread the greatest of things can hang by."[32]

KEEP CALM AND CARRY ON

The idea that so much could depend on men with no obvious enthusiasm for war; that men completely untested in battle would be asked to defend a nation at its darkest hour; that even the youngest among them were called upon to risk all to resist evil—this was the ethos of the England of 1940–45.

After Dunkirk, Churchill compared the RAF pilots to the Arthurian knights of the Round Table. "These young men, going forth every morn to guard their native land and all that we stand for, holding in their hands these instruments of colossal and shattering power, of whom it may be said that 'Every morn brought forth a noble chance / And every chance brought forth a noble knight,' deserve our gratitude."[33] After the Battle of Britain, he praised them for "turning the tide of the World War by their prowess and by their devotion. Never in the field of human conflict has so much been owed by so many to so few."[34]

In between these speeches, Lewis wrote an essay called "The Necessity of Chivalry," in which he, too, extolled the bravery of the RAF pilots, "to whom we owe our life from hour to hour." He warned that if the modern world could not produce men who possessed the virtues of the medieval knight, then "all talk of any lasting happiness or dignity in human society is pure moonshine."[35]

As a medieval scholar, Lewis was thoroughly aware of the vices of medieval Europe. Nevertheless, he argued, the concept of chivalry brought together essential qualities that were in tension: courage and the warrior spirit alongside humility and forbearance. Against the charge of escapism, he insisted that the recovery of this ideal "offers the only possible escape from a world divided between wolves who do not understand, and sheep who cannot defend, the things which make life desirable."[36]

The wolves were at the door. Although the RAF had prevailed, Hitler's determination to crush Great Britain only intensified. On August 14, 1940, Germany announced a total blockade of the country. The rationing of food and raw materials, already underway, accelerated. Reductions in meals at Magdalen College, including the announcement of meatless Fridays, prompted Lewis, in a tone of exaggerated pathos, to denounce it as "the most genuinely alarming piece of war news I have heard since the surrender of France."[37]

Hitler now planned to demoralize the British people by terrorizing them from the air. The Germans had attempted something like this during the First World War, when it converted its zeppelins, commercial airships used for pleasure, into bomb-dropping juggernauts that appeared over the skies of London.

"My grandmother told me this story—we're east Londoners—about when she was a little girl being sent out to get some potatoes by her mum," recalls author Julia Golding. "She ran down the street and then coming over the top of the roofs of Wellsley Road where she lived was this enormous German zeppelin, totally silent. It was like seeing a shark in the sky fly overhead. And she remembers seeing the German officer with his binoculars looking down. It was a very surreal moment."[38]

It could not approach the surreal quality of terror that was about to envelop the city. Hitler ordered a massive bombing campaign against the city of London: the Blitz. Beginning on September 7, 1940, the *Luftwaffe* attacked London every night, save one, for seventy-six consecutive nights. "This is London," announced CBS newsman Edward R. Murrow on the first night of the Blitz. "Never in the long history of this old city beside the Thames has there been such a night as this."

An average of two hundred aircraft filled the skies every evening, dropping explosive and incendiary bombs on London, Bristol, Birmingham, and other major cities. "They were nights of fire and ruin," writes historian John Lukacs. "The people became accustomed to the new landscape of jagged blackness, to the awful smell of pulverized brick, to the swift onrush of death."[39] Civilians and the cities they lived in became the front lines of the war.

Every available RAF fighter plane was sent to meet the onslaught, but they had few night fighters and only primitive air interception radar. At the sound of the air raid sirens, Londoners scurried into basements, shelters, and subway stations. Fires burned all over the city. As the Blitz continued, the weekly death toll hit nearly 1,000. When the campaign was finally called off, about 43,000 British civilians were dead, 139,000 injured, and many left homeless.[40]

Michael Tolkien was thrust into the antiaircraft-gun defenses in the thick of the battle. His father wrote to him in the first week of October 1940, when 2,000 civilians were killed in London and other cities by German bombing.

Tolkien knew what it felt like to have one's life, in its prime, suspended by the "waste" of war. "One war is enough for any man," he wrote. The important thing, he added, was not what we planned to do or to become, but rather what we actually were doing and becoming in the present moment. "But I cannot pretend that I myself found that idea much comfort against the waste of time and militarism of the army," he confessed.[41]

Two weeks later Tolkien wrote to Christopher, studying at university—he would join the RAF in 1943—to report that several bombs exploded near Oxford and that he could no longer leave Edith and Priscilla alone in the evenings. "I caught a quick pint with Lewis in the course of 'business' yesterday morning, and that has been the sum total of last week's amusements!"[42] Tolkien was not amused to learn that a bombing raid on London destroyed the remaining stock of the second printing of *The Hobbit*, which dealt a blow to book sales.

On November 14, while working in his study, Tolkien saw "an ever-increasing fiery glow on the horizon."[43] It was the city of Coventry, just forty miles away, devastated by incendiary bombs. The raid, involving five hundred *Luftwaffe* bombers drawn from airfields all over Europe, lasted eleven hours, making it the most concentrated attack on a British city during the war. The bombardment left at least 554 people dead and destroyed or damaged 43,000 homes, half of the city's housing stock.

"LONDON CAN TAKE IT!"

As terrible as was the assault on Coventry, the December 29 raid on London was worse. The *Luftwaffe* dropped an astonishing 100,000 exploding bombs, setting off nearly 1,500 fires that ravaged the city. The Nazis sought to destroy the capital, targeting train stations, bridges, and communication centers. "The whole of London seemed alight!" said B. J. Rogers, watching from the rooftop of the Bank of England. "We were hemmed in by a wall of flame in every direction." It became known as the Second Great Fire of London because it devastated a larger area of the city than the Great Fire of 1666.

Nevertheless, London's firefighters, demonstrating courageous indifference to the bombs falling around them, saved much of the city from utter ruin.[44]

Incredibly, through it all, Londoners managed to get on with their daily routines. Shops stayed open, and factories operated through the night. Journalist Bruce Lockhart was amazed to see office secretaries who "came early and left late to the cacophonous chorus of bombs and guns and sirens. Poorly paid, they never complained. They rarely, if ever, arrived late."[45]

After the 1938 Munich Pact, the Nazi leadership viewed Great Britain with a mixture of contempt and loathing. Many saw British society as decadent, run by self-indulgent plutocrats. But the valor of the RAF and the resilience of the citizens of London surprised many. Irene Byers, who worked at the Central Telegraph Office, captured their resolve: "There is not the slightest feeling of defeat in the air or on the faces of the clerks and shopkeepers," she said, "only a stern and grim determination to hold on to the end—Hitler's end."[46] London's motto—"We can take it!"—became a symbol of Britain's defiance of the Nazi regime.

"Lancelot is not irrecoverable," wrote Lewis. "To some of us this war brought a glorious surprise in the discovery that after twenty years of cynicism and cocktails the heroic virtues were still unimpaired in the younger generation and ready for exercise the moment they were called upon."[47] Or, as Tolkien described his hobbits: "Soft as butter they can be, and yet sometimes as tough as old tree-roots."[48]

Nevertheless, for many the creeping terror created by the raids—the sudden whoosh of incendiary bombs exploding nearby—was not easily shaken off. The sound of the air raid sirens was enough to bring on a sense of panic. As Tolkien confessed to his son Michael: "I often have a sudden horrible fear that we shall all perish."[49] The assaults on London, Coventry, and other cities bear at least some resemblance to scenes such as the Siege of Gondor in *The Lord of the Rings.*

> The Nazgûl came again, and as their Dark Lord now grew and put forth his strength, so their voices, which uttered only his will and his malice, were filled with evil and horror. At length even the stout-hearted would fling themselves to the ground as the hidden menace passed over them . . . while into their minds a blackness came, and they thought no more of war; but only of hiding and of crawling, and of death.[50]

Although Oxford was never bombed, the university was ordered to take the same precautions against air raids as in London and other cities vulnerable to attack. The university created a fire brigade, placing a trailer pump in every college and huge water tanks in the quadrangles.[51] Before the war, students who climbed up college roofs for amusement faced disciplinary action; now it became a patriotic obligation to man the rooftops, with ladders provided. "The most time-consuming war work for undergraduates was fire-watching," writes Robin Darwall-Smith. "Every night they took turns sitting on its roofs looking out for passing airplanes, some sitting in boredom, others enjoying plane-spotting."[52]

In the evenings Lewis went on weekly patrol with the Home Guard, typically with another Local Defence Volunteer (L.D.V.). He sometimes managed to steer the conversation to topics other than the war and the weather.

During a midnight patrol, Lewis and another member of the Home Guard told a third volunteer that they didn't expect the war to put an end to war, or that human misery would ever be abolished. "I shall never forget that man standing still in the moonlight for at least a whole minute, as this entirely novel idea sank in," he recalled, "and at last breaking out, 'Then what's the good of the ruddy world going on?'" The distractions and falsehoods of the modern world—the facile belief in inevitable "progress"—often prevented people from facing unpleasant realities.[53]

Lewis was not shy in pointing them out. "In the small hours of this morning," he wrote to a friend, "I succeeded in making my L.D.V. fellow sentry realize for the first time in his life that 'nature' can't have 'purposes' unless it is a rational substance, and if it is you'd much better call it God, or the gods, or a god, or the devil."[54] Although he didn't elaborate, Lewis was battling against a philosophy of life that he himself once shared, what George Bernard Shaw and others called the Life Force. Under this view, man's upward evolutionary development was not the result of blind chance but rather some purposeful force in nature, left undefined.[55] The fact that his fellow sentry had never considered the implications of his beliefs, Lewis remarked, was another example of "the great fog of nonsense spread over all nations."[56]

With relentless determination, Lewis set out to pierce the fog of muddled thinking that held so many minds in its sway. In this task, the war created a profound sense of urgency.

As Lewis explained in his sermon at University Church of St. Mary the Virgin, all of man's schemes for happiness that centered on this world were destined for a final frustration. "In ordinary times only a wise man can realize it. Now the stupidest of us knows."[57] The first literary fruits of his attempt to translate Christian concepts for his generation included *The Ransom Trilogy* and *The Screwtape Letters*, works of fantasy. But as the war continued, and as the political situation became increasingly desperate for Great Britain, Lewis delivered a more direct apologetic, beginning with *The Problem of Pain*.

He was soon called upon to make a straightforward defense of the Christian faith for a national audience.

GOD AND THE BBC

Modern consumers of the BBC might be surprised to learn that the secular broadcasting company had deep roots in Christianity. Broadcasting House, completed in 1931, was inscribed with a dedication to "the almighty God" and with a prayer that its programming might encourage its listeners to "tread the path of wisdom and righteousness."[58] Its founding general director, Sir John Reith, was a devout Scotsman, and he ensured that the BBC broadcasted daily religious services and music and meditations during the week.

This was consistent with Britain's self-identity as a Christian nation with an established church, the Church of England. Most Britons identified themselves as members of the Anglican Church. Nevertheless, the director of the BBC's Religious Broadcasting Department, Reverend J. W. Welch, guessed that perhaps two-thirds of BBC listeners went about their lives without any reference to God.[59] Welch wanted to support the war effort, and he knew that millions of people faced the daily terrors of air raids, the news of family members killed in combat, and the possibilities of a German invasion.

As a pious Anglican, Welch believed that the BBC audience could find strength and inspiration in the Christian faith—but only if the faith was explored in a fresh way, in terms they could grasp. Welch was candid about his aim: "In a time of uncertainty and questioning it is the responsibility of the Church—and of religious broadcasting as one of its most powerful voices—to declare the truth about God and His relations to men." He was certain that Christian doctrines could "be applied to present-day society during these difficult times."[60]

Most Anglican ministers, however, either lacked the skills for this task or showed little interest in defending the orthodox faith. Welch had read Lewis's book *The Problem of Pain*—reprinted in the fall of 1940—and knew he had found the voice for the occasion. He wrote to Lewis on February 7, 1941, suggesting that he offer a series of short talks on something like "The Christian Faith as I See It—by a Layman." Though he rarely even listened to the radio, Lewis agreed.

The war had stirred up interest in the consolations of religion, which Lewis saw firsthand at his church in Headington Quarry. "One unexpected feature of life at present is that it's quite hard to get a seat in church—every local family, apparently taking the view that whether they go or not, at any rate their evacuees *shall*," he observed.[61] Yet Lewis knew that most people were largely illiterate with regards to the Bible and the gospel message. The New Testament writers, he told Welch, took for granted that people were conscious of their unworthiness before God. "In modern England, we cannot at present assume this," he said, "and therefore most apologetic begins a stage too far on. The first step is to create, or recover, the sense of guilt."[62]

True to his word, in the opening line of his first broadcast over the BBC in August 1941, Lewis offered the most disarming of introductions: "Everyone has heard people quarreling." For the next fifteen minutes, from 7:45 to 8:00 p.m., the self-described "amateur" and former atheist introduced the BBC audience to the concept of a universal Moral Law. At a moment in world history when the moral foundations of Western civilization seemed to be disintegrating, here was someone trying to reverse the rot.

People everywhere held a common set of beliefs about how they ought to treat one another, Lewis explained, alongside the knowledge that they failed to live up to their own standards. The struggle against fascism, he said, made it impossible to defend the notion that all ethical systems were relative. As bombs rained down on British cities, there was nothing abstract about this argument. "If no set of moral ideas was truer or better than any other, there would be no sense in preferring civilized morality to savage morality, or Christian morality to Nazi morality."[63] This shared sense of right and wrong offered a "clue to the meaning of the universe."

Lewis traveled by train from Oxford to London to record his talks, and his trips were not without risk. Nazi bombing raids continued throughout the war, and the BBC's Broadcasting House was struck several times, killing and wounding many of its staff.

One of the most provocative talks was called "The Invasion," in which Lewis used the war setting as a metaphor for the spiritual conflict raging in everyday life. The Christian faith, he said, teaches that the struggle between Light and Darkness is not a war between independent powers. "It thinks it is a civil war, a rebellion, and that we are living in a part of the universe occupied by the rebel. Enemy-occupied territory—that is what this world is," he explained. "Christianity is the story of how the rightful king has landed, you might say landed in disguise, and is calling us all to take part in a great campaign of sabotage."

Here is an image drawn from bitter flesh-and-blood reality and the shock and horror of a European war, deployed to great effect. "At a quarter to eight, the bartender turned the radio up for Lewis," recalled George Sayer, who heard a live broadcast in a pub filled with soldiers. "'You listen to this bloke,' he shouted: 'He's really worth listening to.'"[64] And for the next fifteen minutes the soldiers listened intently, as did millions of other Britons. "The war, the whole of life, everything tended to seem pointless," recalled Air Chief Marshal Sir Donald Hardman. "We needed, many of us, a key to the meaning of the universe. Lewis provided just that. Better still, he gave us back our old traditional Christian faith."

The broadcasts were edited into a book, *Mere Christianity*, which has become one of the most widely quoted works of Christian apologetics ever written.

BRITAIN ALONE

1941 was a year of destitution for Great Britain. Even after the collapse of democracy in Europe, the Nazi domination of over half the continent, the fall of France, the devastating bombing raids on London—after all of this, the most powerful democracy in the world, the United States, remained on the sidelines of the conflict. Franklin Roosevelt had spent much of 1940 seeking an unprecedented third term in office as president. At the height of the Blitz, FDR was on the campaign trail, repeatedly promising the American people that he would keep the United States out of another European war: "The United States of America shall and must remain unentangled and free."

Roosevelt kept up his rhetoric as the devoted champion of peace throughout the last days of the 1940 presidential campaign. In Boston, October 30: "I have said this before, but I shall say it again and again and again: Your boys are not going to be sent into any foreign wars." In Brooklyn, November 1: "I am fighting to keep our people out of foreign wars. And I will keep on fighting." On November 2, the voters of Buffalo were assured that "your President says this country is not going to war." And in Cleveland on November 3: "The first purpose of our foreign policy is to keep our country out of war."[65]

FDR told the American people, still in an isolationist mood, exactly what they wanted to hear. And the message that the United States communicated to the watching world—to the dictators as well as to the democracies—was unequivocal. The war against totalitarianism in Europe was not America's fight. No assistance to Great Britain would be given. Joseph Kennedy, the US ambassador to Britain, concluded in November 1940: "Democracy is finished in England." Britain was alone.

Thus, 1941 looked like it might be the year of collapse. Tolkien suggested as much in a letter to Michael in January: "But plain reasoning seems to show that Hitler must attack this country direct and very heavily soon, and before the summer."[66]

Tolkien's letters to his sons are at times deeply personal, filled with advice about marriage, family, and faith. Writing again to Michael, in March 1941, he admitted that his son's fear that he might not survive the war was not unfounded. "None of us may: not even Priscilla," he wrote. "I often have a sudden horrible fear that we shall all perish."[67] Tolkien recalled the dread that engulfed him as he left as a soldier for the Western Front: the fear that he would be denied the chance to leave his mark on the world. "I never expected to survive; and the intense emotion of regret, the vivid (almost raw) perception of the young man who feels himself doomed to die before he has 'said his word,' is with me still: a cloud, a patch of sun, a star, were often more than I could bear."[68]

Near Tolkien's home in north Oxford was the RAF Abingdon airfield, a training center for young pilots. On Sunday afternoon, May 4, a Whitley V bomber was flying over New Marston with three crew members on board. Priscilla was playing outside with her friends in the garden adjacent to the Tolkien home at 20 Northmoor Road. Christopher was tracking the plane with his telescope when they saw "black smoke pouring from its engines." One of its engines was misfiring and the plane, with a full load of fuel, was struggling to maintain altitude. Tolkien's children could see that it was going to crash.[69]

The plane hit the western bank of the River Cherwell and slid up Linton Road, hitting a farm cottage and "exploding in a ball of black smoke, followed by the crackle of exploding ammunition."[70] Tolkien rushed to the scene, joined by policemen and a member of the Home Guard. Tolkien later told his children that there were "great acts of heroism by local people" who braved the fire before official help arrived. All three crew members perished, as well as one of the local residents.

A man, unnamed, "climbed into the burning house to rescue a boy trapped in an upstairs room."[71] Though Tolkien would have been too modest to acknowledge it, he almost certainly played a role in the rescue efforts that afternoon.

A WORLD ON FIRE

The war news that came in June 1941 must have made it look as if the whole world was on fire: Germany had invaded the other great rival to its mastery of Europe, the Soviet Union.

Hitler announced his invasion plans to his inner circle not long after the start of the Blitz. Germany's failure to defeat Britain accelerated his timetable. He never intended to honor the Nazi-Soviet Pact. The Führer was determined to destroy "Jewish-Bolshevism" and create a German empire in the east. He also needed raw materials—especially oil from the Caucasus—to prosecute the war against Britain and, if necessary, the United States.

On the eve of the invasion, the Soviet Union was the most repressive totalitarian state in the world. Thanks to Stalin's coercive industrial policies, the regime already had killed far more people—at least six million peasants—than the Third Reich. The cult-like status of the communist party and Stalin's image of infallibility matched that of Hitler and the Nazis. With the help of the Red Army and the KGB, Stalin effectively controlled the movements of hundreds of millions of people spread across eleven time zones. He knew how to put down internal threats to his authority.

Yet, somehow, Stalin did not anticipate that Nazi Germany would turn its rage east. Hitler effectively controlled all of Europe from the English Channel to the Soviet border. Stalin had kept his part of the bargain in the Nazi-Soviet Pact, providing Hitler with oil, grain, and other goods. What else could he want? Would he really gamble everything he had achieved by attacking the Soviet Union? Stalin ignored numerous intelligence reports of an impending Nazi assault. When it arrived, on June 22, 1941, the Soviets were unprepared.

Codenamed Operation Barbarossa, the assault sent three-fourths of Germany's military juggernaut into Soviet territory. It was the largest invasion force in European history: 3.6 million troops, 3,600 tanks, and 2,700 aircraft. On the first day of the invasion, half of the Soviet Air Force was destroyed.

It looked as if Hitler could bring his blitzkrieg to the doorsteps of Moscow. The German *Wehrmacht* seized more ground in a week than the Imperial German Army had managed in three years during World War I.

Soviet soldiers surrendered by the tens and hundreds of thousands; many were simply executed by the Nazis. "Everyone, even the last doubter, knows today that the battle against these sub-humans, who've been whipped into frenzy by the Jews, was not only necessary but came in the nick of time," a panzer gunner wrote to his father in August. "Our Führer has saved Europe from certain chaos."[72] Deeply shaken by the stunning success of Hitler's army, Stalin initially retreated to his dacha outside of Moscow.

From the vantage point of the British people, the entire European continent—including their own island nation—had been turned into a war zone. During the 1914–18 war, the front lines were clear and mostly immovable; the trenches along the Western Front defined them for both sides of the conflict. Not in this war. The new technologies, the "lightning war" strategy of the Nazis, the ruthless disregard for civilian life—all of it meant that any population center could become a target for destruction.

THE INDIVIDUAL IN THE FOG OF WAR

It is no wonder, then, that some of the most striking images in the novels of Tolkien and Lewis are the battle scenes: the Siege of Gondor, the Battle of the Pelennor Fields, the Fight at Anvard, the High King in Command. All possess an unmistakable realism.

"Fires leaped up. Great engines crawled across the field," Tolkien writes in *The Lord of the Rings*. "All before the walls on either side of the Gate the ground was choked with wreck and with bodies of the slain; yet still driven as by a madness more and more came up."[73] In *Prince Caspian* Lewis captures the unexpected vagaries of combat as someone who knew them firsthand. "And as so often happens, the enemy turned out stronger than they had reckoned," he writes. "At last there came a night when everything had gone as badly as possible, and the rain which had been falling heavily all day had ceased at nightfall only to give place to raw cold. . . . It was a gloomy company that huddled under the dripping trees to eat their scanty supper."[74]

"The Chronicles of Narnia is, after all, a series of books for children," observes Alister McGrath, "but it contains some of the most vivid, realistic descriptions of warfare that you find in children's literature."[75] Niall Ferguson notes that although Tolkien and Lewis served faithfully in defense of their country, neither yearned for combat. "Both were appalled by war, and I think depict battle with a degree of insight as fundamentally frightening," he says. "And one gets a good sense from both authors of the frightening quality of battle and the smallness the individual feels. Hobbits are small: It's the defining characteristic of the hobbit. And that means that all the battles that rage around Frodo and Sam in *The Lord of the Rings* are purposefully huge, events that are beyond the control of the tiny, individual hobbit."[76]

The lives of these authors were framed by two devastating global conflicts. They fought in the First World War and survived, only to endure a Second World War. They began writing their epic stories "when the darkest shadow of modern history was cast over the West and, for a crucial part of that time, over England in particular."[77] Thus the onset of the 1939–45 war not only unleashed a flood of memories from the earlier conflict. Both wars were now working powerfully on their imagination:

moments of terror, suffering, and loss, as well as experiences of raw grit and heroic sacrifice.

All of these qualities were on display among the British people, soldier and civilian alike, as the shadow of Nazism threatened to devour them. It is inconceivable that their determination to persevere and resist tyranny played no part in how Tolkien and Lewis depicted their heroic characters.

In *The Lord of the Rings*, the survival of Middle-earth seems bound up with the decision of a fearful yet determined hobbit: "I will take the Ring," Frodo announces at the Council of Elrond, "but I do not know the way." When Frodo and Sam journey into Mordor in their attempt to destroy the Ring of Power, they are exhausted and nearly overwhelmed by the black skies and painful fumes. As Frodo casts himself upon the ground, Sam resolves his internal debate about what he must do. "He knew all the arguments of despair and would not listen to them," Tolkien writes. "His will was set, and only death would break it."[78]

The scene that follows seems an intimation of the stubborn, selfless valor that had thus far preserved Britain from utter ruin:

> Sam looked at him and wept in his heart, but no tears came to his dry and stinging eyes. "I said I'd carry him, if it broke my back," he muttered, "and I will! Come, Mr. Frodo!" he cried. "I can't carry it for you, but I can carry you and it as well. So up you get! Come on, Mr. Frodo dear! Sam will give you a ride. Just tell him where to go, and he'll go."[79]

This theme—the necessity of individual courage to combat evil—animates Lewis's space trilogy. Ransom, we are told, had fought honorably at the Battle of the Somme. But he doubts his own physical courage as he and the *hrossa* join forces to confront the monstrous *hnakra* on the planet Perelandra. After a fierce struggle, they emerge the victors. Lewis describes the solidarity of soldiers—regardless of their social or racial backgrounds—drawn together in combat. "He was one of them," Lewis writes. "They had stood shoulder to shoulder in the face of an enemy, and the shape of their heads no longer mattered. And he, even Ransom, had come through it and not been disgraced. He had grown up."[80]

Later in the story, in his confrontation with the Un-Man, Ransom wonders how it was possible that the fate of Perelandra could hang on "such a man of straw" as himself. He tries, for a moment, to evade his responsibility to resist the force of evil that had invaded the world. In the end, he realizes the shocking freedom that was put into his hands—to choose to fight or flee. "And at that moment, far away on Earth, as he now could not help remembering, men were at war, and white-faced subalterns and freckled corporals who had but lately begun to shave, stood in horrible gaps or crawled forward in deadly darkness, awaking, like him, to the preposterous truth that all really depended on him."[81]

In the works of both authors, obedience—to the Moral Law, to an unseen Guardian of the Shire, to Aslan the Lion—is the keynote. Or, as George MacDonald expressed it, "obedience is the key to every door." In the perennial struggle between duty and desire, it is the presence of courage that settles the matter.

IN THE FRAY WITH THE RAF

With the success of his BBC broadcasts, Lewis was asked by the assistant director of the BBC if he would also deliver talks for the armed forces during their Sunday program. He politely declined. "I'm talking already to the RAF, to the general public, to nuns, to undergraduates, to societies. The gramophone will wear out if I don't take care! With thanks and much regret."[82]

Earlier in the year, the Chaplain-in-Chief of the RAF had asked Lewis if he would give short talks about the Christian faith to the airmen. "The Battle of Britain had had an extraordinary effect on the nation and a quite miraculous effect on the status of the Royal Air Force," recalled Charles Gilmore, the RAF Commandant of the Chaplain's School. The RAF became the branch of the British military that many men—the "cream of the nation"—wanted to join. "Only those who lived through those days can understand this feeling."[83]

Lewis was hesitant, still worried that, at forty-two, he might be called up for service. "This assignment represented a new task for Lewis," said Gilmore. "He was a teacher to his bones . . . but I don't think that he was, for all his kindness, the plodder's teacher. How would it all work out when he was talking to an audience who had never, for the most part, contemplated an academic life at a university level?"[84] Nevertheless, Lewis agreed to lend a hand.

Over the next few years, Lewis slipped away from his other obligations, traveling by train across the English countryside through villages such as Perthshire, Shrewsbury, and Cumberland to speak to the airmen.

For the first time in many months, he was able "to see and smell the sea and hear the sound of the gulls again," he wrote to Arthur on December 23, 1941, "which otherwise I would have been pining for."[85] He traveled for two or three days at a time before returning home, exhausted. "It was immensely demanding, but clearly he felt that this was his war work," says Simon Horobin. "This is what he was being called to do in the war. And he traveled the whole length of the country."[86]

Although Lewis struggled at first with his talks—"As far as I can judge," he said, "they were a complete failure"—he soon learned to connect with the men.[87] "I know that he had a profound effect," recalls Gilmore. "There were, so to speak, no headlines in the morning papers, but as a result of hearing Lewis there were handfuls of young people all gaining quite new concepts of how they fitted into the life that immediately lay before them." The life that lay before the men of the RAF was, of course, a life in peril.

Lewis understood precisely what they faced, and his audience knew instinctively that "his thoughts had been hammered out in the furnace rather than stored inside a glacier." He knew his words might represent the last opportunity for these young airmen to hear a defense of the Christian faith before becoming a casualty of war. "He could light it up with such grace and clarity," writes Gilmore, "that, long after what he actually said had been forgotten, the memory of many who heard him was that he had shown to them a sterling and direct purpose, where before they had found only the confusion of a whirlpool."[88]

The Inklings continued to meet every week amid the blackouts and air raids. In addition to Tolkien and Lewis, the most faithful participants during this time appear to have been Charles Williams, R. E. Havard, Hugo Dyson, and Warnie Lewis. In December, Lewis wrote to Dom Bede Griffiths and explained something of the importance of their gatherings and their friendship. "We meet on Friday evenings in my rooms," he explained. "What I owe them is incalculable. Dyson and Tolkien were the immediate human causes of my own conversion. Is any pleasure on earth as great as a circle of Christian friends by a good fire?"[89]

Most every week someone had a work in progress to share with the rest. Tolkien continued to make progress on his sequel to *The Hobbit*. He had taken the story up to the scene of the Bridge of Khazad-dûm, when the Company hears a deathly noise—"doom, doom"—as if the caverns of Moria had become a vast drum.[90] John Garth suspects that Tolkien was recalling his experience in the trenches on the Western Front, half buried in the earth. "I think when Tolkien is describing underworld dangers in Moria—we hear the doom, doom of the drums in the deep—I don't think that's far off from what the artillery would have sounded like when you were down in a dugout."[91]

Probably in December 1941, Tolkien picked up the story after Gandalf's apparently fatal struggle with the Balrog, when the Company is nearly overwhelmed by his loss. Thoughts of his friends who perished in the First World War could not have been far from his mind. "Grief at last wholly overcame them, and they wept long: some standing and silent, some cast upon the ground."[92] Nevertheless, the Company must soldier on. They head toward the Elvish forest of Lothlórien and learn of the Dark Days when the Dwarves had awakened an ancient evil that threatened the forest. Tolkien kept at it, and before Christmas he had sketched two more chapters: "The Great River" and "The Breaking of the Fellowship."

Wartime economies had created paper shortages, forcing Tolkien to write portions of the latter chapter in between the lines of the examination scripts of his students—as if moved by a creative force he dare not ignore.

THE "WAR OF THE MACHINES"

The overriding message of "The Breaking of the Fellowship" is the danger of the desire for power. That desire seizes Boromir, one of the Company, who becomes ensnared by his craving for the Ring and tries to take it from Frodo by force. "If any mortals have claim to the Ring, it is the men of Númenor, and not Halflings," says Boromir. "It is not yours save by unhappy chance. It might have been mine. It should be mine. Give it to me!"[93]

The theme of power insinuates itself in countless ways in Tolkien's story. For many years Tolkien had been fascinated by the myth of Atlantis, a tale of national corruption and pride dating back to Plato:

> Slowly, the wisdom and temperance of Atlantis gave way to arrogance, folly, and a lust for ever-greater power and wealth. All moderation was lost, and she warred incessantly with her neighbors and, eventually, with herself. . . . The final verdict was that Atlantis must be destroyed as a warning, an object lesson, to all future nations and races of men.[94]

The myth of Atlantis formed the basis for the history of Númenor, the island given in reward to mortal men who fought with the Elves against Morgoth in the Elder Days.[95] Its people became imperialistic as they established a maritime empire, however, much like nineteenth-century Britannia. Like the fall of Atlantis, the island was destroyed by hubris and sank into the sea.

The Ring of Power, of course, is the matrix for all the hatred and wickedness that threatens Middle-earth. The Ring not only grants invisibility to the person who wears it; Sauron invested much of his own strength into the One Ring, allowing it to rule over all the other rings. It is the motive force behind his attempt to enslave or destroy any living thing that stands in his way. "He brooked no freedom nor any rivalry," writes Tolkien, "and he named himself Lord of the Earth."[96]

Yet the story operates at a deeper psychological level. It is not only about the abuse of power but about *the corrupting quality of power*, no matter who possesses it. The Ring involves a two-sided danger: It represents an objective evil, existing outside of the individual. But it also finds an ally within the heart of everyone who seeks it—the evil within. "The very desire of it corrupts the heart," warns Elrond Half-Elven. "If any of the Wise should with this Ring overthrow the Lord of Mordor, using his own arts, he would then set himself on Sauron's throne, and yet another Dark Lord would appear."[97]

Closely associated with the desire for power is the misuse of science and technology to achieve it, a theme, as we have seen, which also appears in Lewis's Ransom series. Sauron's power depends upon machinery: His realm is choked with furnaces, iron wheels in constant motion, hammers pounding, steam rising.[98] The inevitable result, Tolkien implies, is the subjugation and destruction of nature. Even the outskirts of the land of Mordor are a wasteland. "What pestilence of war or evil deed of the Enemy had so blasted all the region even Aragorn could not tell."[99]

Landscapes made desolate by the machinery of war were familiar to any soldier who had fought at the Western Front, especially at the Somme, as Tolkien had. "It really was an alien landscape, and I think anybody who saw this landscape, it would have affected them," explains Michael Sheil, author of *Fields of Battle, Lands of Peace: 1914–1918*. "Tolkien was a man of real sensitivity and imagination, so it obviously had a great impact upon him."[100] Autumn rains filled the trenches and shell craters at the Somme, where the dead would lie submerged until someone discovered them unexpectedly—just as Sam Gamgee encountered dead bodies in the Dead Marshes. "When you read a passage like the passage of the Dead Marshes, your first response to it is this is a fantastical scene without basis in reality," says John Garth. "But when we know what Tolkien went through, we know it had an absolute basis in reality."[101] Tolkien himself acknowledged that his descriptions of the Dead Marshes as Frodo and Sam make their way to Mordor "owe something to Northern France after the Battle of the Somme."[102]

It also seems likely that the realm of Mordor owes something to the war being fought as Tolkien wrote of the struggle for Middle-earth: a war that involved lethal applications of science and technology unimagined in the previous conflict. The physical destruction of European cities during the Second World War simply had no historical parallel. The "first War of the Machines," as Tolkien described it, was leaving "everyone the poorer, many bereaved or maimed and millions dead, and only one thing triumphant: the Machine."[103]

The works of both Tolkien and Lewis were conceived amid the forces of annihilation unleashed during World War II. They were written under the shadow of totalitarian regimes that threatened the very survival of Western civilization. It is thus unsurprising that their stories identify the Will to Power as the chief source of the evil in the world that must be resisted. "For the generation of Oxonians we're talking about, it was obvious that power corrupts, and that absolute power corrupts absolutely," observes Niall Ferguson. "In both *The Chronicles of Narnia* and

The Lord of the Rings we see exquisite portrayals of temptation, and near fatal corruption."[104]

"A LAND OF IDOLS"

By the end of 1941, the corruption must have seemed complete. On December 7, the empire of Japan bombed Pearl Harbor in a surprise attack on the United States. Within hours, 8 US battleships, 3 destroyers, 3 light cruisers, and 177 planes were destroyed or rendered useless. The Japanese lost 55 men, compared to US fatalities of 3,297. General Hideki Tojo, Japan's wartime prime minister, had declared: "Our empire stands at the threshold of glory or oblivion." The Japanese vision of glory—nourished by a theory of racial superiority—depended upon their complete dominance of Asia.

On his writing pad, Tolkien made a reference to the Japanese assault on Malaya that same day. Ninety minutes before the attack on Pearl Harbor, a Japanese fleet of transport ships, cruisers, and destroyers landed at the port of Kota Bharu in northeast Malaya, a British colony. Japanese aircraft sank two British ships, the battle cruiser *Repulse* and the battleship *Prince of Wales*, killing 840 sailors and dealing a withering blow to British prestige throughout Asia. Hong Kong fell on Christmas Day, with reports of the rape and massacre of many civilians. Japan was now at war with America and Great Britain.

Like the British and French in May 1940, the Americans were unprepared for war. The conduct of American leadership, writes Max Hastings, "reflected an institutional failure of imagination which extended up the entire US command chain to the White House, and inflicted a trauma on the American people."[105] The failure to imagine the likelihood of this act of aggression, given Japan's brutal war on China—indeed, the reluctance to believe in the capacity for human wickedness on a vast scale—remains one of the enigmas of the Second World War. As Tolkien expressed it in *The Lord of the Rings*: "And the Elves deemed that evil was ended forever, and it was not so."

On December 11, Hitler declared war on the United States, ordering the German Navy to immediately begin attacking US ships. American neutrality came to an end, and the European war was transformed into a global conflict overnight.

Writing to his daughter as Father Christmas, Tolkien began his annual letter by noting that fewer children had written to him than in previous years. "I expect it's because of this horrible war, and that when it is over things will improve again, and I shall be as busy as ever. But at present so terribly many people have lost their homes or have left them; half the world seems in the wrong place."[106] A more poignant note of realism could hardly be written: *half the world seems in the wrong place.* And the marauding darkness of war was spreading, even to previously safe regions of the North Pole:

> I expect you remember that some years ago we had trouble with the Goblins; and we thought we had settled it. Well, it broke out again this autumn, worse than it has been for centuries. We have had several battles, and for a while my house was besieged. In November it began to look likely that it would be captured and all my goods, and that Christmas Stockings would all remain empty all over the world. . . . It has not happened—and that is largely due to the efforts of Polar Bear.[107]

Remarkably, what Tolkien alluded to as Father Christmas—in a greeting that should have been filled with nothing but whimsy—was the persistence of radical evil in the world. The West had tried to take a holiday from history. The holiday was over: The tragedy of the human condition could no longer be ignored; not even children could avoid the knowledge of it.

The nightmare that had descended upon Europe—from both a military and moral perspective—was almost beyond comprehension.

Committed to spreading atheistic communism by force, Joseph Stalin, in a pact with Hitler, had ruthlessly dismembered Polish society. Nevertheless, once the Soviet Union was attacked by Nazi Germany, Stalin immediately became an ally of the United States and Great Britain: The democracies of the West could not defeat Germany without his help.

It was a Faustian bargain. On Stalin's orders, 14,700 Polish officers languishing in Soviet-controlled POW camps—"uncompromising enemies of Soviet authority"—had been shot. The executions were systematic: Each officer was shot with a single bullet through the base of the skull. Four thousand bodies alone were discovered in a mass grave in the Katyn Forest by the advancing German army. Wherever Soviet occupation forces went, Polish political leaders, officers, and intellectuals "ceased to exist."[108] For Stalin, the Sovietization of eastern Poland was "a matter of world revolution."[109]

In Germany, plans to implement the "Final Solution" to the Jewish problem—the Nazi euphemism for mass murder—were well underway.

German Jews were forced to wear the yellow star, and in October 1941 they began receiving orders to appear at collection points for "evacuation" to an unspecified location. Their property, they were informed, had been confiscated. "The people concerned had lost their civic identity," writes Michael Burleigh. "Now they could be deported and murdered."[110] In German-occupied Poland, two million Polish Jews had been forced into ghettos, where many thousands starved to death. As Nazi forces pushed east toward the Soviet Union, the mass murder of Jews began on an industrial scale. In Bialystok, the first eastern Polish city to be overrun, *Wehrmacht* soldiers locked hundreds of Jews into the main synagogue and set it on fire. By December, as many as a million Jews had been murdered in the occupied areas of the Soviet Union.[111]

The pattern would be repeated throughout the war. By the end of 1941, Hitler effectively had under his control 8.7 million Jews, scattered across the occupied states of Europe.

It is a sobering thing to remember that the scourge of totalitarianism was not something imported from outside the West. It emerged from within Western civilization, like a cancer, ravaging the politics and culture of entire societies. Perhaps this is what Lewis had in mind in a scene from *Prince Caspian*, when the thought occurs to the Pevensie children that the savagery of the animals at war against Narnia could appear back home: "Wouldn't it be dreadful if someday, in our own world, at home, men started going wild inside, like animals here, and still looked like men, so that you'd never know which were which?"[112]

Joseph Stalin and Adolf Hitler, for all their differences in personality and ideology, shared a common ethos: the doctrine of the Will to Power.

In pursuit of their utopian societies, both leaders believed in radical social engineering; without a twinge of conscience, they were prepared to destroy entire population groups whom they identified as a mortal threat to their historic mission. They bore a striking resemblance to the character of the Un-Man in *Perelandra*: "It did not defy goodness, it ignored it to the point of annihilation," Lewis writes. "Ransom perceived that he had never before seen anything but half-hearted and uneasy attempts at evil. This creature was whole-hearted."[113]

In the Soviet Union no less than in Nazi Germany, a totalitarian society was created and sustained through terror: the knock on the door in the middle of the night. In both nations, the individual had ceased to exist as a person, as a moral agent made in the image of God. She had become a commodity, a utensil, easily disposable when she failed to serve the State.

It is a fearsome thing, as well, to realize that tens of millions of people were prepared to lay down their lives in obedience to the political visions of the dictators in Europe and Asia. Each ruler had created a cult of personality: an intensity of devotion among their populations that became a modern form of idol worship. The citizens in each of these totalitarian states were not ignorant of the hatreds and atrocities committed by their leaders. They may not have known the full extent of their crimes, but they knew enough.

And yet they bowed their heads and extended their arms in solidarity, as if in awe of an irresistible Leviathan. "For it is a land of idols," declared the prophet Jeremiah, "idols that will go mad with terror."[114]

PARADISE LOST, REVISITED

How do we make sense of all this? There is a profound mystery to evil that defies a full and satisfying explanation.

In December 1941, when the darkest forces of the world seemed to be on the winning side of history, Lewis launched a probe into the depths of the problem. He delivered a series of lectures on John Milton's *Paradise Lost* to University College of North Wales in Bangor. Lewis insisted that most modern scholars had ignored the great moral of Milton's poem, that "obedience to the will of God makes men happy and that disobedience makes them miserable." The modern outlook, he claimed, could not abide

Milton's teaching about the real nature of the Fall. The critics appear to have succumbed to "a sort of psychological necessity of passing over and hushing it up."[115]

With scholarly detachment, Lewis nonetheless was determined to make Milton's meaning clear. The origin of Satan's Fall, he explained, was the Sense of Injured Merit: He believed himself "impaired" because Messiah had been declared Head of the Angels. "Satan's monomaniac concern for himself and his supposed rights and wrongs," Lewis said, "is a necessity of the Satanic predicament."

The sin of Pride created a rebellion that produced misery for the emotions, corruption of the will, and nonsense in the intellect. Wounded pride may be laughed at when it appears in a child, but it becomes deeply problematic "when it appears armed with the force of millions on the political stage." Lewis's audience would have instantly recognized his thinly veiled reference to the totalitarian states then at war with the West.[116]

In the wake of the Modernist Movement after the First World War, Satan had become something of a noble figure among the literary and intellectual set. They found him to be the best drawn and most compelling of Milton's characters. His defiant battle cry—"Better to reign in Hell than serve in Heaven"—carried a certain appeal. Lewis sought to clarify what it was that many people actually found appealing. "To admire Satan, then, is to give one's vote not only for a world of misery," he said, "but also for a world of lies and propaganda, of wishful thinking, of incessant autobiography."[117]

When Lewis's talks were published under the title *A Preface to Paradise Lost*, it created quite a stir among the Oxford undergraduates. Students love discussing philosophy and literature, of course, but Lewis's work refocused the conversation.

"The *Preface* . . . forced us for the first time since the romantic critics adopted Satan as hero to take Milton's theology as seriously as his poetry and to relate them," recalls Rachel Trickett.[118] "Of all the texts at this time, the one around which most lively debate fizzled was *Paradise Lost*," writes Helen Tyrrell Wheeler. "The *Preface* came out in 1942, and arguments about the moral position of Satan were to be heard in the Kardomah, the Shamrock, on punts, and everywhere that single-minded English literature students congregated."[119]

In a penetrating examination of Milton's concept of evil, Lewis revealed his own sympathy for its staunchly biblical outlook. Hardly a day passes, he warned, without some slight movement towards heaven or hell within each one of us. When the reader of Milton realizes that she is part of this cosmic plot, scholarly indifference is no longer possible: "Our epic holiday is over."[120] Indeed, Milton's understanding of human nature had caused many critics to hold the poem in contempt. "We have all skirted the Satanic island closely enough," Lewis confessed, "to have motives for wishing to evade the full impact of the poem."[121]

In this belief, Lewis had surrounded himself with trusted and talented allies. Tolkien shared his friend's view of the Fall and credited Lewis with strengthening his conviction in the truths embedded in the Genesis story. His own story, Tolkien once said, was mainly about "power, exerted for domination." In man's fallen condition, he cannot help but employ science and technology for "new and horrible evil."[122] What that meant, Tolkien explained, was now blindingly clear: "So we come inevitably from Daedalus and Icarus to the Giant Bomber."[123]

The bombers, terrorizing civilization itself, bore witness to the fact that something resembling the demonic had been set loose upon the world. Milton's message, with help from the Inklings, was getting a new hearing.

CHAPTER 6

IN THE SHADOW OF MORDOR

Wherefore that enemy of man departed humbled, robbed of his triumph, to look upon his house of death.
—*Beowulf*

Then all the Captains of the West cried aloud, for their hearts were filled with a new hope in the midst of darkness.
—J. R. R. Tolkien, *The Lord of the Rings*

The journey you go on is your pain, and perhaps your cure: for you must be either mad or brave before it is ended.
—C. S. Lewis, *Out of the Silent Planet*

Throughout the first half of 1942 the future of Western civilization seemed shrouded in an unforgiving and impenetrable darkness.

Within a week of the attack at Pearl Harbor, Japanese forces stormed across the Pacific and Southeast Asia in a vast offensive that sent British and American troops staggering in defeat and surrender. The Japanese duplicated in Asia what the Germans achieved in Europe: a blitzkrieg that stunned and demoralized the Allied forces. By April 1942, the Japanese lightning war in the Pacific was larger and nearly as devastating as that of the Nazis. The Japanese conquered Guam, Burma, Indonesia, Thailand, Vietnam, and a large arc of Pacific islands. In the battle for the Philippines, 35,000 American troops were captured on the Bataan peninsula, the largest surrender in American military history. Singapore fell in barely seventy days, with 138,000 soldiers taken prisoner. Civilians were systematically massacred. The greater part of eastern China was under Japanese control.

Meanwhile, Nazi Germany seemed destined to achieve the living space imagined by the Führer. Germany and its allies controlled virtually all of Western and Central Europe. Following their invasion of the Soviet Union, German forces conquered Crimea and were pushing toward the Caucasus. Poland, the Baltic states, Ukraine, and Byelorussia were all in Nazi hands. In June 1942, Field Marshal Rommel's Afrika Korps took the British stronghold of Tobruk—thanks to an "ignominious surrender" of British troops—and rolled into Egypt.[1] US military leaders believed that the British campaign for Egypt was lost, and panic swept the country. "In launching war," observes Paul Johnson, "the Germans and the Japanese had pushed the world over the watershed into a new age, outside of anyone's control, full of marvels and unspeakable horrors."[2]

The horrors were multiplying with each Axis victory. The systematic rape and murder of civilians, mass executions, concentration camps, torture, genetic experimentation: Crimes against humanity were being committed on a scale for which the civilized world had no mental category. Here was the future that awaited Great Britain, the United States, and their allies if they could not regain their resolve and take the fight to the enemy. And yet, through the spring and summer of 1942, the tide of war seemed determined to overwhelm them.

Perhaps Tolkien had this horrific possibility in mind when he wrote of Lady Galadriel's warning to the Company in *The Lord of the Rings*: "But this I will say to you. Your Quest stands upon the edge of a knife. Stray but a little and it will fail, to the ruin of all."[3]

Like no other moment in history, Western civilization, with its commitment to the worth of every human soul, stood upon a knife's edge. This was the geopolitical reality as J. R. R. Tolkien and C. S. Lewis struggled to make sense of the world around them. Nevertheless, this was their aim: to aid in the recovery of moral and spiritual truths, in the restoration of a vision of man's dignity that had been stolen away. They possessed an acute sense of the fearsome threats to their civilization: materialism, scientism, collectivism, and totalitarianism. They were determined to expend themselves, in their private and public lives, toward its preservation.

SOCRATES AND THE EXAMINED LIFE

"The war creates no absolutely new situation," Lewis had told an audience at University Church of St. Mary the Virgin in 1939. "It simply aggravates the permanent human situation so that we can no longer avoid it."[4] Part of what Lewis had in mind was the realization of our mortality. Men and women must reckon with the spiritual dimension to life, he advised, while working to renew human culture. Toward this end, neither the war fought on battlefields nor the war for hearts and minds could be ignored: "Good philosophy must exist, if for no other reason, because bad philosophy needs to be answered."[5]

Beginning in January 1942, Lewis helped to create at Oxford a place where bad philosophy would be answered: a gathering of minds to debate the most pressing intellectual questions of the day. It was called the Oxford University Socratic Club, with a founding charter based on Socrates's exhortation to "follow the argument" wherever it would lead.

Lewis the scholar could appreciate the cultural significance of the moment. Socrates, the supreme provocateur of his day, had been accused of mocking the gods of the Greeks and "corrupting the youth" of Athens. At his trial, recorded in Plato's *The Apology*, he was offered a choice: permanent exile or death by poison. Socrates didn't yield an inch. "For I do nothing but go about persuading you all, old and young alike, not to take thought for your persons and your properties, but first and chiefly to care about the greatest improvement of the soul." Evasion and cowardice, whether in war or peacetime, he said, was the easy path. "The difficulty, my friends, is not in avoiding death, but in avoiding unrighteousness; for that runs faster than death."

Lewis thoroughly embraced the Socratic outlook and applied it to his own career, no less so to his other activities, including the Socratic Club. Its purpose was to apply Socratic principles to defend the Christian faith against critics from every corner. "It is a little remarkable that, to the best of my knowledge," Lewis announced, "no society had ever before been formed for such a purpose."[6]

The genesis of the Socratic Club was a conversation at a women's college tea party. In December 1941, Monica Shorten, a student at Oxford's Somerville College, complained to Stella Aldwinckle, a member of the university's pastoral staff, that no one seemed prepared to engage the tough philosophical and moral questions raised by the religious skeptics. They decided to hold a meeting, inviting "all agnostics, atheists, and those disillusioned about religion or think they are" to meet and discuss their questions. After the first gathering, the women asked if they could meet again and bring their boyfriends. When they packed out the room, the organizers turned to Lewis, writing him a letter asking him to serve as president. "Dear Miss Aldwinckle, This club is long overdue," Lewis wrote back. "Come to coffee on Tuesday evening in my rooms to discuss plans."[7]

With Lewis serving as president, the Socratic Club filled a niche at a crucial moment in the life of the university. The onset of war deepened the skepticism about religion that had invaded academic and elite opinion in the 1920s and '30s. Although there were important Christian student organizations such as the Oxford Group, they did not touch the centers of intellectual life at Oxford. Nor did formal academic theology, which remained effectively cut off from other disciplines. As historian F. M. Turner summarizes it, "Oxford philosophy deeply affected Oxford theology."[8]

And the philosophies in vogue at the university tended to invalidate the credibility of biblical religion. Chief among them was logical positivism, promoted by Oxford atheists such as A. J. Ayer in his book *Language, Truth, and Logic*. For philosophers in this school, the only reliable sources of knowledge came from empirical observation or from analytical reasoning. Because religious claims supposedly fit into neither category, they were considered meaningless.[9]

The debate topics for the Socratic Club reveal something of the philosophical landscape: "Is God a Wish Fulfillment?"; "Are There Any *Valid* Objections to Free Love?"; "Can Science Render Religion Unnecessary?"; "Materialism and Agnosticism"; "Marxist and Christian Views of the Nature of Man"; "Has Psychology Debunked Sin?"; and "Did Christ Rise from the Dead?" The weekly evening gatherings, held in a Junior Common Room, drew large crowds, such that "unless one arrived early one was lucky to find a seat on the floor."[10] Although Lewis was not always the representative Christian thinker, he arrived every week to help moderate.

Lewis placed an enormous value on the mere event of opposing philosophical voices listening respectfully to one another's arguments. By inviting some of the most respected academics in the Oxford community, the Socratic Club ensured that each group would hear not the worst, but the best that the other had to offer. "We of the Christian party discovered that the weight of the skeptical attack did not always come where we expected it," Lewis explained. "Our opponents had to correct what seemed to us their almost bottomless ignorance of the Faith they supposed themselves to be rejecting." It had a salutary effect: "At the very least we helped to civilize one another."[11]

At the first meeting of the club, on January 26, 1942, Lewis invited his friend R. E. Havard to deliver a paper addressing the question "Won't Mankind Outgrow Christianity in the Face of the Advance of Science and Modern Ideologies?" A famous wartime encounter involved Lewis and C. E. M. Joad, an Oxford philosopher and BBC broadcaster. "When I opened the door, there were so many people around the door you could hardly get in, and when you got inside, you couldn't move at all," recalled Stella Aldwinckle. It was stifling hot, and Aldwinckle leaned over to Lewis and asked why he didn't take off his jacket. He said in a whisper, "Because my shirt is patched."[12] (Although Lewis made a respectable income, he got into the practice of giving away most of what he earned to charitable causes. He also was notoriously indifferent about his wardrobe.)

A moral philosopher, Joad had been struggling with the problem of suffering. In his book *The Recovery of Belief*, he later credited Lewis for altering his opinion of the plausibility of the Christian worldview. Lewis's arguments "played no small part in preparing my change of view and precipitating the new outlook which it involved."[13] Many others would say the same. Rachel Trickett, who attended the club's meetings, recalled the sincerity and clarity of Lewis's arguments, which had a tremendous effect on the young audience. "Nobody could escape his influence," she recalled.[14] Oriel College philosopher L. W. Grensted thought that the

Socratic Club "was the most important thing that had happened in Oxford during the war."[15]

Though probably an overstatement, Lewis's engagement with these weekly events was critical to their success. "People packed out the meetings. People were sitting on pianos, under pianos. They had to move to larger rooms," says Simon Horobin. "And Lewis was very much the central figure of that."[16] Indeed, many people attended the meetings for one reason: to hear Lewis in debate. "When one met him and had the intention of putting forward something, arguing with him, it was rather like going in to bat in a game of cricket against a very swift bowler," recalled Owen Barfield. "You were so terrified as you walked toward the wicket that every idea in your head completely vanished except that at all costs you must keep a straight bat."[17]

It was an axiom among the academic elite that Christian belief, if it had any place in society at all, must be confined to the private sphere. The Socratic Club was another means for Lewis to consign this notion to the ash heap. "Christianity is not merely what a man does with his solitude," he argued. "It tells of God descending into the coarse publicity of history and there enacting what can—and must—be talked about."[18]

The coarse publicity of history: It was a telling phrase, as apt a description of 1940s Europe as it was of first-century Jerusalem. There was an unpredictability about the events of this period, as if something might happen—at any moment—that could decisively change the course of world history, for good or evil.

A LITTLE MAN CALLED NIGGLE

Responding to a letter from an admirer of *The Hobbit* at about this time, Tolkien informed him that he was writing another story, but this one was "very long" and "very dark."[19] Tolkien began to worry that he would never finish it.

This helps to explain why, unexpectedly, he wrote a short story about a painter who becomes distraught when it appears he will never complete his masterpiece. The story, *Leaf by Niggle*, is by all accounts the most autobiographical of all of Tolkien's works. It was "the only thing I have ever done which cost me absolutely no pains at all," he told his publisher. "Usually I compose only with the greatest difficulty and endless writing. I woke up one morning . . . with that odd thing virtually complete in my head. It took only a few hours to get down, and then copy out."[20]

The story might be called an allegorical autobiography. Niggle is the painter—"not a very successful one"—and Tolkien the writer. Both are perfectionists, easily distracted and somewhat harried by their neighborly obligations. "It would need some concentration, some work, hard uninterrupted work, to finish the picture, even at its present size," Tolkien writes in *Leaf by Niggle*. "But there came a tremendous crop of interruptions."[21]

The "leaf" in the story may be seen as *The Hobbit*, whereas the "tree" is its glorious fulfillment, *The Lord of the Rings*. The "country" in the story might be Middle-earth. And the "other pictures" that are "tacked on the edges of his great picture" are the poems and other stories that Tolkien kept inserting into his greater story.[22] The "garden," which Niggle does not keep up, looks suspiciously like Tolkien's literary life. The war had multiplied his academic obligations and added all-night patrols. Illness seemed to visit his family at regular intervals. "Tolkien is in trouble again, poor fellow, his wife having to have an operation, and some trouble with evacuees which I don't quite understand," Lewis wrote to his brother. "I notice that his trials, besides being frequent and severe, are usually of such a complicated nature as to be impenetrable."[23]

In the story, Niggle, with his painting unfinished, is suddenly forced to leave everything behind and take a train to an undisclosed destination—to face death and judgment. He is sent to a workhouse (purgatory), where he overhears two Voices evaluating his life. "He never got ready for his journey," says the First Voice. "But of course, he is only a little man," says the Second Voice. "He was never meant to be anything very much; and he was never very strong."[24]

Thus, at the age of fifty, with his great literary project still incomplete, Tolkien took humble stock of himself, his ambitions, and his limitations. "I was anxious about my own internal Tree, *The Lord of the Rings*," he admitted. "It was growing out of hand, and revealing endless new vistas—and I wanted to finish it, but the world was threatening."[25]

The point must not be missed: *The world was threatening.* All other distractions aside, it was the disaster of the Second World War—and all that was on the verge of being swept away—that pressed upon his mind so powerfully during the desperate months of 1942. "In addition to my tree-love (it was originally called The Tree)," he explained, "it arose from my own pre-occupation with The Lord of the Rings, the knowledge that it would be finished in great detail or not at all, and the fear (near certainty), that it would be 'not at all.' The war had arisen to darken all horizons."[26]

Leaf by Niggle was Tolkien's self-administered remedy to every man's fear: the fear of death. Not every painting, not every story, will be finished in this life. Death will intervene. Like nowhere else, Tolkien expressed his deepest anxieties over his own mythological Tree. Niggle "saw exactly the way in which to treat that shining spray which framed the distant vision of the mountain," Tolkien writes. "But he had a sinking feeling in his heart, a sort of fear that he would never now get a chance to try it out."[27]

Nevertheless, Niggle makes a courageous and selfless decision before his departure. Although somewhat grudgingly, he agrees to help a bothersome neighbor, Mr. Parish, who interrupts his work on the painting to implore him to fetch a doctor for his ailing wife. Niggle is willing to allow his creative life to effectively come to an end if it means helping—rescuing—another life in need. "It seems plain that this was a genuine sacrifice," said the Second Voice. "Niggle guessed that he was throwing away his last chance with his picture."[28]

This act of giving opens Niggle's mind and heart to a mysterious grace that transforms him. He is allowed to leave the workhouse and journey to the country, where he encounters his painting: completed, sublime in its beauty, a living Tree. "All the leaves he had ever labored at were there, as he had imagined them, rather than as he had made them." He encounters Mr. Parish in the country, and realizes that the most exquisite and beautiful leaves were created "in collaboration with Mr. Parish: there was no other way of putting it."

In this, Tolkien seems to be taking to task the self-absorption of the modern artist. Thanks to his relationship with Lewis, he had learned how unexpected friendships can open up the artist to new sources of beauty and grace.

Here is another instance of what Tolkien meant by the *eucatastrophe*, the undoing of a catastrophe, a theme that would form the redemptive core of *The Lord of the Rings*. Writing *Leaf by Niggle* was an act of defiance:

to use imaginative literature to remind us that the material world, with its temporal aims, is not the sum and substance of our mortal lives. Perhaps Tolkien chose a tree as the object of Niggle's imagination because he had in mind the "tree of life," as described in the Bible, a source of renewal and restoration in the New Jerusalem: "And the leaves of the tree are for the healing of the nations. No longer will there be any curse."[29] Reflecting on the story years later, Priscilla Tolkien viewed it as "a miniature spiritual odyssey" in which "my father expounds his Christian belief that without our lives being seen as a journey to God our artistic or other talents will come to nothing."[30]

THE HIJACKING OF HISTORY

It was the utter negation of the concept of a humble soul in submission to the will of God—and the political elevation of the Will to Power—that had brought about the world catastrophe of 1939–45. A pre-Christian paganism had been revived in Europe.

In *Not Far from Brideshead: Oxford Between the Wars*, Daisy Dunn observes that the Nazis cannibalized the ancient world as a source of Aryan cultural greatness. Sparta was lauded for the success of its brutally militant culture. Monographs such as *The Blond Hair of the Indo-Germanic Peoples of Antiquity* (1935) were routinely published under the Third Reich. "Nazi propaganda," Dunn writes, "would stop at nothing in their efforts to present the German people as the true heirs and descendants of the noble Greeks and their mighty Roman conqueror."[31] These blatant attempts at cultural theft, she argues, heightened the importance of a classical education. "Over the coming years, it would fall to the classicists to repudiate the ideological hijacking of their fields of study by totalitarian thinkers."[32]

Writing in *Time and Tide* magazine in June 1942, Lewis commented on a recent article in the same publication, which reported that the Nazis had chosen the Nordic character of Hagen over that of Siegfried as their national hero. Both figures appear in the Richard Wagner opera *The Ring of the Nibelung*, a blending of Norse mythology with German folklore in a vast story of love and redemption. Lewis was captivated by Wagner's version of this ancient tale as a teenager, when he first heard the opera and saw evocative illustrations of the story by Arthur Rackham.

Hitler absorbed Wagner's music as a youth, and it became the virtual soundtrack for the Third Reich. Wagner's rendering of a heroic Germanic past was appropriated by the regime: By returning to its cultural roots, it was believed, Germany would restore its lost greatness. Wagner was thus a fixture at Nazi ceremonies and rallies. "It was, therefore," Lewis wrote, "a bitter moment when the Nazis took over my treasure and made it part of their ideology."[33]

The Nazi selection of Hagen as a model of Aryan virtues, however, got Lewis thinking. By embracing Hagen, a co-conspirator in the plot against Siegfried, Hitler had elevated a thoroughly pagan notion of power. "Well know I Siegried's conquering strength," says Hagen. "How hard in battle to slay him; but whisper to me some sure device for speeding him to his doom."[34] Likewise, by claiming the Norse god Odin as part of their cultural heritage, Lewis wrote, the Nazis completely misunderstood what Norse religion was about. It had nothing to do with the craving for power but rather the willingness to take heroic stands against hopeless odds. "How is it that the only people in Europe who have tried to revive their pre-Christian mythology as a living faith should also be the people that shows itself incapable of understanding that mythology in its very rudiments?"[35]

Wagner's story, like that of Tolkien's, involves a powerful ring that corrupts those who seek to possess it. Tolkien drew upon some of the same Nordic sources as Wagner for *The Lord of the Rings*. He, too, was attracted to these tales as a young man "when Hitler was, I suppose, dabbling in paint."[36] Most of his academic life was spent studying Germanic literature (broadly understood to include England and Scandinavia), and his admiration for the Germanic spirit ran deep.

Informed by his Catholic faith, Tolkien could distinguish the nobler pagan elements in these stories and bring a Christian ethos to bear in their appropriation. He thus despised the "Nordic nonsense" of the Third Reich. As he put it in a wartime letter to Michael,

> You have to understand the good in things, to detect the real evil. . . . I have in this war a burning grudge—which would probably make me a

> better soldier at 49 than I was at 22: against that ruddy little ignoramus Adolf Hitler. . . . Ruining, perverting, misapplying, and making forever accursed, that noble Northern spirit, a supreme contribution to Europe, which I have ever loved, and tried to present in its true light.[37]

It was a dark coincidence that the Nazi embrace of the mythological figure of Hagen coincided with their elevation of Herbert Hagen, a member of the Security Police of the SS, in their murderous quest for racial purity. In the spring of 1942, Hagen was sent to Paris as the chief aide to General Karl Oberg, the top SS man in France. Hagen's primary role was to hunt down Jews. Tolkien was not off the mark when he said that the Nazi corruption of an otherwise admirable pagan spirit had brought about one of the greatest tragedies of European history, and that behind it lay a "demonic inspiration."

HELL ON EARTH

The persistence of radical evil is a fact that has afflicted the Jewish people for millennia. They have endured persecution under pagan, Christian, and Muslim regimes. Paul Johnson has called anti-Semitism "a disease of the mind." Under Nazi Germany, the disease found its most virulent expression. Although the persecution of the Jews began when Hitler came to power in 1933, it was 1942, the calamitous year for Western civilization, that inaugurated the official start of the Holocaust.

In January, in a villa outside Berlin, Nazi leaders secretly approved a plan to coordinate a European-wide "Final Solution of the Jewish Question," with the goal of killing eleven million Jews.

In March, Nazi police began systematically deporting Jews from the Polish ghettos of Lublin and Lvov, from Slovakia, and from France, sending them to killing centers throughout Europe. In May, the use of the poison gas Zyklon B began at the Auschwitz-Birkenau camp. Before the end of the war, one million Jews alone would be murdered at Auschwitz. In July, the Nazis began deporting Jews from the Netherlands to the death camps. Deportations of Jews from Norway and Austria soon followed. In the same month, 265,000 Jews were shipped from the Warsaw Ghetto to Treblinka, where they were systematically murdered in the newly constructed gas chambers.

In August, Gerhart Riegner, secretary of the World Jewish Congress, sent a telegram to the WJC's offices in London and New York confirming previous reports of Nazi plans to exterminate the Jews. Finally, in December, Great Britain and the United States, on behalf of other Allied nations, issued their first declaration denouncing Germany for engaging in the mass murder of European Jews. They condemned "in the strongest possible terms this bestial policy of cold-blooded extermination." They also resolved to "overthrow the barbarous Hitlerite tyranny" and to "ensure that those responsible for these crimes shall not escape retribution."

British Foreign Secretary Anthony Eden read the statement aloud in the House of Commons. He described how hundreds of thousands of men, women, and children were being transported from German-occupied territory "in conditions of appalling horror and brutality" to Eastern Europe. "None of those taken away," Eden said, "are ever heard of again."[38] What many had dismissed as wartime propaganda was confirmed as fact at the highest levels of government. The racist savagery of Nazism, its heart of darkness, was now impossible to ignore.

Indeed, it is surely significant that in their great works of fiction written during this period, Tolkien and Lewis create characters who expose the problem of race hatred and offer an alternative account of the human family.

In *Out of the Silent Planet*, soon after Ransom arrives in Malacandra, he meets the three species of beings who inhabit the planet: the *hross*, who live a simple agricultural life; the *sorns*, who are scientifically minded; and the *pfifltriggi*, the miners and artisans. To Ransom's amazement, all the races lived in harmony; no one tried to use his unique gifts or strengths to dominate the others. "Ransom turned it over in his mind," Lewis writes. "On Malacandra, apparently, three distinct species had reached rationality, and none of them had yet exterminated the other two. It concerned him intensely to find out which was the real master."[39]

In *The Lord of the Rings*, one of the triumphant arcs of the story is the unexpected friendship between the Elf Legolas and the Dwarf Gimli. The history of antagonism between their races is revealed nearly the moment they find themselves part of the Fellowship to destroy the Ring of Power.

When a company of Elves encounters the Fellowship en route, they bristle upon learning that a Dwarf is among them. "A dwarf!" said Haldir. "That is not well. We have not had dealings with Dwarves since the Dark Days. They are not permitted in our land. I cannot allow him to pass."[40] Only by blindfolding Gimli do Haldir and his guards agree to take the Fellowship to meet the Lady of the Wood. What follows is an exchange with Lady Galadriel that would presage the friendship between Gimli and Legolas.

> She looked upon Gimli, who sat glowering and sad, and she smiled. And the Dwarf, hearing the names given in his own ancient tongue, looked up and met her eyes; and it seemed to him that he looked suddenly into the heart of an enemy and saw there love and understanding. Wonder came into his face, and then he smiled in answer.[41]

Bowing before her—a ruler of the Elves, a race he had learned to despise—the Dwarf declares Lady Galadriel to be "above all the jewels that lie beneath the earth!"[42] Here is Tolkien's vision of the world as it was meant to be, where old hatreds dissolve and are replaced by strong cords of friendship.

THE ABOLITION OF MAN

"Warnie and I are alright," Lewis wrote to Arthur in January 1943. "But it's a weary world, isn't it?"[43] Later that year, Tolkien wrote to his son Christopher, lamenting the all-encompassing nature of the war. "But the special horror of the present world is that the whole damned thing is in one bag. There is nowhere to fly to."[44] It would be hard to overstate the emotional exhaustion that was kept at bay only by great effort—whether through the diversions of work, friendships, family, or other means. The letters of Tolkien and Lewis during this period attest to this fact repeatedly.

Good news arrived for the Allies on January 31–February 1, when the remnants of Hitler's Sixth Army—bogged down by the Russian winter and a ferocious Soviet counteroffensive—surrendered at Stalingrad. It was the most significant Nazi defeat since the start of the conflict. Yet the human costs of this victory were staggering. From August 1942, when the battle began, through February 1943, more than two million troops were drawn into the fighting. Nearly a million people were killed or injured, including tens of thousands of Russian civilians. About one hundred thousand German soldiers were captured, and most were killed by Russian soldiers or left to starve or freeze to death. As one historian describes it, "the contest in barbarism had become unstoppable."[45]

Although the Soviet Union was now an ally of Great Britain and the United States—and Soviet soldiers suffered much higher casualty rates for the remainder of the war—few people had illusions about the nature of Stalin's regime.[46] Like Hitler, he ruled by terror: Purges, secret police, show trials, gulags, and mass murder were the coins of the realm.

These immense and inescapable truths probably helped persuade Lewis to agree to deliver a series of lectures on ethics at Durham University in February 1943. Arriving from Oxford by train with his brother, Lewis spoke to large crowds on three consecutive nights with talks titled "Men Without Chests," "The Way," and "The Abolition of Man." The talks were published later that year under the title *The Abolition of Man*, with the less scintillating subtitle *Or Reflections on Education with Special Reference to the Teachings of English in the Upper Forms of Schools.*

By the time Lewis concluded, he had delivered one of the twentieth century's most trenchant and prophetic warnings against the unholy alliance of moral cynicism, perverted science, and the totalitarian state. As in his other wartime writings, Lewis made it clear that there was a War behind the war: a deeper and more consequential struggle for the human soul.

"I doubt we are sufficiently attentive to the importance of elementary textbooks." With this innocuous opening line, Lewis explained how the concept of truth was being eviscerated by modern educational methods.

Grammar books—like the prototypical *The Green Book* cited by Lewis—were awash with philosophical assumptions that were robbing their readers of the love of virtue and beauty. The attempt to curb certain "unpopular" sentiments was creating a dangerous void. "By starving the sensibility of our pupils," Lewis said, "we only make them easier prey to the propagandist when he comes."[47] By rejecting the idea of a universal Moral Law—what Lewis called "the Tao"—modern educators were subverting the development of character. They were producing "men without chests," a generation of individuals lacking the qualities necessary for a meaningful and virtuous life.

In modern educational policy Lewis discerned the origins of totalitarianism. "The practical result of education in the spirit of *The Green Book*," he said, "must be the destruction of the society which accepts it." To some in his audience, that claim must have sounded like the rantings of a cultural neanderthal. Novelist Ayn Rand, after reading Lewis's book, dismissed him as a "cheap, driveling non-entity!"[48]

Yet for many others, the necessity of the Moral Law would have been agonizingly obvious. Without a solid basis for respecting every human life, for honoring one's moral commitments, the principles of justice and humanity "can be properly swept away" when they clash with other desires. The moment an individual removed himself from the constraints of the Moral Law—launching a rebellion against it—his desires would turn naturally inward, into darkness. "I am not here thinking solely, perhaps not even chiefly, of those who are our public enemies at the moment," Lewis said. "The process goes on apace among Communists and Democrats no less than among Fascists."[49]

Like few thinkers of the hour, Lewis saw the end from the beginning: The roots of totalitarian societies were being planted in English schools by the moral cynics who had come of age in between the world wars.

The final lecture, "The Abolition of Man," was surely the most terrifying for its listeners. Lewis warned that man's desire to "conquer nature"—in the name of "progress" or "happiness"—would become a Faustian bargain. Up until this moment, he said, the common decency of ordinary people had frustrated the wildest schemes of authoritarian elites. "But the man-molders of the new age will be armed with the powers of an omnicompetent state and an irresistible scientific technique." Unrestrained, "the Conditioners" will enlist eugenics, prenatal indoctrination, education, and propaganda to gain mastery over millions.[50]

This critique of the abuse of science to serve a dictatorial cabal was taking shape in Lewis's mind well before he delivered his Durham University lectures. He had begun writing the final installment of his Ransom series, *That Hideous Strength*, in 1942, and he was working on it through the early months of 1943 just as the battle for Stalingrad was raging. For Lewis, the remorseless sacrifice of so many thousands of Russian and German soldiers provided more evidence that the ideology of scientism—with its reduction of man to raw material—opened the door to new barbarisms.

"A large, unintelligent population is now becoming a deadweight. The real importance of scientific war is that scientists have to be reserved," explains Professor Frost, an operative of the N.I.C.E., to Mark Studdock. "It was not the great technocrats of Keonigsberg or Moscow who supplied the casualties in the siege of Stalingrad: it was superstitious Bavarian peasants and low-grade Russian agricultural workers."[51] The "man-molders of the new age," as Lewis put it, were as active in Moscow as they were in Berlin.[52]

There was only one possible result when men stepped outside of the Moral Law: They stepped into the void. "Man's final conquest has proved to be the abolition of Man."[53] In making this argument, Lewis was not creating an imaginary dystopian future, as Aldous Huxley did a decade earlier in *Brave New World*. He was *observing* what the fascist and communist regimes were already doing to their own populations. "For the power of Man to make himself what he pleases means, as we have seen, the power of some men to make other men what *they* please."[54]

Emerging from the social chaos following the First World War, these nations not only functioned as dictatorships that sought to control all aspects of political, economic, and educational life. They also claimed a scientific basis for their political systems.

The Nazis drew upon the racist pseudoscience of social Darwinism and the eugenics movement. Marx and his followers taught a theory of scientific communism to explain the economic history of mankind. "Under modern conditions," Lewis wrote, "any effective invitation to Hell will certainly appear in the guise of scientific planning."[55] Lewis was not being polemical. By 1943, millions of people already had become victims of the most hellish regimes in human history, aided by the tools of modern science.

BEOWULF AND A HOSTILE WORLD

Defeating these powers would require great sacrifice. By the end of 1942, the British government lowered the conscription age to eighteen. More Oxford men were being pressed into military service.

In January 1943, the university created accommodations for Navy and Air Force cadets who wanted to begin their studies before being sent off to fight.[56] Tolkien was tasked with developing a scheme of English courses for a six-month academic program, in which the cadets would take courses while training to be officers. He personally interviewed the cadets, chaired meetings, and arranged for tutors and for substitutes when lecturers became unavailable.[57]

Lewis was part of the roster and apparently became sick in the spring, requiring Tolkien to step in as a substitute lecturer. He wrote Lewis a letter suggesting that he was taking on too many responsibilities and making himself an "easy victim" for illness. "As a mere 'director,' I shall hope very much to persuade you to ease off in travel (if possible), and put some weight into this cadet stuff." Tolkien closed his letter by mentioning that he had lunch at the Air Squadron, where he got the chance to interact closely with the men "and got a brief whiff of an atmosphere now all too familiar to you, I expect."[58]

Tolkien the lecturer was never far removed from his beloved *Beowulf.* When Lewis started a reading club for undergraduates called Beer and Beowulf, Tolkien showed up to help unpack the meaning of the poem. They also unpacked a barrel of beer, which Lewis brought to his rooms in Magdalen. Students and instructors filled their glasses and recited bits of the poem, translating it as they went. "Tolkien would discuss some of the contextual issues, tease out some of the references, talk about the mythology," says Simon Horobin. "And then he and Lewis would compete to blow smoke rings from their pipes."[59]

In the Hilary term of 1943, Tolkien taught on the poem three days a week. He was notorious for entering the classroom silently, fixing his gaze on the audience, and then calling out in a deep voice a few lines from the poem in the original Anglo-Saxon.[60] Although Tolkien spoke quickly and could be difficult to understand, his passion for the subject—and his theatrical talents—won over many of his students. Writer J. I. M. Stuart, a former student, recalled: "He could turn a lecture room into a mead hall in which he was the bard and we were the feasting, listening guests."[61]

Betty Bond studied under Tolkien during the war and was similarly moved by his performance. In a letter of appreciation, she wrote,

> Dear Prof. Tolkien, Some of us among the home students would like to tell you how much we have enjoyed your "Beowulf" lectures this term, and to thank you not only for enlightening but also entertaining us for two hours a week. We hope that we shall now be able to face the terrors of schools [examinations] as fearlessly as Beowulf met Grendel![62]

Poet W. H. Auden, who studied English at Christ Church, also attended the *Beowulf* lectures. They left their mark on him. "I don't think I have ever told you what an unforgettable experience it was for me as an undergraduate, hearing you recite Beowulf," he wrote Tolkien years later. "The voice was the voice of Gandalf."[63]

Humphrey Carpenter believed that Tolkien possessed "a poet's understanding of how language is used." Tolkien had such a love and feel for languages that he could help students understand not only what the words meant but *why* the author had chosen them at that place in the text. "In this respect he almost founded a new school of philology," writes Carpenter. "Certainly there had been no one before him who brought such humanity, one might say such emotion, to the subject."[64] Lewis believed that it was Tolkien's lifelong pursuit as a "linguistic inventor" that accounted for the richness of his lectures and scholarly work. He learned how to put himself "inside language."[65]

Although all this was true, Tolkien's devotion to his *Beowulf* lectures in 1943 seemed to carry a special significance. Perhaps at no time in the two decades that Tolkien taught the poem did its central themes—the existence of radical evil and the heroic sacrifice required to resist it—carry such a contemporary relevance.

As we saw, Tolkien viewed Beowulf as a man "at war with a hostile world," battling monsters that were not peripheral but central to the story. "He had wrapped the dwellers in the land in flame, in fire and burning," writes the author of *Beowulf* of the guardian of the hoard. "He trusted in his barrow, in its wall and his own warlike might, and his trust cheated him."[66] The hubris—the megalomania—of the wicked was no medieval legend. It was alive and well in the twentieth century, on wretched display on the world stage.

LUNCH WITH AN INDEFATIGABLE MAN

"I begin to think that for us to meet on Wednesdays is a duty: there seem to be many obstacles and fiendish devices to prevent it." Thus "Tollers" reminded "Jack," in an April 1943 letter, how important their friendship had become to him.[67]

Lewis was the first person to persuade Tolkien that his love of fantasy, his desire to create "a mythology for England," *must* be pursued. He responded with great enthusiasm—and detailed criticism—when Tolkien dared to share with him the story closest to his heart, the story of Beren and Lúthien. He insisted that Tolkien subject his evolving epic to the scrutiny of the Inklings. He also met with him, one on one, to hear the latest installment in the saga. "He heard all of it, bit by bit, read aloud," recalled Tolkien. "He was for long my only audience. Only from him did I ever get the idea that my 'stuff' could be more than a private hobby. But for his interest and unceasing eagerness for more I should never have brought the Lord of the Rings to a conclusion."[68]

This was not hyperbole. Although Lewis profoundly admired Tolkien and his creative abilities, he also knew that his friend's perfectionism could be his greatest enemy. "He is a very great man," Lewis wrote to Sister Penelope. "His published works (both imaginative and scholarly) ought to fill a shelf by now: but he's one of those people who is never satisfied with a manuscript. The mere suggestion of publication provokes the reply 'Yes, I'll just look through it and give it a few finishing touches'—which means that he really begins the whole thing again."[69]

By the spring of 1944, Tolkien had hit another trough in his effort to finish *The Lord of the Rings*. As he admitted to his publisher around this time, "I have had barely the energy or the time to get through the menial day," and thus "not a line of it was possible for a year."[70]

On March 29, on a Wednesday—the day of the week when he and Lewis met to talk about life and literature despite the "fiendish devices" conspiring against them—the two gathered for lunch, probably at the Eastgate Hotel in Oxford.[71] Lewis must have realized that his friend had dug himself into another pothole of paralysis. Tolkien wrote to Christopher about their meeting. "The indefatigable man read me part of a new story! But he is putting the screw on me to finish mine. I needed some pressure and shall probably respond."[72]

The conversation that day apparently had the desired effect. Tolkien was sending portions of his story to Christopher, who had turned eighteen years old and was serving in the Royal Air Force. Among Tolkien's children, Christopher took the greatest interest in their father's story. Immediately following his lunch with Lewis, Tolkien plunged back into the project. "I have seriously embarked on an effort to finish my book," he wrote on April 5, 1944. "And it is a painful tricky business getting into the swing again. A few pages for a lot of sweat; but at the moment they are just meeting Gollum at the precipice."[73]

Tolkien next wrote a series of letters to his son, usually explaining the progress he was making on the story, sometimes seeking advice on moving forward:

> April 8: Spent part of day (and night) struggling with chapter. Gollum is playing up well on his return. . . . About 2:00 a.m. I was in the warm silver-lit garden, wishing we two could go for a walk.
>
> April 14: Afternoon lawnmowing. Term begins next week. . . . Still I am going to continue "Ring" in every salvable moment.
>
> April 18: I hope to see C.S. Lewis and Charles Williams tomorrow morning and read my next chapter—on the passage of the Dead Marshes and the approach to the Gates of Mordor. . . . The afternoon was squandered on plumbing (stopping overflow) and cleaning out fowls.
>
> April 23: I have neglected too many things to do it. I am just enmeshed in it now, and have to wrench my mind away to tackle exam-paper proofs, and lectures.
>
> April 25: Gave poor lecture, saw the Lewises and Charles Williams for 1/2 hour; mowed three lawns . . . and struggled with recalcitrant passage in "The Ring."
>
> May 14: I saw C.S.L. from 10:45 to 12:30 this morning: heard 2 chapters of his "Who Goes Home?"—a new allegory on Heaven and Hell; and I read my 6th new chapter "Journey to the Crossroads" with complete approval.

Tolkien had arrived at "the nub" of the story, he added, "when the threads must be gathered."

> May 21: Do you think *Shelob* is a good name for a monstrous spider creature?

Tolkien and Lewis continued to meet together on Wednesdays, and Lewis never failed to encourage him to hold fast to his vision for the story. On May 29, Tolkien shared two more chapters with Lewis, which included "The Choices of Master Samwise," a description of Samwise Gamgee battling a giant spider to save his friend, Frodo Baggins, from certain death:

> Sam did not wait to wonder what was to be done, or whether he was brave, or loyal, or filled with rage. He sprang forward with a yell, and seized his master's sword in his left hand. Then he charged. No onslaught more fierce was ever seen in the savage world of beasts, where some desperate small creature armed with little teeth, alone, will spring upon a tower of horn and hide that stands above its fallen mate.[74]

Lewis responded with both praise and emotion. "He approved with unusual fervor," Tolkien wrote, "and was actually affected to tears by the last chapter, so it seems to be keeping up."[75]

BOOKS WITH MEN BEHIND THEM

Here is the quality in literature that Lewis loved when he discovered it: the expression of moral beauty, when an individual, in the face of death itself, forgets himself and expends himself in a struggle to save another soul from a great evil. It was for both men "the mark of the true fairy-story," and produced an experience of deep joy, "the joy of deliverance."[76]

The concept of heroic sacrifice, however, had come under sustained attack in the years after the First World War. The assault came not only from the antiwar poetry and memoirs or the Modernist Movement in literature; it also came from the political and pseudoscientific ideologies that had captured the minds of both elite and popular opinion. At some of the most prestigious universities in England and on the continent, the human person had become degraded, debased, and destined for servitude to forces beyond his control. As Lewis observed, the men and women of his generation fell prey to the moral agnosticism of their era—and disseminated this frame of mind to the next generation:

> In other words, the sources of unbelief among young people today do not lie in those young people. The outlook which they have—until they are taught better—is a backwash from an earlier period. . . . You may frame the syllabus as you please. But when you have planned and reported ad nauseum, if we are skeptical we shall teach only skepticism to our pupils, if fools only folly, if vulgar only vulgarity, if saints sanctity, if heroes heroism.[77]

This is the nature and cultural power of education: to either transmit or negate the wisdom of previous generations. As Lewis summarized it, "A man whose mind was formed in a period of cynicism and disillusion cannot teach hope or fortitude."[78]

Literary critic Edmund Fuller, who surveyed the works of Tolkien, Lewis, and other like-minded authors in an early study, *Books with Men Behind Them*, picked up on this precise theme. Modern literature, he wrote, exhibited the symptoms of a deeply disordered age. "Behind many of the novels and plays of our time there are only weeping, frightened, fretful or rebellious children—or occasionally maimed men," Fuller wrote. "Never has the puerile, the immature, the adolescent (actual or perennial) had such acceptance, or been listened to almost as a sage."[79]

The degeneration of man's moral stature in literature—of his obligations to God and neighbor—occurred at perhaps the worst possible political moment in European history: the age of totalitarianism. To a degree never imagined—much less achieved—in the political history of the West, the individual surrendered her essential humanity to serve the omnicompetent State. As Mussolini declared: *Tutto nello Stato*, that is, Everything for the State.

Near the heart of the literary project of Tolkien and Lewis was their desire to rehabilitate the individual: to restore something of the nobility and responsibilities that God had bestowed on the first man and the first woman, an image of the divinity that was marred by the Fall, yet not obliterated. For these two authors, imaginative literature—fantasy and myth—could help retrieve this dimension of human personality.

REASON AND IMAGINATION

Lewis's approach to this endeavor reflected his own spiritual quest, which had been nourished by many friends and authors who kept pointing him in the same direction: toward beauty, joy, and holiness. "I learned to recognize, like some all too familiar smell, that almost unvarying something which met me, now in Puritan Bunyan, now in Anglican Hooker, and now in Thomist Dante."[80] His discovery caused him to repudiate the materialistic outlook that dominated his age. As Fuller summarized it, "His war is upon the diminishers of humanity."[81]

In "The Decline of Religion," a short but revealing essay written just after the war, Lewis explained his basic conceptual approach as a Christian scholar and author: "If the intellectual climate is such that when a man comes to the crisis at which he must either accept or reject Christ, his reason and imagination are not on the wrong side, then his conflict will be fought out under favorable conditions."[82] In the words of Malcolm Guite, Lewis preserved a "double fidelity" to these faculties: His task was to hold them together, an obligation made urgent by the existential crisis of his day.[83] Modern life was awash in competing ideologies, yet nearly all agreed on one thing: The imaginative mind had nothing to say to the "real" world, the world of "facts" and "rationality." Against this view, Lewis sought to *put reason and imagination on the right side of the struggle for the human soul.* In achieving this goal in both his scholarly and fictional works, he emerged as arguably the most influential defender of the faith in modern times.

In his apologetic works, such as *Mere Christianity, The Problem of Pain*, and *The Abolition of Man*, the emphasis is on recovering the use of reason to make the case for the Christian faith. In his works of fiction, however, the faculty of reason also plays an indispensable role in piercing the Darkness. In *The Ransom Trilogy*, for example, it is the use of reason that often guides the protagonist forward or leads him out of great harm. "The rational part of my mind," writes Lewis in *Perelandra*, "even at that moment, knew perfectly well that even if the whole universe were crazy and hostile, Ransom was sane and wholesome and honest. And this part of my mind in the end sent me forward."[84]

Likewise, in the opening lines of *The Screwtape Letters*, Lewis mocks the irrationality of the modern age, which had become a tool of the Devil to lead people away from faith. "Your man has been accustomed, ever since he was a boy, to have a dozen incompatible philosophies dancing about together inside his head," Screwtape tells his junior demon. "Jargon, not argument, is your best ally in keeping him from the Church." Rational argument, Screwtape explains, moves the struggle onto the Enemy's territory. "By the very act of arguing, you awake the patient's reason," Screwtape says, "and once it is awake, who can foresee the results?"[85]

With characteristic modesty, Lewis admitted that the cultural effort to unite reason and imagination may come to nothing. "Far higher than they stands that character whom, to the best of my knowledge, the present Christian movement has not yet produced—the Preacher in the full sense, the Evangelist, the man on fire, the man who infects."[86] No one is led into the kingdom of heaven through sweet reason. Christian conversion, Lewis believed, involved the alteration of the will, which "does not occur without the intervention of the supernatural."[87]

A THEORY OF COURAGE

In his 1936 lecture on *Beowulf*, Tolkien said explicitly that he hoped to restore a "theory of courage" by his interpretation of the poem. As we've seen, his view of courage was bound up with "that noble northern spirit," the grim defiance of a solitary soul against the forces of evil. Tolkien viewed this outlook as "a supreme contribution to Europe, which I have ever loved, and tried to present in its true light."[88] Indeed, in many ways, this ambition defined his academic and literary life.

Tolkien had begun to accomplish this goal with the success of *The Hobbit*. The coming-of-age moment for Bilbo Baggins occurs when, against all his impulses, he moves forward in the darkness toward the dragon

Smaug. "Going on from there was the bravest thing he ever did," writes Tolkien. "The tremendous things that happened afterward were as nothing compared to it. He fought the real battle in the tunnel alone, before he ever saw the vast danger that lay in wait."[89]

This is one of the great achievements of *The Lord of the Rings*: to make the qualities of courage and fortitude deeply attractive to an otherwise skeptical generation. How did Tolkien do it?

In *The Lord of the Rings,* Tolkien presents us with two kinds of heroes in wartime. There is the extraordinary man, the hidden king determined to fight for his people against a great enemy. But there is also the ordinary man, the hobbit, the person like us, who is "not made for perilous quests." Tolkien acknowledged that hobbits were based on the soldiers he fought alongside in the Great War: shopkeepers, bartenders, clerks, farmers, fishermen, and gardeners. "I think what he saw in the First World War in the trenches was just how heroic the small person can be, who was just thrown into this," explains Stuart Lee. "They were conscripted, and they had to fight in these unbelievable conditions."[90]

Tolkien witnessed, as he described it, the "indomitable courage of quite small people against impossible odds," and he never forgot it. Neither did Lewis, who later wrote about the valor and decency of the soldiers in his battalion: "I came to know and pity and reverence the ordinary man."[91]

The foundation for Tolkien's theory of courage, though, is found in the moral universe in which all his characters reside. He assumes the existence of radical evil. And yet, at the center of his world is an unnamed power of Goodness. Thus, the moral and spiritual growth—or ruin—of the inhabitants of Middle-earth depends upon their choices. Unlike the myths of the ancient world, the heroism of Tolkien's story is rooted in a universe of moral purpose, in which every individual must choose the light over the darkness. "The two powers strove in him," writes Tolkien. "For a moment, perfectly balanced between their piercing points, he writhed, tormented. Suddenly he was aware of himself again, Frodo, neither the Voice nor the Eye: free to choose, and with one remaining instant in which to do so. He took the Ring off his finger."[92]

In all of this, Tolkien was repudiating the disenchantment of his generation. In his review of *The Fellowship of the Ring,* Lewis observed that with Tolkien's story "heroic romance, gorgeous, eloquent, and unashamed, has suddenly returned at a period almost pathological in its anti-romanticism." Moral cynicism had produced a longing for *moral beauty*. It was this quality that Tolkien evoked in the quest to destroy the Ring: "beauties which pierce like swords or burn like cold iron; here is a book that will break your heart."

Yet Tolkien's story would not leave the heart without hope or strength. Just the opposite: "As we read," Lewis explained, "we find ourselves sharing their burden; when we have finished, we return to our own life not relaxed but fortified."[93]

Both authors understood how difficult it was for men and women in the modern age to hold on to these ideals. Yet without them residing in our hearts and minds, life is immeasurably degraded.[94] They encountered the debasement of human personality and rebelled against it. Indeed, they placed an immense value on the individual: on her responsibility to do everything in her power to resist the dark powers set against her.

Toward this end, they found support not only from their faith traditions but also from their training in the classics. Just as *Beowulf* remained a vital part of Tolkien's creative life, Virgil continued to nourish Lewis's imagination. In a letter to his friend Dorothy Sayers, Lewis drew attention to one of Virgil's chief themes. "I've just re-read the *Aeneid* again. The effect is one of the immense costliness of a vocation combined with a complete conviction that it is worth it."[95] Although Aeneas is helped by the gods in his mission to establish Rome, it almost seems that the fate of a civilization hangs on what he does next. "Wars, horrendous wars, and the Tiber foaming with tides of blood, I see it all!" exclaims the Sibyl. "But never bow to suffering, go and face it, all the bolder, wherever Fortune clears the way."[96]

In Dante's epic poem *The Divine Comedy*, he famously chose Virgil as his guide to the Underworld. Likewise, Lewis incorporated those elements of pagan myths that could advance his stories of virtue, heroism, and redemption. "You see in every line that the poet knows, quite as well as any modern, the horrible thing he is writing about," Lewis explained. "He celebrates heroism but he has paid the proper price for doing so. He sees the horror and yet sees the glory."[97] Like Tolkien, Lewis knew from his own experience of combat that the authors of antiquity had expressed fundamental truths about the nature of war.

"That power of taking a great, noble pagan story and realizing that in some way it is related to the story of stories—the capacity to put those things together sensitively—was supremely alive in the later medieval period that Lewis loved," explains Malcolm Guite. "It gave him the ability to freely embrace mythology and imagination. He learned it from the great masters of the Middle Ages, who were more inclusive and comprehensive in their thinking than we are now."[98]

D-DAY AND THE DOWNFALL OF MORDOR

Tolkien and Lewis did not need to invent a force of evil in an imaginary world set in a distant past. Now even a child could see it. The face of evil was there, right in front of them—inhabiting their present world. As Winston Churchill told the British people, they faced a tragedy that "threatened the whole world and might have put out all its lights and left our children and descendants in darkness and bondage—perhaps for centuries."[99]

Yet the great Shadow, which for nearly five years had threatened to overwhelm them, was finally being lifted. "The world has changed since you and I last met," wrote C. S. Lewis to Sister Penelope. "One finds it difficult to keep pace with the almost miraculous mercies we are receiving as a nation. I never in my most sanguine moments dreamed that the invasion of Europe would go quite so well."[100]

In fact, many of the men involved in planning the Allied invasion of northern France on June 6, 1944—D-Day—feared that the assault would go terribly wrong. Dwight D. Eisenhower, the Supreme Commander of the Allied forces in Europe, the person who bore the greatest responsibility for the operation, had prepared for the worst.

Eisenhower wrote two letters on the eve of the invasion. The first, confident of the outcome, was sent to the troops. "The tide has turned. The free men of the world are marching together to Victory!" The second letter was to be released to the press if the invasion failed and the withdrawal of the Allied forces became necessary: "The troops, the air and the Navy did all that Bravery and devotion to duty could do. If any blame or fault attaches to the attempt it is mine alone."

Codenamed Operation Overlord, the cross-Channel assault represented the largest naval, land, and air operation in the history of warfare. It was a multinational force made up of Americans, Brits, Canadians, Poles, and other Allied forces. More than 156,000 troops on 5,000 ships landed on the first day on the beaches of Normandy.

Operation Overlord was two years in the making. Though under American command, the British took the lead in orchestrating an elaborate plan of deception. They constructed a dummy army, leading the Germans to believe that the main assault would come between Dieppe and Calais, not the Normandy coast. Meanwhile, all of southern England had been converted into a vast military camp, cut off from the rest of the country and crowded with soldiers, equipment, and supplies. After crossing the Channel, the Allies still had to penetrate the German line, the "Atlantic Wall": a 2,400-mile fortification of landmines, bunkers, and land obstacles designed to destroy an invading army. "Many held that attack against this type of defense was madness," recalled Eisenhower, "nothing but military suicide."[101]

The other great enemy was the weather. The most carefully planned military operation in history could be undone by the winds and waves of the Channel. A bad storm could drown or immobilize the ships, hinder the air assault, and turn the beaches into a slaughterhouse. In his war memoir, *Crusade in Europe*, Eisenhower acknowledged that he worried deeply about "the stupid, blind sacrifice of thousands of the flower of our youth." If the invasion failed, he added, "the disaster would be far more than local; it would be likely to spread to the entire force."[102]

Like the protagonists in the war stories of Tolkien and Lewis, the soldiers sent to the beaches of Normandy were caught up in this whirlwind in their youth. Most had never before left their homes, much less been tested in battle. In the end, the success of the D-Day invasion depended on the footslogger carrying his rifle and seizing ground. "If he was willing to drive forward in the face of German fire, Overlord would succeed," writes military historian Stephen Ambrose. "If he cowered behind the beached landing craft, it would fail. The operation all came down to that."[103]

The young soldiers did not cower for cover: They stormed the beaches and, with help from the air, overwhelmed the Nazi defenses. Within a few days of their June 6 landing, more than 326,000 troops, 50,000 vehicles, and 100,000 tons of equipment arrived at Normandy to join them in the assault. It was the beginning of the end of Nazism.

THE LINGERING SHADOW

Nevertheless, some of the most lethal battles and highest casualty rates of the war occurred between the Normandy invasion in June 1944 and the Japanese surrender to the Allied forces fifteen months later. "Anxious times, in spite of the rather premature shouting," Tolkien wrote to his son Christopher in September. "The armored fellows are right in the thick of it, and (I gather) think there is going to be a good deal more of the thick yet."[104]

A week after D-Day, the Nazis responded by launching a massive rocket assault on Britain. The V-2 rockets—for *Vergeltungswaffe*, or vengeance weapon—carried a one-ton payload that could destroy entire streets. Once launched, there was no way to stop them. Over the next several months, thousands of V-1 and V-2 rockets descended upon London and southern England, killing nearly 12,000 civilians and servicemen and destroying 107,000 homes.[105]

There would be no walking tours for the Inklings until the Germans were defeated. "The Inklings have already agreed," wrote Tolkien, "that their victory celebration, if they are spared to have one, will be to take a whole inn in the country for at least a week, and spend it entirely in beer and talk, without any reference to a clock!"[106]

Neither the Japanese nor the Germans, despite suffering military defeats and enduring massive casualties, showed any willingness to abandon the war. Just the opposite: The more their strategic situation deteriorated, the more determined they became to fight on, regardless of the cost.

"The news is good today," Tolkien wrote to Christopher. "But when the burst comes in France then will be the time to get excited. How long? And what of the red Chrysanthemum in the East? And when it is all over, will ordinary people have any freedom left . . . or will they have to fight for it, or will they be too tired to resist?"[107] The red chrysanthemum was the emblem of the Japanese imperial family.

Like most everyone else in Britain, Tolkien knew that the war to defeat the Japanese could take a terrible toll in human lives. "Never live to experience shame as a prisoner"—such was the maxim of the Japanese military. They embraced it with religious fervor: In the Pacific theater, the ratio of those killed to captured for the Allies was about 1:4. For the Japanese the ratio was 40:1.[108]

Even after the Yalta Conference in February 1945—which brought together the leaders of Great Britain, the United States, and the Soviet Union as their forces converged on Berlin—the road to final victory looked long and tortuous. "I do not suppose that at any moment in history has the agony of the world been so great or widespread," Churchill told his daughter Sarah. "Tonight the sun goes down on more suffering than ever before in the world."[109]

That was how the world looked to many people in the West: to the prisoners of war, the refugees, the nations subjugated by the Axis powers, the soldiers struggling to stay alive in brutal conditions, the civilians caught up in the bombing raids. And to the families on the home front, hanging upon the latest war news.

"I have just heard the news . . . Russians 60 miles from Berlin," Tolkien wrote to Christopher. "It does look as if something decisive might happen soon. The appalling destruction and misery of this war mount hourly: destruction of what should be (indeed is) the common wealth of Europe, and the world, if mankind were not so besotted. . . . There seem no bowels of mercy of compassion, no imagination, left in this dark diabolical hour." Tolkien also lamented the endless lines of "miserable refugees, women and children pouring West, dying on the way."[110]

There were many thousands of people pouring westward—not only civilians but also German soldiers as they reeled in retreat from the advancing Soviet army. "Everywhere the Soviet victors held sway," writes Max Hastings, "they embarked upon an orgy of celebration, rape and destruction on a scale such as Europe had not witnessed since the seventeenth century."[111]

Nazi brutalities during its failed campaign against the Soviet Union were answered with a vengeance. The Germans knew about the Soviet commitment to murder, rape, and pillage every German they encountered in the march to Berlin.[112] "My father and mother were murdered by the SS because they were Jews," a Soviet Commissar told a terrified German family. "My wife and two children are missing. My home is in ruins. And what has happened to me has happened to millions in Russia. . . . What do you think we want to do, now that we have defeated German armies?"[113] Many Germans committed suicide rather than fall into the hands of the Soviet Army.

In a letter to Christopher, Tolkien lamented the savagery and moral compromises involved in the Allied bombing campaigns. "My sentiments are more or less those that Frodo would have if he discovered some Hobbits learning to ride Nazgûl-birds, 'for the liberation of the Shire.'"[114] Writing to Dom Bede Griffiths two days after Germany surrendered to the Allies, Lewis believed that he and his friends had escaped death "by a series of Providences, some not far short of miracles." Nevertheless, his tone was somber. "And how did you feel on V-Day?" he asked. "I found it impossible to feel either so much sympathy with the people or so much gratitude to God as the occasion demanded."[115]

As expected, the Japanese fought to the bitter end. Among the most notorious was the slaughter of at least one hundred thousand Japanese soldiers in a hopeless battle at Okinawa. Suicide pilots—nearly eight thousand during the course of the war—continued to crash their planes into American ships.

In 1945, the Japanese military still boasted about 5.5 million men, with an air force of roughly nine thousand operational craft.[116] It was only the detonation of two atomic bombs at Hiroshima and Nagasaki—instantly killing more than 140,000 people, mostly civilians—that persuaded the emperor to agree to surrender. In a statement drafted by Churchill, no longer in power, the British government delivered a sober warning to its people: "The revelations of the secrets of nature, long mercifully withheld from Man, should arouse the most solemn reflections in the mind and conscience of every human being capable of comprehension."[117]

Even before the appearance of the A-bomb, Tolkien worried that the end result of the destructive power required to achieve victory was "an ultimately evil job." In several of his letters, he likened it to the struggle over the Ring of Power in his story. "For we are attempting to conquer Sauron with the Ring. And we shall (it seems) succeed. But the penalty is, as you will know, to breed Saurons, and slowly turn Men and Elves into Orcs."[118]

THE INKLINGS SOLDIER ON

For nearly everyone who was forced to endure the blight of 1939–45, the war was the defining experience of their lives. Although Great Britain was never occupied by Nazi Germany, the lives of the British people were filled with anxiety, suffering, and the stalking sense of mortality. For two long and desperate years, Britain stood alone in the fight against Nazism.

Even when victory seemed certain, so much had become uncertain: the idea of right and wrong, the value of human life, the existence of a loving God. As the Sibyl warns the hero of *The Aeneid*, "The descent to the Underworld is easy." Human civilization, it seemed, had descended into darkness, and whether it would emerge was an open question. "Night and day the gates of shadowy Death stand open wide, but to retrace your steps, to climb back to the upper air—there the struggle there the labor lies."[119]

The story of the friendship between J. R. R. Tolkien and C. S. Lewis is a story of how two men helped each other to emerge from their own private darkness and climb back into the daylight. Together with their other friends, the Inklings, they created a haven of sanity and moral health and intense creativity. One gets the sense from their wartime letters that they simply *had* to meet. And they did: weekly, almost without fail—in Lewis's rooms at Magdalen and at the Eagle and Child—through the roughest days of the war.

In November 1944, Tolkien reported "one of our best mornings at the Bird," which brought together Lewis, Warnie, Williams, and Havard. "We had it almost to ourselves. C.S.L. was on excellent form, holding forth like Dr. Johnson to the delight of the worthy landlord," he wrote. "It had to count as C.S.L.'s birthday party: as we've at last discovered that that mysterious date is Nov. 29 today."[120] It was also the date that Lewis arrived in France, on the Western Front, as a second lieutenant with the British Expeditionary Force. The experience of the First World War was something else they all held in common.

On one bright morning, Lewis, Tolkien, and Williams met at the Kilns, which Tolkien described as a "feast of reason and flow of soul, partly because we all agree so."[121] They gathered at other Oxford dining spots when circumstances allowed. When their favorite pub was closed, they drifted over to the King's Arms, where they drank "a passable ale" over conversation. "I hope to see the lads tomorrow," Tolkien reported, "otherwise life is as bright as water in a ditch."[122]

A meeting at the Mitre Hotel brought together Havard, Williams, Barfield, the Lewis brothers, and Tolkien—all, apparently, adequately supplied with stiff drinks. Tolkien observed cheerfully that Barfield "is the only man who can tackle C.S.L." and interrupt his dogmatic pronouncements. "The result was the most amusing and highly contentious evening, on which (had an outsider eavesdropped) he would have thought it a meeting of fell enemies hurling deadly insults before drawing their guns."[123]

Two days after D-Day, on June 8, the Inklings met at Lewis's rooms at Magdalen, from 9 p.m. until 12:30 a.m., an evening crammed with readings from those assembled. There was a long chapter from Warnie's book, *The Splendid Century*, about the government in the *ancien régime* in France, which, according to Tolkien, "he managed to make very amusing." E. R. Edison, a newcomer, had written *The Worm Ouroboros* and other romances and shared a chapter from a new work, *The Mezentian Gate*.

Lewis read an excerpt from his story about people who take a bus ride from hell to the threshold of heaven. He would call it *The Great Divorce*, a moral allegory about the nature of evil, free will, and divine grace. Lewis places himself in the story as one of the travelers and chooses George MacDonald as his Virgil-like spiritual guide. "I don't know what I want, Sir," says Lewis. His Teacher responds: "Son, son, it must be one way or the other. Either the day must come when joy prevails and all the makers of misery are no longer able to infect it: or else for ever and ever the makers of misery can destroy in others the happiness they reject for themselves."[124]

In the midst of a war that had created a bottomless supply of human misery, Lewis returned once again to what he believed was the most urgent question: How does a human soul find joy and peace with God?

Tolkien shared another installment from *The Lord of the Rings*, as he was rewriting his chapter on Shelob and "the disaster" in Cirith Ungol. It is at the Tower of Cirith Ungol that Sam—"the jewel among the hobbits"—rises to his full stature as a truly heroic figure in the story. Desperate to rescue Frodo from the orcs but unable to enter the gate without being discovered, he is seized by the thought of putting on the Ring, which has been in his possession since Frodo's capture. Fantasies invade his mind:

He is Samwise the Strong, Hero of the Age, leading entire armies to defeat the enemy.[125]

"He had only to put on the Ring and claim it for his own, and all this could be," Tolkien writes. "In that hour of trial it was the love of his master that helped most to hold him firm; but also deep down in him lived still unconquered his plain hobbit-sense: he knew in the core of his heart that he was not large enough to bear such a burden."[126] The most convincing stories involving the terrors of death come from those authors who have tasted the experience. The intensity of the war experience was a medium for the imagination.

A FRIENDSHIP FORGED WITH IRON

The scourge of war also made possible a depth and intensity of friendship that was transformative. Some of the most meaningful friendships that Tolkien and Lewis established began in the shadow of the First World War.

Tolkien's "band of brothers"—Christopher Wiseman, Rob Gilson, and Geoffrey Bache Smith—had squared off together on the rugby pitch at King Edward's School. They held in common a passion for literature and poetry and storytelling. They shared Tolkien's youthful ambition to be "a great instrument in God's hands."[127] When war came, it catalyzed something in all of them. "They began to think of themselves as a force to be reckoned with," explains John Garth, "that through visual arts, through poetry, through music, they would somehow be able to change the world for the better."[128] They went off to war together; only two returned.

For Lewis, the loss of Laurence Johnson, whom he met in Oxford while training as an officer, was a grievous blow. "He would have been a lifelong friend," Lewis recalled, "if he had not been killed."[129] They fought alongside each other in the Somerset Light Infantry in France and had "endless arguments" about philosophy, morality, God, and many other topics. It was Johnson who first exposed Lewis's moral hypocrisy and caused him to reexamine his inner life. "The important thing was that he was a man of conscience," Lewis explained in his autobiography, *Surprised by Joy*. "I had hardly till now encountered principles in anyone so nearly my own age and my own sort. The alarming thing was that he took them for granted."[130]

It is hard to overstate the importance of these wartime experiences. In ways that cannot be fully known, they shaped the emotional and intellectual lives of both authors. "Men whom the trenches cast into intimacy entered into bonds of mutual dependency and sacrifice of self stronger than any of the friendships made in peace and better times," writes historian John Keegan. "That is the ultimate mystery of the First World War. If we could understand its loves, as well as its hates, we would be nearer to understanding the mystery of human life."[131]

The same must be said of the wretched sequel to that conflict. Although Tolkien and Lewis were not combatants in the Second World War, they endured its hardships and terrors together. They both feared for the lives of those they loved who were sent as soldiers into the fight. Like nearly all of England, they lived under the constant threat of bombardment and foreign invasion. Outside of the attack at Pearl Harbor, Americans did not experience war on their home front; they did not live with the prospect of starvation or servitude under a Nazi regime; the British people did.

Although much has been written about their friendship, not enough attention has been given to how the catastrophe of another world war drew Tolkien and Lewis together in ways that no other set of circumstances could have achieved. This singular fact frames Lewis's exploration of friendship in *The Four Loves*, in what must rank as one of the most moving and insightful reflections on this neglected dimension of human life ever written.

Friendship, Lewis insisted, must be *about* something, and deep friendships must be about something of real significance. "You will not find the warrior, the poet, the philosopher or the Christian by staring into his eyes as if he were your mistress," he explains. "Better to fight beside him, read with him, argue with him, pray with him." Lewis's discourse on friendship is deeply autobiographical. When he speaks of individuals drawn together because of a common vision, he of course is describing his friendship with Tolkien, Williams, Barfield, Warnie, and the other Inklings:

> Sometimes he wonders what he is doing there among his betters. He is lucky beyond desert to be in such company. Especially when the whole group is together, each bringing out all that is best, wisest, or funniest in all the others. Those are the golden sessions; when four or five of us

> after a hard day's walking have come to our inn; when our slippers are on, our feet spread out towards the blaze and our drinks at our elbows; when the whole world, and something beyond the world, opens itself to our minds as we talk . . . [and] an Affection mellowed by the years enfolds us. Life—natural life—has no better gift to give. Who could have deserved it?[132]

It cannot be emphasized enough that this experience of deep friendship—with Tolkien and Lewis at its heart—was achieved during a period of civilizational crisis.

There was a savage war of aggression devouring the European continent and threatening the survival of Great Britain. Yet there was also an ideological war: the widespread assault on the classical and Christian ideals that had nourished Western civilization for centuries. "It was rather like a huge bank account to which many contributed and which everyone has drawn upon," Lewis explained. "Now you cannot go on writing checks on an account unless you continue to add to its capital. The trouble is that, without adding to that capital, we continue to write checks. One day that capital will run out." Their collective mission was to replenish the account.[133]

In his description of friendship in *The Four Loves*, Lewis admits that a tight circle of friends could become something dark and degraded, a school of vice. But, by God's grace, they also could become a school of virtue and wisdom and love. Authoritarians frown upon friendship, he argues, because it creates a rival to their authority. Like-minded friends can fortify one another against the prejudices, hatreds, and conventional wisdom of the age. "Every real Friendship is a sort of secession," Lewis writes, "even a rebellion." As such, a community of freedom-loving friends offers "the strongest safeguard against complete servitude."[134]

It was the members of the Inklings whom Lewis had foremost in his mind. He intended for them to create a literary counterattack to the materialist, nihilistic, and totalitarian outlook of the age.

"They must have felt that they were standing on a piece of land that was vanishing with the tides all around them," explains author Julia Golding. "They must have felt like King Canute, because these were very strong tides. And I think in a way they rescued these concepts of bravery and self-sacrifice. They helped people to rediscover those beliefs that hold a society together."[135]

This is precisely what the Inklings hoped to achieve. To do so, they took on the role of subversives, provocateurs, rebels, members of the Resistance. As Lewis described them, "The little knots of Friends who turn their backs on the 'World' are those who really transform it."[136]

CONCLUSION

The Far-Off Country

No words can express how much the world owes to sorrow. Most of the Psalms were born in the wilderness. Most of the Epistles were written in a prison. The greatest thoughts of the greatest thinkers have all passed through fire.

—George MacDonald

Unlike the writings of any other authors, the novels of J. R. R. Tolkien and C. S. Lewis exerted a profound influence on the direction of imaginative literature in the twentieth century. They demonstrated that the genres of fantasy, children's literature, satire, and science fiction could be imbued with a deeply Christian outlook and simultaneously possess a narrative power that would appeal to people of all backgrounds.

"They are incredibly important introductions to some of the most profound questions that Western civilization has raised about the human condition," explains Niall Ferguson. "They are universal works that could be read anywhere in the world and appreciated not only as fantasy stories but as tales of profound moral significance. If we lose the ability to communicate the value of these books to the next generation of children, then I shall fear for our civilization."[1]

There are reasons to be anxious. Richly textured fantasy does not emerge from a cultural vacuum. There must be a cumulative heritage from which the author draws.[2] Tolkien and Lewis possessed this literary heritage: from their classical studies, from the great poems and mythologies of medieval Europe, and from the Christian Scriptures, rooted as they are in a complex history of God's redemptive activity.

From all of this, and from the soil of his own imagination, Tolkien was able to construct an immensely detailed and believable history of Middle-earth. The story grew "like a seed in the dark out of the leaf-mold of the mind: out of all that has been seen or thought or read, that has long ago been forgotten, descending into the deeps."[3] The result was a story with a profound moral purpose whose characters are both burdened and inspired by "the memory of vanished civilizations and lost splendor."[4] Lewis achieved something similar, especially with *The Ransom Trilogy* and *The Chronicles of Narnia*, mythic portrayals of the cosmic struggle between the children of Light and the children of Darkness. To accomplish this, both authors not only brought to their craft an intimate knowledge of the great works of Western civilization. They also retained what might be called "the memory of Eden"—a living and powerful sense of the world *as it was meant to be.*

Yet this collective memory has been fading for decades in the West. Its loss was evident even as Tolkien and Lewis embarked on their academic careers: "In our time something which was once the possession of all educated men has shrunk to being the technical accomplishment of a few specialists."[5] With the near-death of the humanities in higher education, young people are being cut off from this cultural inheritance. Tolkien and Lewis were determined to reclaim it for a generation of readers who otherwise might never have encountered it.

HOBBITS AND THE MEMORIES OF WAR

The Lord of the Rings rests on top of Tolkien's mythology, which in turn was rooted in much older mythologies: the old English and Nordic stories that he embraced and studied all his life. "Tolkien pretty much set out a blueprint for how you write a fantasy novel," according to Stuart Lee. "It succeeds because it has depth. Every now and then it will refer back to a legend or a story, of which you don't always see the full details, you just know it's there, that there is a history to this world. Everything in it is believable."[6]

Here is fantasy, washed in myth yet offering insight into our mortal lives. We come to believe that there really is an existential struggle involved in the attempt to destroy the Ring: the survival of everything in the world that is decent and beautiful and humane.

The story is made even more realistic because the quest is undertaken by those who seem least likely to succeed, people all too familiar to us. Thus, the consequence of failure presses upon us at a personal and emotional level. "This quest may be attempted by the weak with as much hope as the strong," says Elrond. "Yet such is oft the course of deeds that move the wheels of the world: small hands do them because they must, while the eyes of the great are elsewhere."[7]

The Lord of the Rings has been called Tolkien's trench memoir. There is some truth in this. He began writing his legendarium while he was under shellfire in the Great War, with the squalor of the trenches and the stench of death all about him. Its descriptions of great battles, of the bodies of dead soldiers piled high, of landscapes blackened by violence—all of this recalls the Somme. "Everyone who remembers a war first-hand knows that the images remain in the memory with special vividness," writes Paul Fussell in *The Great War and Modern Memory*. "When a man imagines that every moment is his next to last, he observes and treasures up sensory details purely for their own sake."[8] For Tolkien, the record of his war experience, expressed in his fiction, initially had a deeper purpose: to prevent his conflicted emotions about the war from festering. "In my case," he wrote, "it generated Morgoth and the History of the Gnomes."[9]

Unlike the antiwar poetry and novels of the postwar period, however, Tolkien's story is totally lacking in cynicism. His hobbits, he explained, were modeled on the surprisingly tough and resilient soldiers with whom he served in France. There was a quality to the British soldier, a dedication to duty, that set him apart. War correspondent Philip Gibbs witnessed their courage firsthand at the Somme. "In each battle there were officers and men who risked death deliberately" and performed "acts of superhuman courage," he wrote. "The heroes of mythology were but paltry figures compared with those who, in the great war, went forward to the roaring devils of modern gunfire."[10]

These facts help explain Tolkien's remark that his taste for fantasy was "quickened to full life by war." He witnessed both the horror and the heroism of trench warfare. By his own admission, the fantasy story became the primary literary outlet for his experience.

The outbreak of war in 1939 drove Tolkien deeper into his story. The shadow of that conflict produced a similar effect on his imagination, whetting his desire to recover the truths and ideals that could best be expressed through fantasy. "One can't really escape a sense of the war of 1939 to 1945 in the text," argues Niall Ferguson. "The way in which Mordor is represented, in which the dark forces are portrayed, in which Sauron is depicted: These seem to me to be influenced by the peculiarly malevolent quality that fascism had."[11] In short, the disaster of the Second World War compelled Tolkien to bring to full maturity the story he had begun during the 1914–18 war. "I believe that in creating his mythology, Tolkien salvaged from the wreck of history much that it is good still to have," writes John Garth, "but that he did more than merely preserve the traditions of Faerie; he transformed them for the modern age."[12]

Tolkien captured in fantasy a dimension of the human story that was felt as vividly in his day as perhaps in any other period of history. For a time, it really did seem that the forces of barbarism would prevail, that the eclipse of Western civilization was at hand. For a time, it really looked as if the survival of England depended upon the choices of "quite small people" who put aside their fears and fought the terror from the skies.

Thus, there is a malignant quality to the forces of darkness in *The Lord of the Rings*—the presence of radical evil—that is almost totally absent in *The Hobbit*. "Evidently I have managed to make the horror really horrible, and that is a great comfort," he wrote his publisher. "For every romance that takes things seriously must have a warp of fear and horror, if however remotely or representatively it is to resemble reality, and not be the merest escapism."[13] Tolkien's achievement is that he persuades his readers that his mythology is very much like reality: It reveals the human condition, facts about man's dignity as well as his shame.

Edmund Fuller insists that what Tolkien created was the antithesis of escapist literature. "Indeed, it may offer temporary refuge and relief from the pressure of an immediate world," he explains. But because Tolkien's story is of such depth, "we are brought to a deeper pondering and insight into central aspects of our actual lives. Our sensitivity is whetted to honor and courage and aspiration and beauty. No one thinking on these things is escaping reality."[14]

No one thinking about these things is escaping reality. By the 1930s, much of the world had ceased to think seriously about these things. Much of the world, in fact, had come under the rule of men who trampled these things underfoot. The result was that entire populations were cast into the deepest darkness.

A LION AND A LITTLE GIRL

"I am not quite sure what made me, in a particular year of my life, feel that not only a fairy tale, but a fairy tale addressed to children, was exactly what I must write—or bust."[15]

The tumultuous period during which Lewis lived offers a clue to the inspiration for his children's books, *The Chronicles of Narnia.* When he was about seven years old, after his family moved to Little Lea on the outskirts of Belfast, he wrote his first story of an imaginary world. He called it Animal Land. It was about a decade later, around 1914, when Lewis said he first saw a mental image of a faun, holding parcels and standing in the snow. "Then one day, when I was about forty, I said to myself: 'Let's try to make a story about it.'"[16]

Thus, an idea that came into his mind during the First World War began to take shape in the shadow of the Second World War. The invasion of children refugees into his home in 1939 opened his mind to how the story might progress.

It is still often assumed that *The Chronicles of Narnia,* like Tolkien's story about Middle-earth, also belongs to the escapist literature that characterizes most of contemporary fantasy. "Part of the reason for the novel's broader appeal, even in an increasingly secular age," writes one critic, "is that it provides escapism and wish-fulfilment aplenty."[17] It could be argued, however, that the exact opposite is the effect of the story on most of its readers. "Lewis invented imaginative worlds," explains Oxford philosopher John Lennox, "and his imagination was concentrated and focused on helping us to get a grip on reality."[18]

In this, both authors owed a debt to Plato's famous "Parable of the Cave" in *The Republic.* Human beings, Plato explained, are like prisoners in a cave whose sense of reality is based on fleeting shadows that flicker on the walls of the cave. Truth—and authentic freedom—lie outside. Plato's intent, he wrote, was to instigate "a conversion, a turning of the soul away from the day whose light is darkness to the true day."[19] Good storytelling possesses a special capacity to bring about a change of heart and mind. "The good kind of escape is the kind that Lewis and Tolkien were trying to generate in their fiction," observes Michael Ward, "showing their readers that there was more to life than wardens, and keys, and locks, and prison walls and barred windows. There were things like beauty, and hope, and goodness, and longing."[20]

In his essay "On Three Ways of Writing for Children," Lewis chastised the well-meaning people who wanted to shield children from life's difficulties, to "keep out of his mind the knowledge that he is born into a world of death, violence, wounds, adventure, heroism and cowardice, good and evil." To do so, he wrote, is to encourage an evasion from reality. To banish life's terrors from children's stories is to banish "all that can ennoble them or make them endurable." Better to help children to face the world as we find it. "Since it is so likely that they will meet cruel enemies, let them at least have heard of brave knights and heroic courage," he argued. "For in the fairy tales, side by side with the terrible figures, we find the immemorial comforters and protectors, the radiant ones."[21]

There is no figure in children's literature as numinous as that of Aslan, the great Lion and true King of Narnia. "It was from the Lion that the light came," Lewis writes. "No one ever saw anything more terrible or beautiful."[22] Even when he is not present, the Lion is the compelling, nearly irresistible presence throughout the seven novels.

The story begins with the four Pevensie children, who slip through a bedroom wardrobe and enter the enchanted world of Narnia, a land of talking beasts, dwarfs, giants, mythological creatures, and wild people of the wood. "I don't know about you, but as a child I used to go all around the doors of my house opening them, just in case the cupboard had become a door to Narnia," admits Julia Golding. "If you've never done that, I'm very sorry for you."[23]

Narnia has fallen under the evil sway of the White Witch, however, and the children are thrust into the war to reclaim the kingdom for its rightful king. Aslan expects much from the Pevensie children and never shields them from the bitter truths of his world—or of theirs. "And soon, very soon, before you are an old man and an old woman, great nations in your world will be ruled by tyrants who care no more for joy and justice and mercy than the Empress Jadis," says Aslan. "Let your world beware. That is the warning."[24]

Throughout the series, the children are confronted with difficult and painful choices in the fight for Narnia. They must learn to listen to the voice of conscience, act decisively, and choose the Good.

A supreme example of this occurs in *Prince Caspian*. A great battle is about to take place, and the children must get themselves ready. The outcome of the war is hanging in the balance, and a little girl is asked to do something that is difficult for her, something that could be costly, something she doesn't want to do. Lucy must decide to put away her fears and obey Aslan.

> "It is hard for you, little one," said Aslan. . . .
>
> Lucy buried her head in his mane to hide from his face. But there must have been magic in his mane. She could feel lion-strength going into her. Quite suddenly she sat up. "I'm sorry, Aslan," she said. "I'm ready now."
>
> "Now you are a lioness," said Aslan. "And now all Narnia will be renewed."[25]

The heroes in the Narnia books, like those in *The Lord of the Rings*, are unlikely candidates to rescue their world from disaster. Tolkien and Lewis had a shared understanding about the meaning of heroism. They both found the works of classical and medieval imagination compelling: The steely determination of Beowulf finds a counterpart in Tolkien's story, just as the Arthurian legends work their way through the Narnia stories.

Nevertheless, the heroic ideal in these older tales had to make room for a more explicitly Christian sensibility. "Lewis is not holding up Achilles or Henry V. He is holding up people like Lucy Pevensie and Reepicheep the mouse: a little girl and a tiny rodent," explains Michael Ward. "These are his heroes: the small, and the despised, and the overlooked. It's a very

Christian approach to leadership—that God has chosen what the world despises to bring the world to its senses."[26]

This moral dimension to their stories was not a literary technique. Rather, it emerged organically from the spiritual roots both authors had nourished over the course of their lives. "The only moral that is of any value," Lewis wrote, "is that which arises inevitably from the whole cast of the author's mind."[27]

Unlike so much of contemporary fantasy, the works of Tolkien and Lewis are not about self-discovery, or going on adventures for their own sake, or the portrayal of clumsy and ignorant adults confounded by their clever children. They are about courage and sacrifice and redemption—in the face of a terrible evil.

"I'll make a frank confession," says Niall Ferguson. "I was reading *The Lion, the Witch and the Wardrobe* a week ago to my six-year-old son. I have lost count of the number of times I've read that book. It still brought tears to my eyes to read the extraordinary sequence in which Aslan, the Christ-like Lion, gives up his life for Edmund. It is one of the most moving pieces of writing in the English language." As Ferguson explains, the bitter experience of war lends the works of both authors a unique emotive power: "What I find deeply reassuring is that children today can still be moved by the intensity of emotion that it seems to me only men who had known great suffering could possibly have expressed."[28]

A FRIENDSHIP FOR THE AGES

It was the storm of suffering created by the First World War that allowed the lives of Tolkien and Lewis to intersect. Their friendship began as they both were trying to make sense of the broken world to which they had returned. "Many people would say that the essential thing which turned the modern world into what it is was the trauma of the First World War," observes Malcolm Guite, "and of course both men were right at the heart of it."[29] They soon found themselves at the center of a second world war, far more devastating than the previous conflict. Remarkably, they used the furnace of these experiences to reassert the moral and spiritual ideals that seemed to be on the brink of extinction.

In the long run, "the artist and the spinner of tales proves the best persuader."[30] Put another way, people are moved more by their imagination than by cold polemics. The modern world had become demoralized and disenchanted. Tolkien and Lewis believed deeply that works of fantasy invite a *re-enchantment*: an opening of the mind and heart to truths that otherwise might not be welcome. "Imagination, given time," writes Russell Kirk, "does rule the world."[31]

Here are the threads that brought Tolkien and Lewis together in friendship: They were war veterans who endured great loss early in their lives, writers with an imaginative life of incredible reach and richness, lovers of the mythopoeic, and guardians of a deep and generous Christian faith. "Imagine a world without *The Lord of the Rings* and *The Chronicles of Narnia,*" says Colin Duriez. "Were it not for the friendship between Tolkien and Lewis, we would have neither."[32] That judgment seems just.

Indeed, much of what remains in modern literature and storytelling that bears some trace of wonder and humanity might not exist without them. "We neither of us expected much success as amateurs," Tolkien recalled. "And after all that has happened since, the most lasting pleasure and reward for both of us has been that we provided one another with stories to hear or read that we really liked—in *large* parts."[33] What they did for each other, however, extended far beyond the boundaries of their private lives. Given the truly global influence of their writing, it is hard to think of a more consequential friendship in the twentieth century.

Their admiration for each other was real and deep. "Also, I must respect his opinion," remarked Tolkien, "as I believed him to be the best living critic until he turned his attention to me, and no degree of friendship would make him say what he does not mean: he is the most uncompromisingly honest man I have met!"[34] It was Lewis's dogged honesty that persuaded Tolkien to turn his private mythology into a compelling, epic fantasy.

Until he met Lewis, Tolkien was more interested in building up languages than writing a sequel to *The Hobbit*. Lewis helped to change his mind. As Tolkien put it to Walter Hooper: "You know, C. S. Lewis was such a boy, he had to have a *story*. And that story, The Lord of the Rings, was written to keep him quiet!" At the very least, as Tolkien himself admitted, without Lewis's great encouragement and demands for more of the story, he never would have completed it.

When he finally did, not long after the Second World War, Tolkien sent it to his friend. "I have drained the rich cup," Lewis wrote to him, "and satisfied a long thirst." With its enormous sense of history and its "upward slope of grandeur and terror," the only work to which Lewis could compare it was *The Aeneid.*[35] "So much of your whole life, so much of our joint life, so much of the war, so much that seemed to be slipping away *spurlos* [without a trace] into the past, is now, in a sort, made permanent."[36]

It is an extraordinary thing to say: Through the use of his imagination, Tolkien captured something of the quality of their common life and the moral and spiritual truths that gave it meaning. He accomplished this only after years of struggle, battling doubts and discouragement, amid the ravages of the most horrifying war in history. Here is what friendship can achieve when it reaches for a high purpose and is watered by the streams of loyalty, sacrifice, and love. "It is written in my life's blood," Tolkien said, "such as that is, thick or thin."[37]

OUR INCONSOLABLE SECRET

This was thick blood, indeed. Unlike any other "quest" story in literature, in *The Lord of the Rings* the hero's supreme objective is not to endure dangers in order to acquire or recover something of value. Instead, the terrible suspense of the story is whether two solitary hobbits, prepared to risk all, can complete their task of *destroying* something of great value: the Ring of Power.

In their quest, they must endure the terrors of Mordor, an image of utter devastation reminiscent of Tolkien's experience at the Somme in 1916. "Frodo and Sam re-enter that horrific landscape, purposefully, in order to do something which, had it been done in our world, would have meant we would have never fought that war," explains Malcolm Guite. "They must let go of the desire for power and domination and send the Ring to the fire."[38]

Here Tolkien departs most radically from the pagan and medieval myths he loved. His heroes do not seek glory for themselves or their kinsmen. Their mission is one of complete renunciation of the self for a noble cause: the redemption of Middle-earth from the designs of the Dark Lord.

Tolkien once said that the "kernel" of his story is found in the final volume of the book, in Frodo's words to Sam when the Ring of Power has been destroyed. After bearing the terrible burden of carrying the Ring, Frodo finds himself changed, unable to resume his life in the Shire: "I have been too deeply hurt. I tried to save the Shire, and it has been saved, but not for me. It must often be so, Sam, when things are in danger: someone has to give them up, lose them, so that others may keep them."[39]

In this, Tolkien discerned the mystery of grace. His concept of the *eucatastrophe*—the introduction of a "sudden and miraculous grace"—has its roots in one of the central themes of the Bible.

Indeed, the broad narrative structure of *The Lord of the Rings* carries the imprint of Tolkien's Christian commitments. It is a story, after all, about the sacrifice of self to rescue others from great harm. Though containing a mythic quality, the gospel narrative—about the God-Man who sacrifices himself to save the human race—has entered history. "Art has been verified. God is the Lord, of angels, and of men—and of elves. Legend and History have met and fused." The Christian must continue to work, suffer, hope, and die, Tolkien explains, "but he may now perceive that all his bents and faculties have a purpose, which can be redeemed."[40]

Self-denial, humility, the rejection of worldly power, the need for redemption: In the immediate context of the Second World War—with nations on all sides equally desperate to obtain weapons of mass destruction—this message could not have been more revolutionary.

These themes were equally important to Lewis throughout his life. When he was sixteen years old, he was smitten by the medieval romance that helped to define England's national character. "My dear Arthur," he wrote to his friend, "Do you ever wake up in the morning and suddenly wonder why you have not bought such-and-such a book a long time ago, and then decided that life without it will be quite unbearable? I do frequently." The book on this occasion was Malory's *Le Morte D'Arthur*.[41]

The concepts of courage and self-sacrifice pulsate through Lewis's works, finding supreme expression in *The Chronicles of Narnia*, in the character of Aslan. In his mission to rescue Narnia from the forces of evil, the great Lion reveals himself as a moral force above and beyond nature.

Like the ideal of the medieval knight, the Lion King combines tenderness with martial strength. Yet he also possesses a splendor and authority—a *gravitas*—that is strongly suggestive of Jesus of Nazareth.

Here is a *Personality* whom Lewis encountered only in the Gospels: a human portrayal of Love and Truth and Holiness that he did not find in the old myths that he knew and loved so well.

> "Oh Aslan," said Lucy. "Will you tell us how to get into your country from our world?"
>
> "I shall be telling you all the time," said Aslan. "But I will not tell you how long or short the way will be; only that it lies across a river. But do not fear that, for I am the great Bridge Builder."[42]

There is a sublime quality to the works of these authors, which reaches across time and across cultures. It speaks to the deepest desires of the human heart and is perhaps the most important reason for their enduring appeal. Tolkien described this quality as "Joy beyond the walls of the world, poignant as grief." Lewis called it "our inconsolable secret," the realization that we have been cut off from the source of all Goodness and Joy in the universe, yet retain a profound longing to be reunited, to be welcomed back into the heart of God.

That J. R. R. Tolkien and C. S. Lewis could create stories of such radiance and nobility—when the world around them was so dark and disfigured—seems itself a mystery of grace. They knew what it was like to live in the Land of Shadow. And yet, like Frodo Baggins and Sam Gamgee on the threshold of Mordor, their courage and faith did not fail them. They pressed on through the darkness and left for us a bright glimpse of the far-off country.

"There, peeping among the cloud-wrack above a dark tor high up in the mountains, Sam saw a white star twinkle for a while. The beauty of it smote his heart, as he looked up out on the forsaken land, and hope returned to him," Tolkien writes. "For like a shaft, clear and cold, the thought pierced him that in the end the Shadow was only a small and passing thing: there was light and high beauty forever beyond its reach."[43]

ACKNOWLEDGMENTS

Every author owes an incalculable debt to the family and friends and others who have nourished his heart and mind with their love and loyalty. My debt is a large one: I am deeply grateful to my brother, Mike, and my sister, Sue, and to their spouses, Ann Marie and Joe, for their steady love and support throughout the years. I want to thank the Loconte and Aiello families for their love and encouragement, and for helping me remember what we owe to our parents and grandparents, who lived through the terrors of the Second World War and sacrificed so much for us.

J. R. R. Tolkien once said of his friend C. S. Lewis, that "friendship with Lewis compensates for much." So, too, does my friendship with the many individuals who have inspired me, challenged me, and lifted my spirits: Kara Callaghan, John and Kelli Baker, Jedd and Rachel Medefind, Charlie and Joanie Catlett, Ken and Marilyn Jackson, Bill and Dana Wichterman, and Lia and Charles Howard. Special thanks to Brendan and Haley McNamera, Tim Schwartz, Pete Peterson, Jay Hein, Cherie Harder, Rob Schwarzwalder, and Fred Ferrara for their enduring friendship. My British comrades have been an endless source of mirth and timely encouragement: Tim Montgomerie, Ben Rogers, and Daniel Johnson.

I am especially grateful to John Bishop, my most zealous advocate in telling the Tolkien-Lewis story; to Os Guinness, who never ceases to encourage and challenge me by his example of intellectual rigor and Christian integrity; and to Rich Lowry, who provided generous editorial space to tell portions of this story on the pages of *National Review*. Mark Noll has offered a model of academic scholarship and a steady diet of editorial encouragement. Many thanks to John Meko, my intellectual patriot-in-arms in Philadelphia, and to Juliarose Childs, my graceful and irreplaceable operative in New York City. Max McLean, Mary Theroux, Joel Woodruff, Andrew Teravskis, and Adam Gregory also deserve special thanks for their encouragement along the way.

I want to thank my publishers at Thomas Nelson/HarperCollins, especially Daniel Marrs, whose enthusiasm for this story opened the door that made the book possible, and Paul Pastor, whose Herculean patience allowed us to navigate the literary permissions process. Natalie Nyquist, whose deft and tireless editing improved the manuscript at numerous points and rescued it (and me) from embarrassing errors, deserves high praise. I also want to thank my students at Grove City College and at New College of Florida for engaging so thoughtfully with the Tolkien-Lewis story during our classes together. Many thanks to my legal team: to Kirk Schroder for his unfailingly wise counsel, and to Ron Dove and Dallin Earl, whose remarkable generosity, graciousness, and sound judgment helped me to navigate into safe harbors.

Many thanks to the Tolkien and Lewis estates for making available such a wealth of resources about these authors. I wish to express my gratitude to all of the Tolkien and Lewis scholars whose work has so deepened my understanding of these authors, and those scholars who gave so generously of their time in my interviews with them: Niall Ferguson, Julia Golding, Simon Horobin, Daisy Dunn, Owen Barfield, Mary Clare Havard, Malcolm Guite, John Garth, Colin Duriez, Stewart Lee, Michael Ward, Robin Darwall-Smith, Joanna Bowring, John Lennox, and Alister McGrath.

Finally, I am grateful beyond words for the grace of Jesus, who sought me and rescued me and has given me a glimpse of that bright Kingdom that lies beyond the Sea.

A REMEMBRANCE

Like J. R. R. Tolkien and C. S. Lewis, the lives of my grandparents were caught up in the fire and fury of two world wars.

My paternal grandfather, Michele (Michael) Loconte, was born in Bitritto, Italy, a small southern town near Bari. When the First World War broke out in August 1914, he was living in the United States and finding work wherever he could—from Henry Ford's assembly line in Detroit, Michigan, to the vineyards of California. The Americans offered Grandpa a choice: Fight for the Italians or, with the promise of a fast-track to citizenship, fight for the United States. At twenty-three years old, Grandpa enlisted in the US Army and joined the 91st Division. He was sent to the Western Front in 1918 and took part in the bloody Meuse-Argonne Offensive, a decisive campaign of the war.

Michele Loconte a soldier in US Army, 91st Division, during World War I.

My maternal grandfather, Giuseppe (Joseph) Aiello, was born in Ventotene, Italy, a tiny island off the coast of Naples. One of ten children, he was too young to serve in the Italian army. He was fortunate: Italy lost more than half a million men in the conflict, and many came home with grievous injuries. During my first visit to the island, I was deeply moved by the white marble monument to the fallen in the Piazza Castello. Among its list of casualties is a member of the Aiello family. The inscription also carries these words:

Con volto al nemico
Con la patria nel cuore
Tempestando la mitraglia
Si votarono
Alla morte
Ed alla gloria
Nella Grande Guerra

Facing the enemy
With their country in their heart
Storming the machine gun
They offered themselves
To death
And to glory
In the Great War

Monuments like this can be found all over Italy (and all over Europe, for that matter), including one in the main piazza in Bitritto, which carries names from the Loconte family. Whatever Italy hoped to achieve in the First World War, the nation was economically devastated by the conflict, especially the poorest regions in the south. Both of my grandfathers apparently decided, either during or shortly after the war, that the future belonged to America.

In 1921, when he was sixteen years old, Giuseppe Aiello boarded the SS Patria in the Bay of Naples and left Ventotene for New York. His timing was excellent: A year later Benito Mussolini came into power, establishing the first fascist government in Europe. Giuseppe found work in New York City as a barber and eventually opened his own barbershop at 247 West 35th Street in Manhattan. He settled in Brooklyn, married Restituta (known as Esther), and raised four children: Vincent, Salvatore, Anne Marie (my mother), and Carmella. During the Second World War,

The Aiello family in Ventotene, Italy (left to right): Candida, Giuseppe, Maria, Antonio, Marianna Lucia, Anna, Ciro, Ciarina, and Civita. Not present are Luigi, Angela Rosa, and Vincenzo (my great grandfather).

Mussolini converted Ventotene into an *isola di confino*: an island of confinement for his political opponents.

Michele Loconte made the final break from his home country in the mid-1930s when he arranged for his wife, Teodora, and two sons (Vito and Michael, my father) to leave Italy and settle in Brooklyn, New York. His timing was also remarkably good: If he had waited a year or so later, Mussolini's invasion of Ethiopia might have left his wife and children stranded in Italy until the end of the war. Two more children, Nardina and Albert, completed the family. By then Grandpa's ice-oil-coal delivery business was in high gear, and he was a confirmed fan of the Brooklyn Dodgers.

Michele and Teodora Loconte

By the time of the war my grandparents had established themselves as US citizens and were raising their children with a deep gratitude for the freedom and opportunity that they experienced in their adopted country—a love for America that they in turn passed on to their children.

Grandpa Loconte at work in the family's wholesale dairy business in Brooklyn, NY, in the 1950s, boasting "the best from the nest."

BIBLIOGRAPHY

Aeschylus. *Prometheus Bound*. Translated by Joel Agee. New York Review Books, 2015.

Aldington, Richard. *Death of a Hero*. Chatto & Windus, 1929. Reprint, Penguin, 2013.

Aldwinckle, Stella. "Socrates Was a Realist." *Socratic Digest* 1, no. 6 (1943): 9.

Ambrose, Stephen. *Eisenhower: Soldier and President*. Simon & Schuster, 1990.

Aston, T. H., ed. *The History of the University of Oxford* Vol. 3, *The Collegiate University*, edited by James McConica. Clarendon Press, 1986.

Barfield, Owen. *Owen Barfield on C. S. Lewis*. Barfield, 2011.

Bartlett, J. W. "Munich Agreement Is Signed." *History Today* 48, no. 9 (1998). https://www.historytoday.com/archive/munich-agreement-signed.

BBC. "December 17, 1942: Britain Condemns Massacre of Jews." BBC: On This Day. http://news.bbc.co.uk/onthisday/hi/dates/stories/december/17/newsid_3547000/3547151.stm.

BBC. "Making Friends with Hitler: Britain's Pre-War Admiration for the Nazi Dictator." *History Extra*, January 28, 2021. https://www.historyextra.com/period/20th-century/britain-adolf-hitler-dictator-admiration-appeasement-relationship-britain-germany/.

Benda, Julien. *The Treason of the Intellectuals*. Translated by David Broder. William Morrow, 1928.

Bosworth, R. J. B. *Mussolini*. Rev. ed. Bloomsbury, 2010.

Bradbury, Malcolm, and James McFarlane, eds. *Modernism: A Guide to European Literature, 1890–1930*. Penguin, 1978.

Brittain, Vera. *Testament of Youth*. Penguin, 2005.

Bunyan, John. *Pilgrim's Progress*. 1678. Reprint, Penguin, 2008.

Burleigh, Michael. *The Third Reich: A New History*. Hill & Wang, 2000.

Burns, C. Delisle. *Modern Civilization on Trial*. MacMillan, 1931.

Carpenter, Humphrey. *The Inklings: C. S. Lewis, J. R. R. Tolkien, Charles Williams, and Their Friends*. Houghton Mifflin, 1979.

Carpenter, Humphrey. *J. R. R. Tolkien: A Biography*. George Allen & Unwin, 1977. Reprint, Houghton Mifflin, 2000.

Chambers, R. W. Review of *Beowulf: The Monsters and the Critics*, by J. R. R. Tolkien. *Modern Language Review* 33, no. 2 (1938): 272–73. https://doi.org/10.2307/3715017.

Chiang Kai-shek, Madame. Radio address. October 10, 1941. Transcript in "Memorandum by Mr. John P. Davies, Jr., of the Division of Far Eastern Affairs." United States Department of State: Office of the Historian. https://history.state.gov/historicaldocuments/frus1941v04/d403.

Churchill, Winston. "Munich Agreement." Speech to the House of Commons. October 5, 1938. Transcript at the International Churchill Society. https://winstonchurchill.org/resources/speeches/1930-1938-the-wilderness/the-munich-agreement/

Churchill, Winston. *Never Give In! The Best of Winston Churchill's Speeches*. Edited by Winston S. Churchill. Hyperion, 2003.

Churchill, Winston. "Never in the Field of Human Conflict Was So Much Owed by So Many to So Few." Speech to the House of Commons. August 20, 1940. Transcript at the UK Parliament. https://www.parliament.uk/about/living-heritage/transformingsociety/private-lives/yourcountry/collections/churchillexhibition/churchill-the-orator/human-conflict/.

Churchill, Winston. "Situation at Bilbao." Debate at the House of Commons. April 14, 1937. Transcript at the UK Parliament. https://hansard.parliament.uk/commons/1937-04-14/debates/fc1f83cc-6d89-4d7f-90e2-645af1cb5dd6/SituationAtBilbao.

Churchill, Winston. "Their Finest Hour." Speech to the House of Commons. June 18, 1940. Transcript at the International Churchill Society. https://winstonchurchill.org/resources/speeches/1940-the-finest-hour/their-finest-hour/.

Churchill, Winston. "We Shall Fight on the Beaches." Speech to the House of Commons. June 4, 1940. Transcript at the International Churchill Society. https://winstonchurchill.org/resources/speeches/1940-the-finest-hour/we-shall-fight-on-the-beaches/.

Churchill, Winston. *The World Crisis*. Abridged and rev. ed. Free Press, 2005.

Como, James T. *C. S. Lewis at the Breakfast Table*. Harcourt Brace Jovanovich, 1992.

Croft, Janne Brennan. *War and the Works of J. R. R. Tolkien*. Praeger, 2004.

Darwall-Smith, Robin. *A History of University College Oxford*. Oxford University Press, 2008.

Dearmer, Percy, ed. *Christianity and the Crisis*. Victor Gollancz, 1933.

Drout, Michael, D. C. "'Beowulf: The Monsters and the Critics': The Brilliant Essay That Broke Beowulf Studies." Lord of the Rings Plaza: Scholars Forum. 2010. https://www.academia.edu/44060261/_Beowulf_The_Monsters_and_the_Critics_The_Brilliant_Essay_that_Broke_Beowulf_Studies.

Drout, Michael D. C., ed. *J. R. R. Tolkien Encyclopedia: Scholarship and Critical Assessment*. Routledge, 2007.

Duhamel, Georges. *Civilization, 1914–1917*. Translated by E. S. Brooks. Century, 1919.

Dunn, Daisy. *Not Far from Brideshead: Oxford Between the Wars*. Weidenfeld & Nicolson, 2022.

Duranty, Walter. "Soviets in 16th Year Calm and Hopeful." *New York Times*, November 13, 1932. E4. https://www.nytimes.com/1932/11/13/archives/soviet-in-16th-year-calm-and-hopeful-industries-are-showing-big.html.

Duriez, Colin. *Bedeviled: Lewis, Tolkien, and the Shadow of Evil.* InterVarsity, 2015.

Eisenhower, Dwight D. *Crusade in Europe: A Personal Account of World War II.* Johns Hopkins University Press, 1997.

Farrell, Nicholas. *Mussolini: A New Life.* Weidenfeld & Nicolson, 2003.

Ferguson, Niall. *The War of the World: Twentieth-Century Conflict and the Descent of the West.* Penguin, 2006.

Freud, Sigmund. *Civilization and Its Discontents.* Translated by James Strachey. 1929. Reprint, W. W. Norton, 2010.

Freud, Sigmund. *The Future of an Illusion.* Translated and edited by James Strachey. 1927. Reprint, W. W. Norton, 1989.

Freud, Sigmund. *The Interpretation of Dreams.* Translated and edited by James Stachey. 1899. Reprint, Basic Books, 2010.

Fuller, Edmund. *Books with Men Behind Them.* Random House, 1962.

Fussell, Paul. *The Great War and Modern Memory.* Oxford University Press, 2013.

Gallately, Robert. *Stalin's Curse: Battling for Communism in War and Cold War.* Vintage Books, 2013.

Garth, John. *Tolkien and the Great War: The Threshold of Middle-earth.* Houghton Mifflin, 2003.

Garth, John. *Tolkien at Exeter College: How an Oxford Undergraduate Created Middle-earth.* Exeter College, 2015.

Gibb, Jocelyn, ed. *Light on C. S. Lewis.* Harcourt Brace Jovanovich, 1976.

Gibbs, Philip. *Now It Can Be Told.* Compass Circle, 2020.

Gilbert, Martin. *Churchill: A Life.* Henry Holt, 1991.

Gilbert, Martin. *The Righteous: The Unsung Heroes of the Holocaust.* Henry Holt, 2003.

Gilbert, Martin. *The Second World War: A Complete History.* Henry Holt, 2004.

Glyer, Diana Pavlac. *The Company They Keep: C. S. Lewis and J. R. R. Tolkien as Writers in Community.* Kent State University Press, 2007.

Graham, David, ed. *We Remember C. S. Lewis.* Broadman & Holman, 2001.

Green, Roger Lancelyn, and Walter Hooper. *C. S. Lewis: A Biography.* HarperCollins, 2003.

Guite, Malcolm. "Yearning for a Far-Off Country." In *C. S. Lewis and His Circle: Essays and Memoirs from the Oxford C.S. Lewis Society.* Edited by Roger White, Judith Wolfe, and Brendan N. Wolfe. Oxford University Press, 2015.

Haig, Douglas. "Our Backs to the Wall." Special Order of the Day to British troops. April 11, 1918. The British Library. https://blogs.bl.uk/untoldlives/2018/04/with-our-backs-to-the-wall-sir-douglas-haigs-special-order-1918-.html.

Hansen, Lilian. "The Great Evacuation." Archived on "Poem About Evacuation from London, 1940." Imperial War Museums. Accessed November 1, 2024. https://www.iwm.org.uk/collections/item/object/1030002181.

Harrison, Brian, ed. *The History of the University of Oxford.* Vol. 8, *The Twentieth Century.* Clarendon Press, 1994.

Hastings, Adrian. *A History of English Christianity: 1920–1990.* Trinity Press International, 1991.

Hastings, Max. *Inferno: The World at War, 1939–1945.* Vintage, 2012.

Havard, R. E. "Professor J. R. R. Tolkien: A Personal Memoir." *Mythlore: Journal of*

J. R. R. Tolkien, C. S. Lewis, Charles Williams, and Mythopoeic Literature 17, no. 2 (1990).

Heck, Joel D. *Irrigating Deserts: C. S. Lewis on Education*. Concordia, 2006.

Helms, Randel. *Tolkien's World*. Thames and Hudson, 1975.

Henderson, Arthur. "Opening Speech by the President." Speech at the World Disarmament Conference. February 2, 1932. Geneva, Switzerland. Transcript at the United Nations of Geneva Library. https://libraryresources.unog.ch/londisarmament/world-disarmament-conference.

Hibbert, Christopher. *Mussolini: The Rise and Fall of Il Duce*. St. Martin's Griffin, 2008.

Hitler, Adolf. *Mein Kampf*. 1925. Translated by Ralph Manheim. Harper, 1998.

Hitler, Adolf. Speech to the Reichstag. March 7, 1936. "Translation of Document 2289-PS." Translated by C. Virginia von Schon. Nürnberg Krupp Trial Papers of Judge Hu C. Anderson. Vanderbilt University. https://krupp.library.vanderbilt.edu/node/1043.

Hodin, J. P. *The Dilemma of Being Modern: Essays on Art and Literature*. Noonday Press, 1959.

Hooper, Walter, ed. *The Collected Letters of C. S. Lewis*. Vol. 1, *Family Letters, 1905–1931*. HarperSanFrancisco, 2000.

Hooper, Walter, ed. *The Collected Letters of C. S. Lewis*. Vol. 2, *Books, Broadcasts, and the War, 1931–1949*. HarperSanFrancisco, 2004.

Hooper, Walter, ed. *The Collected Letters of C. S. Lewis*. Vol. 3, *Narnia, Cambridge, and Joy, 1950–1963*. HarperSanFrancisco, 2007.

Hooper, Walter, *C. S. Lewis: A Companion and Guide*. Fount, 1997.

Huxley, Julian. *Brave New World*. Chatto & Windus, 1932. Reprint, Harper Perennial, 2006.

Huxley, Julian. "The Case for Eugenics." *The Sociological Review* a18, no. 4 (1926): 279–90. https://doi.org/10.1111/j.1467-954X.1926.tb01590.x.

Huxley, Julian. *Religion Without Revelation*. Watts, 1945.

Inge, William Ralph. *The Fall of the Idols*. Putnam, 1940.

Inge, William Ralph. "Some Moral Aspects of Eugenics." *The Eugenics Review* 1, no. 1 (1909): 26–36. https://pmc.ncbi.nlm.nih.gov/articles/PMC2990368/.

Jacobs, Alan. *The Narnian: The Life and Imagination of C.S. Lewis*. HarperOne, 2006.

Jankowski, Paul. *All Against All: The Long Winter of 1933 and the Origins of the Second World War*. HarperCollins, 2020.

Jenkins, Stephanie. "Crew of the Whitley V Aircraft." Oxford War Memorials. Accessed November 1, 2024. https://oxfordhistory.org.uk/war/wolfson_flight/index.html.

Joad, C. E. M. *The Recovery of Belief: A Restatement of Christian Philosophy*. Faber & Faber Limited, 1952.

Johnson, Bruce R. "The Efforts of C. S. Lewis to Aid British Prisoners of War During World War II." *Sehnsucht: The C.S. Lewis Journal* 12, no. 1 (2018): 41–76. https://www.jstor.org/stable/48579685.

Johnson, Paul. *A History of the American People*. Weidenfeld & Nicolson, 1997.

Johnson, Paul. *Modern Times: The World from the Twenties to the Nineties*. Rev. ed. Harper Perennial Modern Classics, 2001.

Jones, Ernest. *What Is Psychoanalysis?* George Allen & Unwin, 1949.

Jordan-Smith, Paul. "The Silver Trumpet." *Los Angeles Times*, July 27, 1986. https://www.latimes.com/archives/la-xpm-1986-07-27-bk-1425-story.html.

Keegan, John. *The First World War*. Vintage, 2000.

Kershaw, Ian. *To Hell and Back: Europe, 1914–1949*. Penguin, 2015.

Keys, David. "Revealing a WWI Drama: How Modern Technology Is Shedding New Light on the Horrors of Submarine Warfare." *Independent*, August 7, 2020. https://www.independent.co.uk/news/science/archaeology/ww1-german-submarine-uc47-navy-flamborough-head-yorkshire-north-sea-archaeology-history-a9655336.html.

King, Don W., ed. *Collected Poems of C. S. Lewis: A Critical Edition*. Kent State University Press, 2020.

Kirk, Russell. *Enemies of the Permanent Things: Observations of Abnormality in Literature and Politics*. Arlington House, 1969.

Kotkin, Stephen. *Stalin: Waiting for Hitler, 1929–1941*. Penguin, 2017.

Krabbe, Henning, ed. *Voices from Britain: Broadcast History 1939–45*. George Allen & Unwin, 1947. https://www.worldradiohistory.com/BOOKSHELF-ARH/History/Voices-from-Britain-1939-1945-Krabbe-1937.pdf.

Krutch, Joseph Wood. "The Modern Temper." *Atlantic*, February 1927. https://www.theatlantic.com/magazine/archive/1927/02/the-modern-temper/649130/.

Lawlor, John. *C. S. Lewis: Memories and Reflections*. Spencer, 1998.

Leishman, J. B. "Rehabilitations and Other Essays." *The Review of English Studies* 16, no. 61 (January 1940): 109–13. https://www.jstor.org/stable/510045.

Lewis, C. S. *Abolition of Man*. Oxford University Press, 1943. Reprint, HarperOne, 2015.

Lewis, C. S. *All My Road Before Me: The Diary of C. S. Lewis, 1922–1927*. Mariner, 2002.

Lewis, C. S. *Allegory of Love*. Clarendon Press, 1936. Reprint, Cambridge University Press, 2013.

Lewis, C. S. *Christian Reflections*. Edited by Walter Hooper. Geoffrey Bles, 1967. Reprint, Eerdmans, 2014.

Lewis, C. S. *The Chronicles of Narnia*. 1950–56. Reprint, HarperCollins, 2004.

Lewis, C. S. *C. S. Lewis's Lost Aeneid: Arms and the Exile*. Edited by A. T. Reyes. Yale University Press, 2011.

Lewis, C. S. *De Descriptione Temporum: An Inaugural Lecture*. Cambridge University Press, 1955.

Lewis, C. S. *The Discarded Image*. Cambridge University Press, 1964.

Lewis, C. S. *Essay Collection: Faith, Christianity and the Church*. Edited by Lesley Walmsley. HarperOne, 2002.

Lewis, C. S. *The Four Loves*. Geoffrey Bles, 1960. Reprint, Harcourt Brace Jovanovich, 1988.

Lewis, C. S., ed. *George MacDonald: An Anthology*. Geoffrey Bles, 1946. Reprint, HarperOne, 2001.

Lewis, C. S. *God in the Dock*. 1970. Reprint, Eerdmans, 2014.

Lewis, C. S. *The Great Divorce*. Geoffrey Bles, 1945. Reprint, HarperOne, 2001.

Lewis, C. S. *Image and Imagination: Essays and Reviews*. Edited by Walter Hooper. Cambridge University Press, 2013.

Lewis, C. S. *Letters of C. S. Lewis*. Edited by Warren Lewis and Walter Hooper. Harcourt Brace & World, 1966.

Lewis, C. S. *Mere Christianity.* Geoffrey Bles, 1952. Reprint, HarperSanFrancisco, 2001.

Lewis, C. S. *Of This and Other Worlds.* Edited by Walter Hooper. Originally published as *Of Other Worlds: Essays and Stories.* Geoffrey Bles, 1966. Reprint, Fount, 1984.

Lewis, C. S. *Out of the Silent Planet.* Bodley Head, 1938. Reprint, Scribner, 2003.

Lewis, C. S. *Perelandra.* Bodley Head, 1943. Reprint, Scribner, 2003.

Lewis, C. S. *The Pilgrim's Regress: An Allegorical Apology for Christianity, Reason, and Romanticism; The Wade Annotated Edition.* Edited by David C. Downing. Eerdmans, 2014.

Lewis, C. S. *Poems.* Edited by Walter Hooper. Harcourt Brace, 1964.

Lewis, C. S. *A Preface to Paradise Lost.* Oxford University Press, 1942. Reprint, HarperOne, 2022.

Lewis, C. S. *Present Concerns: Essays by C. S. Lewis.* Edited by Walter Hooper. Harcourt Brace Jovanovich, 1986.

Lewis, C. S. *The Problem of Pain.* Centenary Press, 1940. Reprint, HarperOne, 1996.

Lewis, C. S. *The Screwtape Letters.* Geoffrey Bles, 1942. Reprint, HarperOne, 1996.

Lewis, C. S. *The Seeing Eye and Other Selected Essays from Christian Reflections.* First published as an article in *Show,* 1963. Reprint, Ballantine, 1986.

Lewis, C. S. *Spirits in Bondage: A Cycle of Lyrics.* Harcourt Brace & Jovanovich, 1919.

Lewis, C. S. *Surprised by Joy: The Shape of My Early Life.* Geoffrey Bles, 1955. Reprint, Harcourt Brace Jovanovich, 1984.

Lewis, C. S. *That Hideous Strength.* Bodley Head, 1945. Reprint, Scribner, 2003.

Lewis, C. S. "On Three Ways of Writing for Children." In *On Stories: And Other Essays on Literature.* Edited by Walter Hooper. Geoffrey Bles, 1966. Reprint, Harcourt Brace, 1982.

Lewis, C. S. *Till We Have Faces.* Geoffrey Bles, 1956. Reprint, HarperOne, 2017.

Lewis, C. S. "Universities of Captivity." *The Christian News-Letter,* February 4, 1942, back page. https://archive.org/details/christian-news-letter_1942-02-04_119.

Lewis, C. S. *The Weight of Glory.* First published as a sermon in *Theology,* 1941. Reprint, HarperOne, 2015.

Lippmann, Walter. *A Preface to Morals.* Routledge, 1982.

Lonnrot, Elias. *Kalevala: The Epic of the Finnish People.* Penguin, 2021.

Lukacs, John. *The Last European War.* Yale University Press, 2001.

MacDonald, George. *Lilith.* Chatto & Windus, 1895. Reprint, Eerdmans, 1988.

MacDonald, George. *What's Mine's Mine.* Routledge & Sons, 1886. Reprint, Forgotten Books, 2018.

Markos, Louis. *The Myth Made Fact: Reading Greek and Roman Mythology Through Christian Eyes.* Classical Academic Press, 2020.

Marsden, George M. *C. S. Lewis's* Mere Christianity*: A Biography.* Princeton University Press, 2016.

Marx, Karl. *The Difference Between the Democritean and Epicurean Philosophy of Nature.* Translated by Andy Blunden. 1841. Progress, 1902.

Masefield, John. *Gallipoli.* MacMillan, 1916.

McIlwaine, Catherine, ed. *Tolkien: Maker of Middle-earth.* Bodleian Library Publishing, 2018.

Mendelsohn, Daniel. "Is the Aeneid a Celebration of Empire—or a Critique?" *New*

Yorker, October 8, 2018. https://www.newyorker.com/magazine/2018/10/15/is-the-aeneid-a-celebration-of-empire-or-a-critique.

Mitchell, Christopher. "University Battles—C. S. Lewis and the Oxford University Socratic Club." C. S. Lewis Institute. January 7, 2010. https://www.cslewisinstitute.org/resources/university-battles-c-s-lewis-and-the-oxford-university-socratic-club/.

Murray, Gilbert. *The Ordeal of This Generation*. Harper & Brothers Publishers, 1929.

New York Times Wireless. "Four-Power Pact Is Signed in Rome." *New York Times*, July 16, 1933. https://www.nytimes.com/1933/07/16/archives/fourpower-pact-is-signed-in-rome-mussolini-receives-envoys-of.html.

New York Times Wireless. "Mines Sink Five More Ships, Four Owned by Neutrals." *New York Times*, November 20, 1939.

Nicholi, Armand. "The Question of God: Why Freud & Lewis?" PBS. September 15, 2004. https://www.pbs.org/wgbh/questionofgod/why/index.html.

Ordway, Holly. *Tolkien's Faith: A Spiritual Biography*. Word on Fire Academic, 2023.

Orwell, George. *Collected Essays, Journalism and Letters*. 4 vols. Harmondsworth, 1966–80.

Orwell, George. *Why I Write*. Penguin, 2005.

Overy, Richard. *The Twilight Years: The Paradox of Britain Between the Wars*. Penguin, 2010.

Plato. *The Republic*. Translated by William C. Scott and Richard W. Sterling. W. W. Norton, 1996.

Poe, Harry Lee, and Rebecca Whitten Poe, "C. S. Lewis as Christian and Scholar." Chap. 1 in *C. S. Lewis Remembered: Collected Reflections of Students, Friends and Colleagues*. Edited by Harry Lee Poe and Rebecca Whitten Poe. Zondervan, 2006.

Reynolds, David. *The Long Shadow: The Legacies of the Great War in the Twentieth Century*. W. W. Norton, 2015.

Roberts, Andrew. *Churchill: Walking with Destiny*. Viking, 2018.

Rook, Alan. *These Are My Comrades*. Routledge, 1943.

Roosevelt, Franklin D. "Address at Chautauqua, N.Y." August 14, 1936. Transcript at The American Presidency Project. https://www.presidency.ucsb.edu/documents/address-chautauqua-ny.

Roosevelt, Franklin D. "Appeal for World Peace by Disarmament and for Relief from Economic Chaos." May 16, 1933. Transcript at The American Presidency Project. https://www.presidency.ucsb.edu/documents/appeal-for-world-peace-disarmament-and-for-relief-from-economic-chaos.

Roosevelt, Franklin D. "Campaign Address at Cleveland, Ohio." November 2, 1940. Transcript at The American Presidency Project. https://www.presidency.ucsb.edu/documents/campaign-address-cleveland-ohio.

Ryrie, Alec. *Protestants: The Faith That Made the Modern World*. Penguin, 2017.

Sale, Roger. *Modern Heroism: Essays on D. H. Lawrence, William Empson, and J. R. R. Tolkien*. University of California Press, 1973.

Sanger, Margaret. *The Pivot of Civilization*. Brentano's, 1922.

Sayer, George. *Jack: A Life of C. S. Lewis*. Crossway, 2005.

Schofield, Stephen, ed. *In Search of C. S. Lewis*. Bridge Logos Foundation, 1983.

Scull, Christina, and Wayne G. Hammond, eds. *The J. R. R. Tolkien Companion and Guide*. Vol. 1, *Chronology*. Houghton Mifflin, 2006.

Scull, Christina, and Wayne G. Hammond, eds. *The J. R. R. Tolkien Companion and Guide*. Vol. 2, *Reader's Guide*. Houghton Mifflin, 2006.

Sewell, Rob. "1920: When Britain Came Close to Revolution." *In Defence of Marxism*, March 18, 2022. https://www.marxist.com/1920-when-britain-came-close-to-revolution.htm.

Shippey, Tom. *J. R. R. Tolkien, Author of the Century*. Houghton Mifflin, 2001.

Shippey, Tom. "The Lewis Diaries: C. S. Lewis and the English Faculty in the 1920s." In *C. S. Lewis and His Circle: Essays and Memoirs from the Oxford C.S. Lewis Society*. Edited by Roger White, Judith Wolfe, and Brendan N. Wolfe. Oxford University Press, 2015.

Shirer, William L. *Berlin Diary*. Alfred A. Knopf, 1941. Reprint, RosettaBooks, 2011.

Shirer, William, L. *The Rise and Fall of the Third Reich: A History of Nazi Germany*. 1960. Reprint, Simon & Schuster, 2011.

Smith, Eden A. "Notable Debates." The Oxford Union. Accessed November 11, 2024. https://oxford-union.org/pages/notable-debates.

Spacks, Patricia Meyer. "Power and Meaning in *The Lord of the Rings*." In *Understanding* The Lord of the Rings*: The Best of Tolkien Criticism*. Edited by Rose A. Zimbardo and Neil D. Isaacs. Houghton Mifflin, 2004.

Spengler, Oswald. *The Decline of the West*. A. A. Knopf, 1926.

Spurgeon, M. R. "Wireless in Wartime." BBC: World War II People's War. September 6, 2005. https://www.bbc.co.uk/history/ww2peopleswar/stories/86/a5547486.shtml.

Stalin, Joseph V. "The Tasks of Economic Executives." Speech at the First All-Union Conference of Leading Personnel of Socialist Industry. February 4, 1931. Moscow, Russia.

Strong, Archibald, trans. *Beowulf*. Constable, 1925.

Taylor, A. J. P. *The First World War: An Illustrated History*. Penguin, 1966.

Tearle, Oliver. "A Summary and Analysis of *The Lion, the Witch and the Wardrobe* by CS Lewis." *Interesting Literature*. Accessed May 6, 2024. https://interestingliterature.com/2021/04/lewis-lion-witch-wardrobe-summary-analysis/.

Thompson, George H. "Early Review of Books by J. R. R. Tolkien." *Mythlore: Journal of J. R. R. Tolkien, C. S. Lewis, Charles Williams, and Mythopoeic Literature* 11, no. 2 (1984), article 8. https://dc.swosu.edu/mythlore/vol11/iss2/8/.

Tillotson, Kathleen. Review of *The Allegory of Love: A Study in Medieval Tradition* by C. S. Lewis. *The Review of English Studies* 13, no. 52 (1937): 477–79. https://www.jstor.org/stable/509612.

Tolkien, J. R. R. *Battle of Maldon: Together with the Homecoming of Beorhtnoth*. Edited by Peter Grybauskas. William Morrow, 2023.

Tolkien, J. R. R. *Beowulf: A Translation and Commentary Together with Sellic Spell*. Edited by Christopher Tolkien. Houghton Mifflin Harcourt, 2015.

Tolkien, J. R. R. *Beren and Lúthien*. Edited by Christopher Tolkien. William Morrow, 2017.

Tolkien, J. R. R. "Dragons." Christmas Lectures for Children. Ashmolean Natural History Society. January 1, 1938. Oxfordshire.

Tolkien, J. R. R. *The Fall of Arthur*. Edited by Christopher Tolkien. William Morrow, 2014.

Tolkien, J. R. R. *The Fall of Gondolin*. Edited by Christopher Tolkien. Houghton Mifflin Harcourt, 2018.

Tolkien, J. R. R. *The Lay of Beowulf*. In *Beowulf: A Translation and Commentary*, edited by Christopher Tolkien. HarperCollins, 2014.

Tolkien, J. R. R. *Letters from Father Christmas*. Centenary Edition. Edited by Baillie Tolkien. Houghton Mifflin Harcourt, 2020.

Tolkien, J. R. R. *The Letters of J. R. R. Tolkien*. Rev. ed. Edited by Humphrey Carpenter. William Morrow, 2023.

Tolkien, J. R. R. *The Lord of the Rings*. George Allen & Unwin, 1954. Reprint, William Morrow, 2012.

Tolkien, J. R. R. *The Monsters and the Critics and Other Essays*. Edited by Christopher Tolkien. George Allen & Unwin, 1983.

Tolkien, J. R. R. *The Silmarillion*. 2nd ed. Edited by Christopher Tolkien. George Allen & Unwin, 1977. Reprint, William Morrow, 2001.

Tolkien, J. R. R. *Sir Gawain and the Green Knight*. Edited by Christopher Tolkien. George Allen & Unwin, 1975.

Tolkien, J. R. R. *Tales from the Perilous Realm*. Mariner, 2021.

Tolkien, J. R. R. *Tree and Leaf*. George Allen & Unwin, 1964. Reprint, HarperCollins, 2001.

Trevor-Roper, H. R. *Men and Events*. Harper, 1957.

Tuchman, Barbara W. *The Guns of August*. Random House, 2014.

Virgil. *The Aeneid*. Translated by Robert Fagles. Penguin Classics, 2008.

Wagner, Richard. *The Ring of the Niblung*. Translated by Margaret Armour. William Heinemann, 1911.

Ward, Michael. *After Humanity: A Guide to C. S. Lewis's* The Abolition of Man. Word on Fire Catholic Ministries, 2021.

Webb, Sidney, and Beatrice Webb. *The Decay of Capitalist Civilization*. George Allen & Unwin, 1923.

Weiss, John. *Ideology of Death: Why the Holocaust Happened in Germany*. Ivan R. Dee, 1996.

Wells, H. G. *The New World Order*. Secker & Warburg, 1940.

Wells, H. G. *The Outline of History: Being a Plain History of Life and Mankind*. Vol. 1. Review of Reviews, 1923.

Wells, H. G. *The Shape of Things to Come*. MacMillan, 1933.

White, Roger, Judith Wolfe, and Brendan N. Wolfe, eds. *C. S. Lewis and His Circle: Essays and Memoirs from the Oxford C. S. Lewis Society*. Oxford University Press, 2015.

Williams, Charles. *The Place of the Lion*. Read Books, 2019.

Zaleski, Philip, and Carol Zaleski. *The Fellowship: The Literary Lives of the Inklings: J. R. R. Tolkien, C. S. Lewis, Owen Barfield, and Charles Williams*. Farrar, Straus & Giroux, 2016.

Ziegler, Philip. *London at War: 1939–1945*. Alfred A. Knopf, 1995.

NOTES

Introduction: Minds Lit By Fire

1. Masefield, *Gallipoli*, 104. Poet John Masefield served in the British Army.
2. Ferguson, *War of the World*, 646.
3. Kershaw, *To Hell and Back*, 348.
4. Fuller, *Books with Men Behind Them*, 3.
5. Hooper, *Collected Letters*, vol. 3, 1396.
6. Garth, *Tolkien and the Great War*, 309.

Chapter 1: The End of Illusions

1. Hibbert, *Mussolini*, 69.
2. Sewell, "1920: When Britain Came Close to Revolution."
3. Hooper, *Collected Letters*, vol. 1, 502.
4. Kershaw, *To Hell and Back*, 93.
5. Hooper, *Collected Letters*, vol. 1, 458.
6. Hooper, *Collected Letters*, vol. 1, 449.
7. Daisy Dunn, interview with the author, March 4, 2024.
8. Overy, *Twilight Years*, 12.
9. Tuchman, *Guns of August*, 483.
10. See Taylor, *First World War*, 22.
11. Harrison, *History of the University of Oxford*, 18.
12. Churchill, *World Crisis*, 841.
13. Brittain, *Testament of Youth*, 404.
14. Aldington, *Death of a Hero*, 261.
15. Tolkien, *Letters*, 73.
16. Garth, *Tolkien at Exeter College*, 33.
17. Garth, *Tolkien at Exeter College*, 52–53.
18. Garth, *Tolkien at Exeter College*, 44.
19. Duhamel, *Civilization, 1914–1917*, 274–75.

20. Tolkien, *Letters*, 62.
21. Garth, *Tolkien and the Great War*, 247.
22. Lewis, *Surprised by Joy*, 188.
23. Robin Darwall-Smith, interview with the author, July 29, 2024.
24. Hooper, *Collected Letters*, vol. 1, 388.
25. Walter Hooper, interview with the author, November 8, 2018.
26. Simon Horobin, interview with the author, March 11, 2024.
27. Hooper, *Collected Letters*, vol. 1, 428.
28. Hooper, *Collected Letters*, vol. 1, 108.
29. Scull and Hammond, *Tolkien Companion*, vol. 1, 118.
30. Tolkien, *Letters*, 73.
31. Tolkien, *Fall of Gondolin*, 178.
32. Garth, *Tolkien at Exeter College*, 50.
33. Scull and Hammond, *Tolkien Companion*, vol. 1, 118. In February 1950, Tolkien wrote to George Allen & Unwin to say that the manuscript was finished: "My work has escaped from my control, and I have produced a monster: an immensely long, complex, rather bitter, and rather terrifying romance, unfit for children (if fit for anybody); and it is not really a sequel to *The Hobbit*, but to *The Silmarillion*." Tolkien, *Letters*, 193.
34. MacDonald, *Lilith*, xi.
35. Lewis, *George MacDonald*, xxxviii–xxxix.
36. Alister McGrath, interview with the author, July 25, 2017.
37. Hooper, *Collected Letters*, vol. 1, 397.
38. Lewis, *Spirits in Bondage*, 27–28.
39. Lewis, *Spirits in Bondage*, 92.
40. Hooper, *Collected Letters*, vol. 1, 555.
41. Johnson, *Modern Times*, 6.
42. Hooper, *Collected Letters*, vol. 1, 605.
43. Hooper, *Collected Letters*, vol. 1, 605.
44. Freud, *Future of an Illusion*, xxiii.
45. Freud, *Future of an Illusion*, 40.
46. Freud, *Future of an Illusion*, xxiii.
47. Hooper, *Collected Letters*, vol. 1, 231.
48. Lewis, *Pilgrim's Regress*, 49–51. I am indebted to David Downing's annotated edition of *The Pilgrim's Regress*.
49. Overy, *Twilight Years*, 138.
50. Freud, *Future of an Illusion*, 71.
51. Johnson, *Modern Times*, 6.
52. "All the features of modernism were present in avant-garde culture before the war," writes Ian Kershaw, "but the horrors of 1914–18 greatly accentuated the artistic assault on rationality." Kershaw, *To Hell and Back*, 168.
53. Kershaw, *To Hell and Back*, 168.
54. Bradbury and McFarlane, *Modernism*, 27.
55. Hodin, *Dilemma of Being Modern*, 3.
56. Bradbury and McFarlane, *Modernism*, 27.

57. Lippmann, *Preface to Morals*, 89.
58. Lippmann, *Preface to Morals*, 88.
59. Hodin, *Dilemma of Being Modern*, 3.
60. Reynolds, *Long Shadow*, 196.
61. Hodin, *Dilemma of Being Modern*, 3.
62. Sale, *Modern Heroism*, 3.
63. Carpenter, *Inklings*, 29.
64. Michael Ward, interview with the author, March 11, 2024.
65. Lewis, *All My Road Before Me*, 409–10.
66. Lewis, *All My Road Before Me*, 411.
67. Tolkien, *Letters*, 328.
68. Garth, *Tolkien and the Great War*, 293.
69. Tolkien, "On Translating Beowulf," in *Monsters and the Critics*, 55.
70. Scull and Hammond, *Tolkien Companion*, vol. 2, 1195.
71. Tolkien, *Monsters and the Critics*, 73. Tolkien delivered his lecture at the University of Glasgow in 1953.
72. Tolkien, *Monsters and the Critics*, 88–89.
73. Tolkien, *Sir Gawain and the Green Knight*, 18–19.
74. Tolkien, *Monsters and the Critics*, 93.
75. Scull and Hammond, *Tolkien Companion*, vol. 2, 963–64.
76. Tolkien, *Beowulf*, 34.
77. Strong, *Beowulf*, xxii. In the foreword, "Beowulf and the Heroic Age," R. W. Chambers quotes from Klaeber to strengthen his point: "The Christian elements are, almost without exception, so deeply ingrained in the very fabric of the poem that they cannot be explained away as the work of a reviser or later interpolator. Whilst the episodes are all but free from these modern influences, the main story has been thoroughly imbued with the spirit of Christianity." Strong, *Beowulf*, xxv.
78. Stuart Lee, interview with the author, July 25, 2024.
79. Tolkien, *Battle of Maldon*, xvi.
80. Tolkien, *Letters*, 348–49.
81. Mendelsohn, "Is the Aeneid a Celebration of Empire—or a Critique?"
82. Hooper, *Collected Letters*, vol. 1, 362.
83. Hooper, *Collected Letters*, vol. 1, 490.
84. Lewis, *Preface to Paradise Lost*, 37.
85. Lewis, *Lost Aeneid*, 11.
86. Lewis, *Preface to Paradise Lost*, 38–39.
87. Daisy Dunn, interview with the author, March 4, 2024.
88. Tolkien, *Letters*, 13.
89. Tolkien, *Tales from the Perilous Realm*, xv.
90. Scull and Hammond, *Tolkien Companion*, vol. 1, 141.
91. Tolkien, *Letters*, 74.
92. Keys, "Revealing a WWI Drama."
93. Lewis, *All My Road Before Me*, 234.
94. Hooper, *Collected Letters*, vol. 1, 601.
95. Hooper, *Collected Letters*, vol. 1, 610.

96. Daisy Dunn, interview with author, March 4, 2004.
97. Lewis, *All My Road Before Me*, 358.
98. Hooper, *Collected Letters*, vol. 1, 642–46.
99. Green and Hooper, *C.S. Lewis: A Biography*, 63.
100. Hooper, *Collected Letters*, vol. 1, 642.
101. Garth, *Tolkien and the Great War*, 208.
102. Hitler, *Mein Kampf*, 290, 305.
103. Brittain, *Testament of Youth*, 463.
104. Dearmer, *Christianity and the Crisis*, 28–29.
105. Hodin, *Dilemma of Being Modern*, 3.
106. Dearmer, *Christianity and the Crisis*, 95.
107. Lippmann, *Preface to Morals*, 91.
108. Tolkien, *Tree and Leaf*, 56.
109. Tolkien, *Tree and Leaf*, 56.
110. Hooper, *Collected Letters*, vol. 1, 649.
111. Lewis, *Till We Have Faces*, 86.

Chapter 2: Enemies of the Permanent Things

1. Hooper, *Collected Letters*, vol. 1, 649.
2. Webb and Webb, *Decay of Capitalist Civilization*, 165, 166–67.
3. Lewis, *Surprised by Joy*, 216.
4. Scull and Hammond, *Tolkien Companion*, vol. 1, 149. Behind their disagreement, it seems, was a deeper divide between the teaching of language and literature at Oxford. Tom Shippey discusses this in his essay "The Lewis Diaries: C. S. Lewis and the English Faculty in the 1920s," in White et al., *C. S. Lewis and His Circle*, 142–47.
5. Although there is no record of Tolkien having spoken these precise words, it is a reasonable postulation from Lewis's record of the meeting.
6. Dearmer, *Christianity and the Crisis*, 9.
7. Spengler, *Decline of the West*, 31.
8. Spengler, *Decline of the West*, 383.
9. Spengler, *Decline of the West*, 30.
10. Spengler, *Decline of the West*, 31.
11. Overy, *Twilight Years*, 16.
12. Overy, *Twilight Years*, 14.
13. Reynolds, *Long Shadow*, 198.
14. Wells, *Outline of History*, 1087.
15. Wells, *Outline of History*, 954.
16. Trevor-Roper, *Men and Events*, 320, 322.
17. Overy, *Twilight Years*, 42.
18. Tom Shippey, "Tolkien and 'That Noble Northern Spirit,'" in McIlwaine, *Tolkien: Maker of Middle-earth*, 58–59.
19. Tolkien, *Monsters and the Critics*, 17. In Tolkien's reference to "their backs to the wall," he seems to have in mind the famous directive from Field Marshall Sir Douglas Haig (see note 21).

20. Tolkien, *Fall of Gondolin*, 84.
21. Haig, "Our Backs to the Wall."
22. Lewis, *Discarded Image*, 100.
23. See Scull and Hammond, *Tolkien Companion*, vol. 2, 858–59; Carpenter, *Inklings*, 29. Interest in the "Northern" heritage of Europe had been on the rise since the nineteenth century, when scholars began to emphasize England's Nordic ancestry in contrast with the classical traditions of Greece and Rome.
24. They began reading the work on February 18, 1927.
25. Tolkien, "On Fairy Stories," cited in Scull and Hammond, *Tolkien Companion*, vol. 2, 858.
26. Garth, *Tolkien and the Great War*, 16. In some respects, he said, it was on a par with the works of Homer. "There is no scene in Homer like the final tragedy of Sigurd and Brynhild." Scull and Hammond, *Tolkien Companion*, vol. 1, 28.
27. Barfield, *Owen Barfield on C. S. Lewis*, 4.
28. Simon Horobin, interview with the author, March 11, 2024.
29. Hooper, *Collected Letters*, vol. 1, 701.
30. Overy, *Twilight Years*, 93.
31. Sanger, *Pivot of Civilization*, 86.
32. Sanger, *Pivot of Civilization*, 118.
33. Sanger, *Pivot of Civilization*, 100.
34. Huxley, "Case for Eugenics," 280.
35. Huxley, "Case for Eugenics," 283. Even Christian ministers, anxious about the health of England's racial stock, jumped on the eugenics bandwagon. "I cannot say that I am hopeful about the near future," wrote the Reverend W. R. Inge, dean of St. Paul's Cathedral in London. "I am afraid that the urban proletariat may cripple our civilization, as it destroyed that of ancient Rome." Inge warned that unless eugenics measures were applied, "these degenerates, who have no qualities that confer a survival value, will probably live as long as they can" by relying on the state's welfare system. Inge, "Some Moral Aspects of Eugenics."
36. Lewis, *That Hideous Strength*, 40.
37. Hibbert, *Mussolini*, 28.
38. Julia Golding, interview with the author, March 4, 2024.
39. Tolkien, *Lord of the Rings*, 521.
40. Overy, *Twilight Years*, 176.
41. Murray, *Ordeal of This Generation*, 118, 115.
42. Brittain, *Testament of Youth*, 650.
43. Scull and Hammond, *Tolkien Companion*, vol. 1, 436–47.
44. Tolkien, *Battle of Maldon*, 65.
45. John R. Holmes, "The Battle of Maldon," in Drout, *J. R. R. Tolkien Encyclopedia*, 52–54.
46. Tolkien, *Battle of Maldon*, 55.
47. Malcolm Guite, interview with the author, March 5, 2024.
48. Aeschylus, *Prometheus Bound*, line 505.
49. Marx, *Difference Between the Democritean and Epicurean Philosophy of Nature*, draft of new preface.

50. See Markos, *Myth Made Fact*, 77. Louis Markos explains that for Percy Shelley, "Prometheus was the noble rebel who throws off all unjust authority that would hold man back from unlimited growth and self-expression. He is the one who will serve no master other than himself and who will set others free to do the same."
51. Aeschylus, *Prometheus Bound*, xi, xxxiii.
52. See Barfield, *Owen Barfield on C. S. Lewis*, 17. The two first met in November 1919, the month when each turned twenty-one.
53. Poe and Poe, "C. S. Lewis as Christian and Scholar," 26.
54. Owen Barfield, interview with the author, March 14, 2024.
55. Gibb, *Light on C. S. Lewis*, xviii.
56. As assistant editor of the Oxford-based journal *The Beacon*, Barfield published Lewis's poem "Joy" in 1922. Their friendship was long and deep. As Barfield summarized it: "C. S. Lewis was for me, first and foremost, the absolutely unforgettable friend, the friend with whom I was in close touch for over forty years, the friend you might come to regard hardly as another human being, but almost as a part of the furniture of my existence." Barfield, *Owen Barfield on C. S. Lewis*, 1.
57. Lewis, *All My Road Before Me*, 438.
58. Lewis, *All My Road Before Me*, 438–39. Before dinner, Lewis showed Barfield a portion of a poem he had been working on, "The Queen of Drum," in an effort to reconcile the ideals of the pagan world with Christianity. Barfield thought the story "a very promising one," and Lewis worked on the poem for the next twenty years.
59. Lewis, *All My Road Before Me*, 439–40.
60. C. S. Lewis, annotation to personal copy of Henri Bergson, *L'Evolution Creatrice* (Paris, 1917), 60. Part of the Wade Center Collection, Wheaton College, Wheaton, Illinois.
61. Lewis, *Surprised by Joy*, 228–29.
62. According to the *Tolkien Companion*, Tolkien and Lewis attended a society meeting together on one of three Mondays in November: the 11th, 18th, or 25th, after which Tolkien returned with Lewis to his rooms in Magdalen. I have selected November 18 as a likely date.
63. Lewis, *Surprised by Joy*, 17.
64. Lewis, *George MacDonald*, xxix.
65. Tolkien, *Silmarillion*, 162.
66. Tolkien, *Beren and Lúthien*, 12.
67. Tolkien, *Silmarillion*, xvii.
68. Tolkien, *Beren and Lúthien*, 12.
69. Julia Golding, interview with the author, March 4, 2024.
70. Lewis's letter to Tolkien was dated December 7, 1929, and is discussed in Scull and Hammond, *Tolkien Companion*, vol. 1, 161.
71. The interpretation of Christopher Tolkien in Scull and Hammond, *Tolkien Companion*, vol. 1, 650. When Tolkien submitted "The Lay of Leithian" to George Allen & Unwin for publication, he got a chilly reception from reader Edward Crankshaw: "Would there be any market for a long, involved, romantic verse-tale of Celtic elves and mortals? I think not." Scull and Hammond, *Tolkien Companion*, vol. 1, 650.

72. Carpenter, *Inklings*, 56n.
73. Scull and Hammond, *Tolkien Companion*, vol. 2, 955.
74. Hooper, *Collected Letters*, vol. 2, 9.
75. Malcolm Guite, interview with the author, March 5, 2024.
76. Louis Markos views Tolkien's insight as crucial to Lewis's conversion. "It is no exaggeration to say that Tolkien's suggestion revolutionized Lewis's interactions with and understanding of the great myths of the pre-Christian Mediterranean world," helping to convince Lewis that "Christianity, far from being a foreign idea imposed upon the world by a small Middle Eastern tribe, was the one true answer to a universal human need." Markos, *Myth Made Fact*, xviii.
77. Lewis, *George MacDonald*, xxxviii.
78. Hooper, *Collected Letters*, vol. 1, 934–36.
79. MacDonald, *What's Mine's Mine*, 106–7.
80. Hooper, *Collected Letters*, vol. 1, 950.
81. Hooper, *Collected Letters*, vol. 1, 955.
82. Lewis, *George MacDonald*, xxxii.
83. Lewis, *George MacDonald*, xxx.
84. Just before his conversion, Lewis wrote a poem expressing what it would be like to reconcile the faculties of reason and imagination—and thus embrace the Christian faith. It contains these closing lines: "Who make in me a concord of the depth and height? / Who make imagination's dim exploring touch / Ever report the same as intellectual sight? / Then could I truly say, and not deceive, / Then wholly say, that I BELIEVE." Lewis, "Reason," in *Poems*.
85. Lewis, *Surprised by Joy*, 212.
86. Lewis, *Surprised by Joy*, 230.
87. Hooper, *Collected Letters*, vol. 1, 974.
88. Hastings, *History of English Christianity*, 231.
89. Hastings, *History of English Christianity*, 231–32.
90. *Oxford Magazine*, February 19, 1931, 486–87, quoted in Harrison, *History of the University of Oxford*, 314.
91. Lippmann, *Preface to Morals*, 8.
92. Bertrand Russell, quoted in E. A. Burroughs, "Vindication," in Dearmer, *Christianity and the Crisis*, 24.
93. Krutch, "Modern Temper."
94. Colin Duriez, interview with the author, July 2017.
95. Kirk, *Enemies of the Permanent Things*.
96. Burns, *Modern Civilization on Trial*, 305.
97. Inge, *Fall of the Idols*, 17–18.
98. Stalin, "The Tasks of Economic Executives."
99. Duranty, "Soviets in 16th Year Calm and Hopeful."
100. Johnson, *Modern Times*, 275.
101. Orwell, *Collected Essays*, vol. 1, 559. Quoted in Harrison, *History of the University of Oxford*, 399.
102. Burleigh, *Third Reich*, 382.
103. Lippmann, *Preface to Morals*, 9.

104. Tolkien, *Lord of the Rings*, 51.
105. Genesis 3:5, emphasis added.

Chapter 3: When Dragons Roam the Earth

1. Harrison, *History of the University of Oxford*, 167.
2. Smith, "Notable Debates."
3. Historian Paul Jankowski argues that "national delusions," which had become ingrained in mass politics, reached a tipping point in 1933. "These yielded Hitler, the flight from collective commitments, the passivity of the Western powers, Japanese defiance, the Soviet persecution mania, and much else besides." Jankowski, *All Against All*, xvii.
4. Johnson, *History of the American People*, 777.
5. Ferguson, *War of the World*, 290.
6. *New York Times* Wireless, "Four-Power Pact Is Signed in Rome."
7. Bosworth, *Mussolini*, 367.
8. Hooper, *Collected Letters*, 128.
9. Ryrie, *Protestants*, 272.
10. Ryrie, *Protestants*, 269.
11. Burleigh, *Third Reich*, 257.
12. Burleigh, *Third Reich*, 257.
13. Benda, *Treason of the Intellectuals*, 29.
14. Shirer, *Rise and Fall of the Third Reich*, 241.
15. Shirer, *Rise and Fall of the Third Reich*, 241.
16. Ironically, the fresh outbreak of political repression and militarism across the globe was occurring simultaneously with an international conference on disarmament. When delegates to the World Disarmament Conference first met in Geneva in February 1932, the mood was anxious but hopeful, even bombastic. "Mankind is looking to this Conference," declared Arthur Henderson, the conference president, "with its unrivalled experience and knowledge, its unchallengeable representative authority and power, its massed wisdom and capacity, to bestow the gift of freedom from the menace to peace and security that the maintenance of huge national armaments must ever be." Henderson, "Opening Speech by the President."
17. According to Christopher Tolkien, his father began writing an alliterative poem, "The Fall of Arthur," in the early 1930s. The theme of war seemed to be at the forefront of his mind. The opening line of the poem, which he never completed, reads thus: "How Arthur and Gawain went to war and rode into the East." Tolkien, *Fall of Arthur*, 10–11.
18. Carpenter, *J. R. R. Tolkien: A Biography*, 175.
19. Scull and Hammond, *Tolkien Companion*, vol. 1, 509.
20. Hooper, *Collected Letters*, vol. 2, letter to Arthur Greeves, February 4, 1933.
21. Scull and Hammond, *Tolkien Companion*, vol. 1, 509.
22. Lewis's review appeared on October 8, 1937.
23. Tolkien, *Hobbit*, 85.
24. Shippey, *J. R. R. Tolkien, Author of the Century*, 28. However, in a February 20, 1938, letter to the *Observer*, Tolkien acknowledges that there were important sources of

inspiration for his story, including the works of George MacDonald and Beowulf. "Beowulf is among my most valued sources; though it was not consciously present to the mind in the process of writing. . . . My tale is not consciously based on any other book—save one, and that is unpublished: the 'Silmarillion,' a history of the Elves, to which frequent allusion is made." Tolkien, *Letters*, 31.

25. Shippey, *J. R. R. Tolkien, Author of the Century*, 29.
26. Tolkien, *Hobbit*, 144.
27. Tolkien, *Letters*, 105.
28. Garth, *Tolkien and the Great War*, 308.
29. Tolkien, *Hobbit*, 59.
30. Tolkien, *Hobbit*, 260.
31. Garth, *Tolkien and the Great War*, 307.
32. Helms, *Tolkien's World*, 33.
33. In his afterword to the book, Lewis writes that "Romanticism" was for him "a particular recurrent experience which dominated my childhood and adolescence." It was the experience of longing: He labeled it "romantic" because "inanimate nature and marvelous literature were among the things that evoked it." Lewis, *Pilgrim's Regress*, 45.
34. In the afterword to the book, Lewis explains the sometimes-tough tone of his work. "After this explanation the reader will more easily understand (I do not ask him to condone) the bitterness of certain pages in this book. He will realize how the Post-War period must have looked to one who had followed such a road as mine." Lewis, *Pilgrim's Regress*, 45.
35. Lewis, *Pilgrim's Regress*, 45.
36. Lewis, *Pilgrim's Regress*, 45.
37. Carpenter, *Inklings*, 49.
38. Armand Nicholi writes, "On the morning of September 26, 1939, in northwest London, a group of friends and family gathered to mourn the death of Sigmund Freud. The *New York Times* article mentioned Freud's 'worldwide fame and greatness,' referring to him as 'one of the most widely discussed scientists,' mentioning that 'he set the entire world talking about psychoanalysis' and noting that his ideas had already permeated our culture and language." Nicholi, "The Question of God: Why Freud & Lewis?"
39. Freud, *Civilization and Its Discontents*, 39.
40. Dearmer, *Christianity and the Crisis*, 61.
41. Lewis, *Surprised by Joy*, 203.
42. Lewis, *Pilgrim's Regress*, 49–50.
43. Lewis, *Pilgrim's Regress*, 102.
44. Lewis, *Pilgrim's Regress*, 106.
45. Lewis, *Pilgrim's Regress*, 105. Lewis is explicit about his references to fascism and communism in a letter to Arthur Greeves, dated November 5, 1933: "For the German people as a whole we ought to have charity: but for dictators, 'Nordic' tyrants and so on—well, read the chapter about Mr. Savage in the *Regress* and you have my views." Hooper, *Collected Letters*, vol. 2, 128.
46. Bunyan, *Pilgrim's Progress*, xx.

47. Bunyan, *Pilgrim's Progress*, 152.
48. Lewis, *Letters of C. S. Lewis*, 44.
49. Lewis wrote the book during his stay, from August 15 to 19, 1932.
50. C. S. Lewis, letter to Arthur Greeves, March 25, 1933.
51. Malcolm Guite, interview with the author, March 5, 2024.
52. Guite, interview.
53. Lewis, *Pilgrim's Regress*, 12.
54. Lewis, *Surprised by Joy*, 19.
55. Carpenter, *Inklings*, 52.
56. Carpenter, *Inklings*, 55.
57. Scull and Hammond, *Tolkien Companion*, vol. 1, 569. Letter on September 11, 1967.
58. Scull and Hammond, *Tolkien Companion*, vol. 1, 569–570.
59. Lewis, *Letters of C. S. Lewis*, 13–14, quoted in Scull and Hammond, *Tolkien Companion*, vol. 1, 574.
60. Hooper, *Collected Letters*, vol. 2, 198.
61. Jordan-Smith, "Silver Trumpet." Jordan-Smith summarized the importance of the book in his review: "The fortitude of the young prince and the courage of the princess in Barfield's tale betoken the heroism of each, and this appeals to children because the heroic is what they wish for themselves. And why not? Why do we adults not wish it for ourselves, and worse, why do we not always wish it for our children?"
62. Owen Barfield, interview with the author, March 14, 2024.
63. Zaleski and Zaleski, *Fellowship*, 448.
64. Colin Duriez, interview with the author, July 2017.
65. Jacobs, *Narnian*, 203.
66. John Wain, quoted in Zaleski and Zaleski, *Fellowship*, 3.
67. Lawlor, *C. S. Lewis: Memories and Reflections*, 96. Although Lawlor is referring to Lewis in this passage, his other writings suggest he thought of Tolkien in the same light.
68. Lawlor, *C. S. Lewis: Memories and Reflections*, 96.
69. Tolkien, *Lay of Beowulf*, 417.
70. Chambers, review of *Beowulf*, 272–73.
71. Drout, "'Beowulf: The Monsters and the Critics.'"
72. Helms, *Tolkien's World*, 12–13.
73. Helms, *Tolkien's World*, 12.
74. Tolkien, *Monster and the Critics*, 17.
75. Italics added.
76. Shippey, *J. R. R. Tolkien: Author of the Century*, 40–41.
77. Tolkien, *Monster and the Critics*, 28.
78. Lawlor, *C. S. Lewis: Memories and Reflections*, 96.
79. Leishman, "Rehabilitations and Other Essays," 109.
80. Ifor Evans, quoted in Sayer, *Jack*, 243.
81. Tillotson, review of *The Allegory of Love*, 477.
82. Jacobs, *Narnian*, 161.
83. Jacobs, *Narnian*, 161.

84. Tillotson, review of *The Allegory of Love*, 477.
85. Lewis, *Allegory of Love*, 11.
86. Lewis, *Allegory of Love*, 5.
87. Tillotson, review of *The Allegory of Love*, 448–49.
88. Zaleski and Zaleski, *Fellowship*, 184.
89. Dearmer, *Christianity and the Crisis*, 67–68.
90. Burleigh, *Third Reich*, 255.
91. Farrell, *Mussolini*, 344.
92. Hibbert, *Mussolini*, 68.
93. Bosworth, *Mussolini*, 252.
94. Kershaw, *To Hell and Back*, 281.
95. Farrell, *Mussolini*, 342.
96. Farrell, *Mussolini*, 2.
97. Kershaw, *To Hell and Back*, 255.
98. Ferguson, *War of the World*, 261.
99. Hitler, "Translation of Document 2289-PS."
100. Roosevelt, "Address at Chautauqua, N.Y."
101. Kershaw, *To Hell and Back*, 288–99.
102. Chiang Kai-shek, "Memorandum by Mr. John P. Davies, Jr."
103. Johnson, *Modern Times*, 190.
104. Colin Duriez, interview with the author, July 2017.
105. Thompson, "Early Reviews of Books," 56.
106. Lewis, *Of This and Other Worlds*, 94.
107. Tolkien, "Dragons."
108. Tolkien, "Dragons."
109. Lewis, "On Three Ways of Writing for Children."
110. Hooper, *Collected Letters*, vol. 2, 180–81.
111. Hooper, *Collected Letters*, vol. 2, 183.
112. Hooper, *Collected Letters*, vol. 2, 183.
113. Williams, *Place of the Lion*, 180.
114. Hooper, *Collected Letters*, vol. 2, 184.
115. Roosevelt, "Appeal for World Peace."
116. Tolkien, *Letters from Father Christmas*, 116–21.
117. Tolkien, *Letters*, 30.
118. Garth, *Tolkien and the Great War*, 283.
119. White, *C. S. Lewis and His Circle*, 142.
120. Orwell, *Why I Write*, 8.
121. Lewis, *Pilgrim's Regress*, 110.
122. Churchill, "Situation at Bilbao."
123. Tolkien, *Letters*, 30.

Chapter 4: The Inklings Go to War

1. Hooper, *Collected Letters*, vol. 2, 225.
2. Hooper, *Collected Letters*, vol. 2, 225, 232, 234.
3. Tolkien, *Letters*, 52.

4. Krabbe, *Voices from Britain*, 12.
5. Ferguson, *War of the World*, 367.
6. Bartlett, "Munich Agreement Is Signed."
7. Churchill, "Munich Agreement."
8. Brittain, *Testament of Youth*, 218.
9. Daisy Dunn, interview with the author, March 4, 2024.
10. Graham, *We Remember C. S. Lewis*, 62.
11. Schofield, *In Search of C. S. Lewis*, 62.
12. Graham, *We Remember C. S. Lewis*, 52.
13. Lewis, *God in the Dock*, 202.
14. Malcolm Guite, interview with the author, March 5, 2024.
15. Tolkien, *Letters*, 222–227.
16. Ferguson, *War of the World*, 374.
17. Tolkien, *Lord of the Rings*, 5.
18. Kershaw, *To Hell and Back*, 340.
19. Kershaw, *To Hell and Back*, 339.
20. Tolkien was asked whether in the event of a national emergency (i.e., war) he would be willing to work in the cryptographical department of the Foreign Office. Tolkien, *Letters*, 54, 611n.
21. Hooper, *Collected Letters*, vol. 2, 239.
22. Hooper, *Collected Letters*, vol. 2, 240.
23. Hooper, *Collected Letters*, vol. 2, 258.
24. Also known as the Molotov-Ribbentrop Pact, since it was negotiated by Soviet foreign minister V. I. Molotov and German foreign minister Joachim von Ribbentrop.
25. Both Nazi Germany and the Soviet Union intended to effectively wipe Poland off the political map. In the secret protocol, writes William Shirer, "Hitler and Stalin agreed to institute in Poland a regime of terror designed to brutally suppress Polish freedom, culture and national life." Shirer, *Rise and Fall of the Third Reich*, 632.
26. Ferguson, *War of the World*, 379.
27. Tolkien, *Letters*, 51–52.
28. Tolkien, *Letters*, 54.
29. Tolkien, *Letters*, 55.
30. Scull and Hammond, *Tolkien Companion*, vol. 2, 898.
31. Tolkien, *Tree and Leaf*, 3.
32. Tolkien, *Tree and Leaf*, 9.
33. Tolkien, *Tree and Leaf*, 8.
34. Tolkien, *Tree and Leaf*, 54.
35. Tolkien, *Tree and Leaf*, 56.
36. Lewis, *God in the Dock*, 66.
37. Tolkien, *Lord of the Rings*, 274.
38. Even before the Norwegian leader, Vidkun Quisling, famously disgraced himself by welcoming a Nazi-installed regime, his surname had become synonymous with betrayal.
39. Tolkien, *Tree and Leaf*, 68.

40. Tolkien, *Tree and Leaf*, 68–69.
41. Tolkien, *Tree and Leaf*, 55–56.
42. Tolkien, *Tree and Leaf*, 62.
43. Hooper, *Collected Letters*, vol. 2, 262.
44. Hooper, *Collected Letters*, vol. 2, 262. Elsewhere, Lewis explains his motivation for writing his Space Trilogy in similar terms. "It was against this outlook on life, this ethic, if you will, that I wrote my satiric fantasy, projecting in my Weston a buffoon-villain image of the 'metabiological' heresy." Lewis, *Of This and Other Worlds*, 122.
45. Hooper, *Collected Letters*, vol. 2, 236–37.
46. Wells, *Shape of Things to Come*, 420.
47. Wells, *New World Order*, 67.
48. Wells, *New World Order*, 189.
49. Lewis, *Seeing Eye*, 173.
50. Lewis, *Out of the Silent Planet*, 37. The other authors that Lewis had in mind include scientists such as J. B. S. Haldane, a biochemist, agnostic, and disillusioned Marxist who had written an essay defending interplanetary colonization. It was, Lewis wrote, a "desperately immoral outlook." Hooper, *Collected Letters*, vol. 2, 236.
51. Lewis, *Out of the Silent Planet*, 137.
52. Lewis, *Out of the Silent Planet*, 121–22.
53. Shirer, *Berlin Diary*, 582. I am indebted to Michael E. Conklin for bringing Shirer's insight, and its relationship to C. S. Lewis's Space trilogy, to my attention in his paper, "A Bent People: Germany Under National Socialism," delivered at the Intercollegiate Studies Institute on November 4, 2024.
54. Weiss, *Ideology of Death*, 325.
55. See Lewis in *Mere Christianity* and "Dogma and the Universe," in *The Seeing Eye*.
56. Lewis, *Perelandra*, 111.
57. Lewis, *That Hideous Strength*, 7.
58. Lewis, *That Hideous Strength*, 200.
59. Churchill, "Their Finest Hour."
60. Lewis, *Of This and Other Worlds*, 121.
61. Hooper, *Collected Letters*, vol. 2, 262.
62. *New York Times* review, quoted in Hooper, *Collected Letters*, vol. 2, 240.
63. Tolkien, *Letters*, 47–48.
64. Tolkien, *Letters*, 47–48.
65. Scull and Hammond, *Tolkien Companion*, vol. 1, 244.
66. A similar war council is held in *Prince Caspian*, when Glenstorm the centaur announces that the company must hold a war council to drive the wicked King Miraz out of Narnia. "He spoke with such a voice that neither Caspian nor the others hesitated for a moment: it now seemed to them quite possible that they might win a war and quite certain that they must wage one." Lewis, *Chronicles of Narnia*, 352.
67. Tolkien, *Lord of the Rings*, 266.
68. Gilbert, *Churchill*, 617.
69. Shirer, *Rise and Fall of the Third Reich*, 597.

70. Shirer, *Rise and Fall of the Third Reich*, 625.
71. Carpenter, *Inklings*, 68–69.
72. Carpenter, *Inklings*, 68–69.
73. Roberts, *Churchill*, 458.
74. Scull and Hammond, *Tolkien Companion*, vol. 1, 246.
75. Tolkien, *Letters*, 56.
76. Tolkien, *Letters*, 56.
77. Scull and Hammond, *Tolkien Companion*, vol. 1, 246–47.
78. Hooper, *Collected Letters*, vol. 2, 274.
79. Hooper, *Collected Letters*, vol. 2, 280.
80. Hooper, *Collected Letters*, vol. 2, 274, 276.
81. Kotkin, *Stalin*, 723.
82. Hastings, *Inferno*, 32.
83. Scholars debate the relationship of the Kalevala to Finnish national identity. See Lonnrot, *Kalevala*, vii-xxv.
84. Scull and Hammond, *Tolkien Companion*, vol. 1, 35.
85. Joanna Bowring, interview with the author, July 2017.
86. Bowring, interview.
87. Scull and Hammond, *Tolkien Companion*, vol. 1, 35.
88. Tolkien, *Lord of the Rings*, 365.
89. Hooper, *Collected Letters*, vol. 1, 235.
90. Walter Hooper, interview with the author, November 8, 2018.
91. Lewis, *Problem of Pain*, 86.
92. Lewis, *Problem of Pain*, 90, 93–94.
93. McIlwaine, *Tolkien: Maker of Middle-earth*, 154.
94. Hooper, *Collected Letters*, vol. 1, 291.
95. Aston, *History of the University of Oxford*, vol. 3, 170–71.
96. Lewis, *Weight of Glory*, 47.
97. Lewis, *Weight of Glory*, 49.
98. Lewis, *Weight of Glory*, 57.
99. Lewis, *Weight of Glory*, 60.
100. Lewis, *Weight of Glory*, 61.
101. Lewis, *Weight of Glory*, 58–59.
102. Hansen, "The Great Evacuation."
103. Harrison, *History of the University of Oxford*, 171.
104. Harrison, *History of the University of Oxford*, 171.
105. Hooper, *Collected Letters*, vol. 2, 451.
106. Hooper, *Collected Letters*, vol. 2, 270.
107. Schofield, *In Search of C. S. Lewis*, 53.
108. Schofield, *In Search of C. S. Lewis*, 57.
109. White, *C. S. Lewis and His Circle*, 151.
110. Schofield, *In Search of C. S. Lewis*, 57.
111. Hooper, *C. S. Lewis: A Companion and Guide*, 758–59.
112. Hooper, *C. S. Lewis: A Companion and Guide*, 402.
113. Hooper, *C. S. Lewis: A Companion and Guide*, 306.

114. *New York Times* Wireless, "Mines Sink Five More Ships."
115. Hooper, *Collected Letters*, vol. 2, 290.
116. *New York Times* Wireless, "Mines Sink Five More Ships."
117. Hooper, *Collected Letters*, vol. 2, 305.
118. Hooper, *Collected Letters*, vol. 2, 303.
119. Hooper, *Collected Letters*, vol. 2, 368.
120. Hooper, *Collected Letters*, vol. 2, 290.
121. Hooper, *Collected Letters*, vol. 2, 310–11.
122. McIlwaine, *Tolkien: Maker of Middle-earth*, 26.
123. Owen Barfield, interview with the author, March 14, 2024.
124. Carpenter, *Inklings*, 118.
125. Carpenter, *Inklings*, 114–15.
126. Hooper, *Collected Letters*, vol. 1, 918.
127. Hooper, *Collected Letters*, vol. 2, 501.
128. See Diana Glyer, *The Company They Keep*.
129. Daisy Dunn, interview with the author, March 4, 2024.
130. Havard, "Professor J. R. R. Tolkien," 61.
131. Como, *C. S. Lewis at the Breakfast Table and Other Reminiscences*, 216.
132. Mary Clare Havard, interview with the author, November 2022.
133. Lewis, *Problem of Pain*, 161–62.
134. Hastings, *Inferno*, 41.
135. Kershaw, *To Hell and Back*, 347.
136. Gilbert, *Second World War*, 1.
137. Tolkien, *Letters from Father Christmas*, 180.
138. Tolkien, *Letters*, 571.
139. Tolkien, *Lord of the Rings*, 318.
140. Ferguson, *War of the World*, 429.
141. Ferguson, *War of the World*, 429.

Chapter 5: No Holiday from History

1. Tolkien, *Lord of the Rings*, 259.
2. Gilbert, *Churchill*, 651.
3. Hooper, *Collected Letters*, vol. 2, 406.
4. Janet Brennan Croft writes that "the fortification of the Rammas Echor, the outwall of Minas Tirith, is a reminder of the futility of the Maginot Line, which gave France a false sense of security against German invasion." Croft, *War and the Works of J. R. R. Tolkien*, 61.
5. Gilbert, *Churchill*, 651.
6. Rook, *These Are My Comrades*, 17. Rook was safely evacuated at Dunkirk. His wartime poems were published in a slim volume, *These Are My Comrades* (1943), which he later sent as a gift to Tolkien.
7. Churchill, "Their Finest Hour."
8. Hastings, *Inferno*, 78–79.
9. Tolkien, *Lord of the Rings*, 847. The name Éomer, which means "Horse-famous" in Old English, is found in *Beowulf*.

10. Churchill, *Never Give In!*, 216.
11. Lewis, *Present Concerns*, 41.
12. Tolkien, *Lord of the Rings*, 83.
13. Lewis, *Chronicles of Narnia*, 707.
14. Hooper, *Collected Letters*, vol. 2, 425.
15. Hooper, *C. S. Lewis: A Companion and Guide*, 276.
16. Lewis, *Screwtape Letters*, 133.
17. Lewis, *Screwtape Letters*, 60.
18. Lewis, *Screwtape Letters*, 76–77.
19. Lewis, *Of This and Other Worlds*, 129.
20. Ferguson, *War of the World*, 423.
21. Lewis made a similar point in his rejoinder to an essay published by J. B. S. Haldane, who criticized Lewis's science fiction trilogy. "The first of these tendencies is the growing exaltation of the collective and the growing indifference to persons. . . . Secondly, we have the emergence of 'the Party' in the modern states—the Fascists, Nazis, or Communists. What distinguishes this from the political parties of the nineteenth century is the belief of its members that they are not merely trying to carry out a program but are obeying an impersonal force: that Nature, or Evolution, or the Dialectic, or the Race is carrying them on. . . . In this state of mind men can become devil-worshippers in the sense that they can now honor, as well as obey, their own vices." Lewis, *Of This and Other Worlds*, 132–33.
22. Ferguson, *War of the World*, 150–151. The dismissive quote, "History is bunk," is attributed to Henry Ford.
23. Huxley, *Brave New World*, 40.
24. Huxley, *Religion Without Revelation*, viii.
25. Hooper, *C. S. Lewis: A Companion and Guide*, 276.
26. Hastings, *Inferno*, 77.
27. Ferguson, *War of the World*, 414–15.
28. Tolkien, *Letters*, 340.
29. Tolkien, *Letters*, 61.
30. Hastings, *Inferno*, 88.
31. Hastings, *Inferno*, 82.
32. Gilbert, *Churchill*, 670.
33. Churchill, "We Shall Fight on the Beaches."
34. Churchill, "Never in the Field of Human Conflict Was So Much Owed by So Many to So Few."
35. Lewis, *Present Concerns*, 15.
36. Lewis, *Present Concerns*, 14–16.
37. Hooper, *Collected Letters*, vol. 2, 432.
38. Julia Golding, interview with the author, March 4, 2024.
39. Lukacs, *Last European War*, 111.
40. Hastings, *Inferno*, 92.
41. Tolkien, *Letters*, 62.
42. Tolkien, *Letters*, 63.
43. Scull and Hammond, *Tolkien Companion*, vol. 1, 261.

44. Ziegler, *London at War*, 144.
45. Ziegler, *London at War*, 132.
46. Ziegler, *London at War*, 145.
47. Lewis, *Present Concerns*, 16.
48. Tolkien, *Lord of the Rings*, 47.
49. Tolkien, *Letters*, 71.
50. Tolkien, *Lord of the Rings*, 823.
51. Harrison, *History of the University of Oxford*, 175.
52. Darwall-Smith, *History of University College Oxford*, 469.
53. Lewis, *Christian Reflections*, 71.
54. Hooper, *Collected Letters*, vol. 2, 448.
55. Lewis had read Bergson's book *Creative Evolution* while a student at University College and wrote to his father on September 13, 1919, informing him that two important figures were arriving soon in Oxford: W. B. Yeats, who moved to 4 Broad Street, and Henri Bergson, who was coming for a visit. Lewis critiqued this viewpoint in several of his works, including *Mere Christianity*.
56. Hooper, *Collected Letters*, vol. 2, 448.
57. Lewis, *Weight of Glory*, 62.
58. Marsden, *C. S. Lewis's* Mere Christianity, 24.
59. Marsden, *C. S. Lewis's* Mere Christianity, 25.
60. Duriez, *Bedeviled*, 94.
61. Hooper, *Collected Letters*, vol. 2, 277.
62. Hooper, *Collected Letters*, vol. 2, 470.
63. Lewis, *Mere Christianity*, 15.
64. Marsden, *C. S. Lewis's* Mere Christianity, 36. See Sayer, *Jack*.
65. Roosevelt, "Campaign Address at Cleveland, Ohio."
66. Tolkien, *Letters*, 64.
67. Tolkien, *Letters*, 71.
68. Tolkien, *Letters*, 71. In the same letter, Tolkien recalled a conversation with a fellow soldier: "I said, outside Lichfield Cathedral, to a friend of my youth—long since dead of gas-gangrene (God rest his soul: I grieve still)—'Why is that cloud so beautiful?' He said: 'Because you have begun to write poetry, John Ronald.' He was wrong. It was because Death was near, and all was intolerably fair, lost ere grasped. That was why I began to write poetry."
69. Scull and Hammond, *Tolkien Companion*, vol. 1, 264.
70. Jenkins, "Crew of the Whitley V Aircraft."
71. Scull and Hammond, *Tolkien Companion and Guide*, vol. 1, 264.
72. Hastings, *Inferno*, 144.
73. Tolkien, *Lord of the Rings*, 828.
74. Lewis, *Chronicles of Narnia*, 358.
75. Alister McGrath, interview with the author, July 25, 2017.
76. Niall Ferguson, interview with the author, March 5, 2024.
77. Fuller, *Books with Men Behind Them*, 188.
78. Tolkien, *Lord of the Rings*, 940.
79. Tolkien, *Lord of the Rings*, 940.

80. Lewis, *Perelandra*, 81–82.
81. Lewis, *Perelandra*, 126, 121.
82. Hooper, *Collected Letters*, vol. 2, 492.
83. Como, *C. S. Lewis at the Breakfast Table*, 186.
84. Como, *C. S. Lewis at the Breakfast Table*, 187.
85. Hooper, *Collected Letters*, vol. 2, 504.
86. Simon Horobin, interview with the author, March 11, 2024.
87. Hooper, *Collected Letters*, vol. 2, 485.
88. Como, *C. S. Lewis at the Breakfast Table*, 186–88.
89. Hooper, *Collected Letters*, vol. 2, 501.
90. Tolkien, *Lord of the Rings*, 323. Although I cannot be certain when Tolkien reached this chapter in the story, it seems likely, given his progress on it around December 1941.
91. John Garth, interview with the author, July 30, 2017.
92. Tolkien, *Lord of the Rings*, 332.
93. Tolkien, *Lord of the Rings*, 399.
94. Markos, *Myth Made Fact*, 126–27.
95. Note here the Tolkien–Lewis conversation that prompted Tolkien to pursue the Atlantis/Numenor story. Scull and Hammond, *Tolkien Companion*, vol. 2, 874.
96. Tolkien, *Lord of the Rings*, 267.
97. Tolkien, *Silmarillion*, quoted in Scull and Hammond, *Tolkien Companion*, vol. 2, 1094.
98. Spacks, "Power and Meaning in *The Lord of the Rings*," 55.
99. Tolkien, *Lord of the Rings*, 371.
100. Author interview with Michael Sheil, November 11, 2018.
101. John Garth, interview with the author, July 18, 2018.
102. Tolkien, *Letters*, 432.
103. Tolkien, *Letters*, 160–61.
104. Niall Ferguson, interview with the author, March 5, 2024.
105. Hastings, *Inferno*, 193.
106. Tolkien, *Letters from Father Christmas*, 192.
107. Tolkien, *Letters from Father Christmas*, 192–93.
108. Gallately, *Stalin's Curse*, 49.
109. Kotkin, *Waiting for Hitler*, 773.
110. Burleigh, *Third Reich*, 631.
111. Gilbert, *Righteous*, 2.
112. Lewis, *Chronicles of Narnia*, 371.
113. Lewis, *Perelandra*, 95.
114. Jeremiah 50:38.
115. Lewis, *Preface to Paradise Lost*, 71.
116. Lewis, *Preface to Paradise Lost*, 96.
117. Lewis, *Preface to Paradise Lost*, 102–3.
118. Graham, *We Remember C. S. Lewis*, 63.
119. Graham, *We Remember C. S. Lewis*, 49.
120. Lewis, *Preface to Paradise Lost*, 132.

121. Lewis, *Preface to Paradise Lost*, 103.
122. Tolkien, *Letters*, 125.
123. Tolkien, *Letters*, 125.

Chapter 6: In the Shadow of Mordor

1. Hastings, *Inferno*, 354.
2. Johnson, *Modern Times*, 397.
3. Tolkien, *Lord of the Rings*, 357.
4. Lewis, *Weight of Glory*, 49.
5. Lewis, *Weight of Glory*, 58.
6. Lewis, *God in the Dock*, 126.
7. Aldwinckle, "Socrates Was a Realist."
8. Harrison, *History of the University of Oxford*, 308.
9. Heck, *Irrigating Deserts*, 107.
10. Como, *C. S. Lewis at the Breakfast Table*, 140.
11. Lewis, *God in the Dock*, 127.
12. White, *C. S Lewis and His Circle*, 192.
13. Joad, *Recovery of Belief*, 81.
14. Mitchell, "University Battles."
15. White, *C. S Lewis and His Circle*, 193.
16. Simon Horobin, interview with the author, March 11, 2024.
17. Barfield, *Owen Barfield on C. S. Lewis*, 9.
18. Lewis, *God in the Dock*, 128.
19. Scull and Hammond, *Tolkien Companion*, vol. 1, 270.
20. Tolkien, *Letters*, 164.
21. Tolkien, *Tree and Leaf*, 95–96.
22. Scull and Hammond, *Tolkien Companion*, vol. 1, 661.
23. Hooper, *Collected Letters*, vol. 2, 297.
24. Tolkien, *Tree and Leaf*, 105–6.
25. Hooper, *Collected Letters*, vol. 2, September 8–9, 1962.
26. Hooper, *Collected Letters*, vol. 2, June 24, 1957.
27. Tolkien, *Tree and Leaf*, 99.
28. Tolkien, *Tree and Leaf*, 107.
29. Revelation 22:2–3.
30. Scull and Hammond, *Tolkien Companion*, vol. 1, 663. Priscilla Tolkien: "It is also unique in being the most directly autobiographical. . . . It concerns the life of an artist and how an artist is to respond both to the pressures of his absorption in his creative ideas and to the demands of living an ordinary life in the ordinary world; in other words, how is he to enjoy living in the life of the imagination while at the same time remaining a moral being sensitive to the needs of other people."
31. Dunn, *Not Far from Brideshead*, 156.
32. Dunn, *Not Far from Brideshead*, 159.
33. Lewis, *God in the Dock*, 278.
34. Wagner, *Ring of the Niblung*, 154.
35. Lewis, *God in the Dock*, 279.

36. Tolkien, *Letters*, 77.
37. Tolkien, *Letters*, 77.
38. BBC, "December 17, 1942."
39. Lewis, *Out of the Silent Planet*, 70.
40. Tolkien, *Lord of the Rings*, 343.
41. Tolkien, *Lord of the Rings*, 356.
42. Tolkien, *Lord of the Rings*, 356.
43. Hooper, *Collected Letters*, vol. 2, 549.
44. Tolkien, *Letters*, 91.
45. Tolkien, *Letters*, 314.
46. The focus of the war shifted east: For the next four years, for every five German soldiers killed in combat, four died on the Eastern Front. See Roberts, *Churchill*, 662.
47. Lewis, *Abolition of Man*, 27.
48. Ward, *After Humanity*, 3.
49. Ward, *After Humanity*, 81.
50. Lewis, *Abolition of Man*, 71.
51. Lewis, *That Hideous Strength*, 255.
52. Lewis, *That Hideous Strength*, 255.
53. Lewis, *Abolition of Man*, 74.
54. Lewis, *Abolition of Man*, 70.
55. Lewis, *Of This and Other Worlds*, 87.
56. I am indebted to Bruce R. Johnson for bringing to my attention the role of Lewis and Tolkien in developing at Oxford University a special course and examination in English literature for British POWs. He writes: "Lewis worked with J. R. R. Tolkien to create the program while other scholars, such as Neville Coghill, made suggestions regarding bibliography and the final exam scripts." According to Johnson, the Oxford English examination for British POWs "was the first ever examination by the university outside of Oxford." Required primary texts were forwarded by the German authorities to the POWs, and their responses to examination questions were forwarded back to Oxford examiners. Johnson, "Efforts of C. S. Lewis."

    In a letter to the editor of *The Christian News-Letter*, Lewis praised this innovative approach: "On the cultural side I anticipate, along with much bad work, answers of real interest, for I believe that the necessary restriction on bulky works of criticism, literary history, and apparatus, by forcing the students to concentrate on the texts and to digest them more thoroughly and, above all, to find in one great author their chief commentary on another, may have certain positive advantages over the normal procedure." Lewis, "Universities of Captivity," quoted in Johnson, "Efforts of C. S. Lewis."
57. Scull and Hammond, *Tolkien Companion*, vol. 1, 276–77.
58. Tolkien, *Letters*, 81.
59. Simon Horobin, interview with the author, March 11, 2024.
60. Tolkien, *Letters*, 137–38.
61. Letter from Auden, July 28, 1955, in Tolkien family papers, quoted in McIlwaine, *Tolkien: Maker of Middle-earth*, 92.

62. McIlwaine, *Tolkien: Maker of Middle-earth*, 92.
63. Tolkien, *Letters*, 138.
64. Tolkien, *Letters*, 139.
65. Tolkien, *Letters*, 139.
66. Tolkien, *Beowulf*, 80–81.
67. Tolkien, *Letters*, 81.
68. Tolkien, *Letters*, 506. Tolkien made a similar confession to his publisher, Rayner Unwin, when Lewis raised the possibility that his endorsement of Tolkien's book might hurt him in some literary circles. "I should not have wished other than to be associated with him—since only by his support and friendship did I ever struggle to the end of the labor." Zaleski and Zaleski, *The Fellowship*, 422.
69. Hooper, *Collected Letters*, vol. 2, 631.
70. Tolkien, *Letters*, 123.
71. Though I can't be certain, the Eastgate Hotel was a favorite lunch spot for Tolkien and Lewis.
72. Tolkien, *Letters*, 100.
73. Tolkien, *Letters*, 103.
74. Tolkien, *Lord of the Rings*, 728.
75. Tolkien, *Letters*, 119.
76. Tolkien, *Tree and Leaf*, 70–71.
77. Lewis, *God in the Dock*, 116.
78. Lewis, *God in the Dock*, 116.
79. Fuller, *Books with Men Behind Them*, 6–7.
80. Lewis, *God in the Dock*, 203.
81. Fuller, *Books with Men Behind Them*, 167.
82. Lewis, *Essay Collection*, 182.
83. Guite, "Yearning for a Far-Off Country," in White, *C. S. Lewis and His Circle*, 117.
84. Lewis, *Perelandra*, 13.
85. Lewis, *Screwtape Letters*, 1.
86. Lewis, *God in the Dock*, 221–22.
87. Lewis, *God in the Dock*, 221.
88. Quoted in McIlwaine, *Tolkien: Maker of Middle-earth*, 63.
89. Tolkien, *Hobbit*, 197.
90. Stuart Lee, interview with the author, July 25, 2024.
91. Lewis, *Surprised by Joy*, 196.
92. Tolkien, *Lord of the Rings*, 401.
93. Lewis, *Image and Imagination*, 101, 103.
94. Fuller, *Books with Men Behind Them*, 136.
95. Hooper, *Collected Letters*, vol. 1, 750.
96. Virgil, *Aeneid*, 185.
97. Lewis, *Present Concerns*, 70. In this essay, "Talking About Bicycles," Lewis contrasts the disenchanted authors of the post–World War I years, such as Siegfried Sassoon, with authors like himself who retained a belief in the concept of noble sacrifice. "One is not in the least deceived: we remember the trenches too well. We know how much of the reality the romantic view left out. But we also know that heroism

is a real thing, that all the plumes and flags and trumpets of the tradition were not there for nothing." Lewis, *Present Concerns*, 69–70.

98. Malcolm Guite, interview with the author, March 5, 2024.
99. Roberts, *Churchill*, 815.
100. Hooper, *Collected Letters*, vol. 2, 625.
101. Eisenhower, *Crusade in Europe*, 46.
102. Eisenhower, *Crusade in Europe*, 246.
103. Ambrose, *Eisenhower*, 129.
104. Tolkien, *Letters*, 133.
105. Roberts, *Churchill*, 825–26.
106. Tolkien, *Letters*, 134.
107. Tolkien, *Letters*, 127.
108. Ferguson, *War of the World*, 538.
109. Roberts, *Churchill*, 862.
110. Tolkien, *Letters*, 160.
111. Hastings, *Inferno*, 605.
112. Hastings, *Inferno*, 604.
113. Hastings, *Inferno*, 606.
114. Tolkien, *Letters*, 167.
115. Hooper, *Collected Letters*, vol. 2, 647–48.
116. Ferguson, *War of the World*, 538.
117. Ferguson, *War of the World*, 890.
118. Ferguson, *War of the World*, 113.
119. Virgil, *Aeneid*, 186.
120. Hooper, *Collected Letters*, vol. 2, 148.
121. Tolkien, *Letters*, 144. From Tolkien's description, the meeting apparently occurred at Lewis's home, not at Magdalen College.
122. Hooper, *Collected Letters*, vol. 2, 131.
123. Hooper, *Collected Letters*, vol. 2, 145–46.
124. Lewis, *Great Divorce*, 136. Tolkien records this meeting of the Inklings in his June 10, 1944, letter to Christopher. Although he does not cite the work that Lewis read to the Inklings, he records a May 31 Inklings meeting in which Lewis read excerpts from "Who Goes Home?"—Lewis's original title for *The Great Divorce*. It seems likely, though not certain, that Lewis read another excerpt from the story at the June 8 meeting.
125. Tolkien, *Lord of the Rings*, 901.
126. Tolkien, *Lord of the Rings*, 901.
127. Tolkien, *Letters*, 6.
128. John Garth, interview with the author, November 2018.
129. Lewis, *Surprised by Joy*, 191.
130. Lewis, *Surprised by Joy*, 192.
131. Keegan, *First World War*, 427.
132. Lewis, *Four Loves*, 105.
133. Lewis, *Christian Reflections*, vii.
134. Lewis, *Four Loves*, 114–15.

135. Julia Golding, interview with the author, March 4, 2004.
136. Lewis, *Four Loves*, 101.

Conclusion: The Far-Off Country

1. Niall Ferguson, interview with the author, March 5, 2024.
2. Fuller, *Books with Men Behind Them*, 140.
3. Carpenter, *J. R. R. Tolkien: A Biography*, 131.
4. Fuller, *Books with Men Behind Them*, 103.
5. Lewis, *De Descriptione Temporum*.
6. Stuart Lee, interview with the author, July 25, 2024.
7. Tolkien, *Lord of the Rings*, 262.
8. Fussell, *Great War and Modern Memory*, 354.
9. Tolkien, *Letters*, 113. Tolkien wrote those words in a letter to his son Christopher, dated May 6, 1944, in which he encouraged his son, then training in the RAF, to find his own voice in writing. "I think if you could begin to write, and find your own mode, or even (for a start) imitate mine, you would find it a great relief. I sense amongst all your pains (some merely physical) the desire to express your feeling about good, evil, fair, foul in some way: to rationalize it, and prevent it from just festering."
10. Gibbs, *Now It Can Be Told*, 168, 247.
11. Niall Ferguson, interview with the author, March 5, 2024.
12. Garth, *Tolkien and the Great War*, xv.
13. Tolkien, *Letters*, 174.
14. Fuller, *Books with Men Behind Them*, 136.
15. Lewis, *Of This and Other Worlds*, 49.
16. Lewis, *Of This and Other Worlds*, 64.
17. Tearle, "Summary and Analysis of *The Lion, the Witch and the Wardrobe*."
18. John Lennox, interview with the author, July 20, 2018.
19. Plato, *The Republic*, 215.
20. Michael Ward, interview with the author, March 11, 2024.
21. Lewis, *Of This and Other Worlds*, 48–49.
22. Lewis, *Chronicles of Narnia*, 282.
23. Julia Golding, interview with the author, March 4, 2024.
24. Lewis, *Chronicles of Narnia*, 102.
25. Lewis, *Chronicles of Narnia*, 381.
26. Michael Ward, interview with the author, March 11, 2024.
27. Lewis, *Of This and Other Worlds*, 51.
28. Niall Ferguson, interview with the author, March 5, 2024.
29. Malcolm Guite, interview with the author, March 5, 2024.
30. Fuller, *Books with Men Behind Them*, 146.
31. Kirk, *Enemies of the Permanent Things*, 114.
32. Colin Duriez, interview with the author, July 2017.
33. Tolkien, *Letters*, 531.
34. Tolkien, *Letters*, 28.
35. Hooper, *Collected Letters*, vol. 3, 990–91. Writing to Tolkien again after rereading

the first volume of *The Lord of the Rings*, Lewis was effusive with praise: "I have been trying—like a boy with a bit of toffee—to take Vol. 1 slowly, to make it last, but appetite overmastered me and it's now finished: far too short for me. The spell does not break. The love of Gimli and the departure from Lothlorien is still almost unbearable. What came out stronger at this reading than on any previous one was the gradual coming of the shadow—step by step—over Boromir." Hooper, *Collected Letters*, vol. 3, 384.

36. Hooper, *Collected Letters*, vol. 3, 250.
37. Tolkien, *Letters*, 176.
38. Malcolm Guite, interview with the author, March 5, 2024.
39. Tolkien, *Lord of the Rings*, 1029.
40. Tolkien, *Tree and Leaf*, 73.
41. Hooper, *Collected Letters*, vol. 1, 94.
42. Lewis, *Chronicles of Narnia*, 540–41.
43. Tolkien, *Lord of the Rings*, 922.

ABOUT THE AUTHOR

Joseph Loconte, PhD, is an author, historian, and filmmaker. He serves as Director of The Rivendell Center in New York City. He is a Presidential Scholar at New College of Florida and a Senior Fellow at the Sagamore Institute. Mr. Loconte's commentary appears in outlets such as *The New York Times, The Wall Street Journal, National Affairs, The New Criterion, National Geographic, Law and Liberty, The National Interest,* and *National Review.* For ten years Mr. Loconte served as a commentator for National Public Radio's *All Things Considered.* A native of Brooklyn, New York, he divides his time between Washington, DC, and New York City.